I0649259

Conversations with William T. Vollmann

Literary Conversations Series
Monika Gehlawat
General Editor

Conversations with William T. Vollmann

Edited by Daniel Lukes

University Press of Mississippi / Jackson

The University Press of Mississippi is the scholarly publishing agency of
the Mississippi Institutions of Higher Learning: Alcorn State University,
Delta State University, Jackson State University, Mississippi State University,
Mississippi University for Women, Mississippi Valley State University,
University of Mississippi, and University of Southern Mississippi.

www.upress.state.ms.us

The University Press of Mississippi is a member
of the Association of University Presses.

Copyright © 2020 by University Press of Mississippi
All rights reserved
Manufactured in the United States of America

First printing 2020
∞

Library of Congress Cataloging-in-Publication Data available

LCCN 2019052095
Hardback ISBN 978-1-4968-2669-5
Trade paperback ISBN 978-1-4968-2670-1
Epub single ISBN 978-1-4968-2671-8
Epub institutional ISBN 978-1-4968-2672-5
PDF single ISBN 978-1-4968-2673-2
PDF institutional ISBN 978-1-4968-2674-9

British Library Cataloging-in-Publication Data available

Books by William T. Vollmann

You Bright and Risen Angels. London: André Deutsch, 1987.

The Rainbow Stories. London, André Deutsch, 1989.

The Ice-Shirt. London, André Deutsch, 1990.

Thirteen Stories and Thirteen Epitaphs. London, André Deutsch, 1991.

Whores for Gloria. London: Picador, 1991.

Fathers and Crows. New York: Viking, 1992.

An Afghanistan Picture Show: Or, How I Saved the World. New York: Farrar, Strauss and Giroux, 1992.

Butterfly Stories. New York: Grove Press, 1993.

The Rifles. New York: Viking, 1994.

The Atlas. New York: Viking, 1996.

The Royal Family. New York: Viking, 2000.

Argall: The True Story of Pocahontas and Captain John Smith. New York: Viking, 2001.

Rising Up and Rising Down: Some Thoughts on Violence, Freedom and Urgent Means. New York: McSweeney's, 2003.

Europe Central. New York: Viking, 2005.

Uncentering the Earth: Copernicus and the Revolutions of the Heavenly Spheres. New York: Atlas / W.W. Norton, 2006.

Poor People. New York: Ecco, 2007.

Riding Toward Everywhere. New York: Ecco, 2008.

Imperial. New York: Viking, 2009.

Kissing the Mask: Beauty, Understatement and Femininity in Japanese Noh Theater. New York: Ecco, 2010.

Into the Forbidden Zone: A Trip Through Hell and High Water in Post-Earthquake Japan. San Francisco: Byliner, 2011.

The Book of Dolores. New York: powerHouse, 2013.

Last Stories and Other Stories. New York: Penguin, 2014.

The Dying Grass. New York: Viking, 2015.

No Immediate Danger: Volume One of Carbon Ideologies. New York: Viking, 2018.

No Good Alternative: Volume Two of Carbon Ideologies. New York: Viking, 2018.

The Lucky Star. New York: Viking, 2020.

Contents

Introduction

I inherited this project from Michael Hemmingson, who died in January 2014, just as Christopher K. Coffman and I were finishing up editing *William T. Vollmann: A Critical Companion* (University of Delaware Press, 2014), to which Hemmingson had contributed an afterword: "Beyond the Book: William T. Vollmann's End Matter (Appendices, Glossaries, and Extra Texts)." Hemmingson had been in touch with me about *Conversations with William T. Vollmann* to include an interview I did with Vollmann for *While You Were Sleeping* magazine in 2004. A while after he died, I contacted University Press of Mississippi to ask about the status of the book, whether it was coming out; they told me that nothing had materialized before Hemmingson's death and asked whether I would be interested in taking on the project. I felt that the job had found me, and there was no question of my turning the opportunity down. I asked if Hemmingson had given any indication as to what he intended to include, and the answer was no. I assume his research for the book is in his laptop, and who knows where that is? So I started from scratch. This is thus a different book from the one Michael Hemmingson would have edited: one haunted by Hemmingson and his book that will never be.

My initial impulse was to reproduce the interviews published by Hemmingson in his own book *William T. Vollmann: A Critical Study and Seven Interviews* (McFarland, 2009); but as my research progressed both online and in the Vollmann archives at the Ohio State University Library in Columbus, Ohio, where I encountered lots of long-dormant and foreign-language interviews, it soon became clear to me that there wouldn't be much room for interviews already republished or easily-available online (or in Scott Rhodes's 2015 *William T. Vollmann: Selected Interviews*). My guiding criterion for *Conversations with William T. Vollmann* has been to privilege hard-to-find, rare, or best yet new and unpublished material. For this reason such classic Vollmann interviews as Madison Smartt Bell's *Paris Review* "William T. Vollmann: The Art of Fiction" (1994), Larry McCaffery's "Pattern Recognitions" (2001) on *Argall*, Kate Braverman's "The Subversive Dialogues" (2006), or

Tom Bissell's fantastic "You Are Now Entering the Demented Kingdom of William T. Vollmann" (2014) are unrepresented here.

Reading dozens of Vollmann interviews reveals various insights into his career. In the early interviews I am struck by the extent of self-fashioning going on. Given that Vollmann was first published in England by André Deutsch, some of the earliest Vollmann coverage is British, and Jonathan Coe's *Guardian* and Paul Oldfield's 1989 *Melody Maker* (a pop music weekly) interviews give a taste of what will be in the canonical Vollmann blazon: troubled genius out slumming, talent out of bounds, wild literary experimentation, and risk-taking tendencies bordering on the suicidal. Early and tabloidish portraits of Vollmann have about them a doomed-young-man vibe, as if he were a mythical creature soon to be snuffed out. Even as late as 2004 Larry McCaffery's *Expelled from Eden* "A William T. Vollmann Chronology" jokes that Vollmann's life would soon end. Kate Braverman memorably writes how Vollmann "elicits the desire to both injure and defend him. You want to beat him and have him arrested and yet, as a magical being, you intuit his vulnerability and do not violate him with a camera. I instinctively feel protective, as if encountering an endangered species at the edge of extinction."

It is compelling to see the construction of a literary legend through the format of the interview, and much is made in these early interviews of Vollmann's physical appearance, described as out of the ordinary. "His eyes squint through thick oblong glasses from a chubby, scrappily shaved face, unflatteringly offset by a vicious crewcut. With a few spots, a backside as wide as his shoulders and an all-over indoor pudginess, he looks like a late-adolescent computer nerd," writes Andy Beckett in 1994. Michael Coffey calls him "an enigma dressed like a schlemiel" (1992), and Elisabeth Sherwin in 1993 describes him as looking like "a well-groomed street person."

Vollmann certainly leans into the making of his own myth, encouraging a tableau of talking points, at the center of which is the death by drowning of his six-year-old sister Julie, under his neglectful watch at age nine at a New Hampshire Pond. This event is arguably the Vollmann foundational myth. Vollmann tells this story over and over: in an early recounting it is a "tortured" moment in the conversation, beset by embarrassment and discomfort, but with Vollmann "gamely" admitting his role in her death, as Coffey writes in 1992. There are two other Vollmann sisters, Ann Louise and Sarah Reed, but we don't hear much about them in his writing or interviews. When Vollmann asks Hannah Jakobsen in 2017 what the saddest event in her life is, after her answer he brings up Julie's death. It is clearly a touchstone he still returns to.

Some of the best interviews here are when the interviewer spends some quality time with Vollmann, getting a more rounded portrait of the writer in his element, in the daily life of Sacramento. A fan-like quality, or awe, permeates some of the pieces, pointing to Vollmann's cult following. Alexander Laurence and Michael Hemmingson's contributions give valuable glimpses into Vollmann negotiating private/public boundaries and a picture of the writer in public; David Boratav and Stephen Heyman's show what it's like to be invited into Vollmann's spaces and hang out with "Bill."

It also must be noted that the category of "Conversations with William T. Vollmann" cuts both ways: Vollmann is of course a journalist and an interviewer, which means there is a whole other parallel field in existence of interviews *by* Vollmann: conversations in which he is the interviewer, not the interviewee. Additionally, Vollmann often turns the tables on his interviewer and starts asking questions, like when he asks Tom McIntyre in 1993 whether *he* has ever been to a prostitute. Vollmann is quite frequently commended by those featuring him for appearing to take genuine interest in their thoughts, treating the encounter not passively, but as a genuine conversation between two people.

As Vollmann becomes less of an edgelord outsider and more of a known quantity and accepted literary writer, coverage becomes less sensationalistic, though certain tropes endure: the George Costanza-like image of Vollmann sleeping under the desk at his Silicon Valley programmer job; his relationship with sex workers and his idea that we are all prostitutes; how he separates between his fiction and his nonfiction, his journalism, his truth-telling, his photography, his storytelling, and his art; the matter of his putting himself in harm's way in the service of his writing, and the question of whether he has a death wish. We witness Vollmann's ability to enter in and out of worlds, to cross the barriers and divides, imaginary, willed, or imposed between humans, and do his part to break them down and question their existence. What emerges across these conversations is a hopeful picture of a writer's life from youthful isolation and alienation, toward an endless outward reach. In 2001, not long after 9/11, Vollmann has this to say to Paul Hunter:

It is so wonderful that in life there are so many things a person can do to go into darkness and discover something new. I remember in my twenties I was really depressed for a while. I thought well, the law of gravity is not going to change, all the human beings are going to look about the same and they'll have the same respiratory functions. Really, it is going to be a very boring life. Fortunately, I was so wrong. I think one of the great things about reading literature or, for that matter, writing it is that you can enter all kinds of new worlds. The more you read and the more you write, the more you discover and the more it becomes really possible to appreciate a lot of things.

A note on the cover photo: it is by Larry McCaffery, who writes,

It was taken in early January 2003 while Bill was conducting research for *Imperial*. Bill is standing amidst the rugged Pichacho Peak Wilderness Area, located on the eastern side of Imperial Valley, not far from the Colorado River. As always, Bill had brought along his trusty notebook, which he used to draw sketches and jot down descriptions, notes, and impressions that he would enter into his laptop every evening. We had driven twenty or thirty miles along a rough dirt road when winter clouds began gathering, producing the ominous, spectacular light-conditions you see in the photo; as is usual in Imperial Valley, though, the clouds never delivered any rain. As I recall, the specific reason we stopped here was to examine traces of one of the many abandoned mines in the area. The photo certainly brings back fond memories from the many trips I did with Bill around Imperial Valley: there's something about Bill's "fierce" expression, and the rugged setting, that seems to capture something essential about Bill.

Finally, I would like to thank Mark Amerika, Eric Allen Been, Madison Smartt Bell, Justin Berton, Tom Bettridge and Miriam-Leah Hess at *032C*, Tom Bissell, David Boratav, Sylvain Bourmeau, Laurie Bouthillier, R.V. Branham, Kate Braverman, Ben Bush, Kevin Cascell and Jeffrey Fuccillo, Christi Cassidy at *Publisher's Weekly*, Carson Chan, Jimmy Cline, Peter Cobus, Christopher K. Coffman for his invaluable research skills, Dennis Cooper, Heather Corcoran, Debbie Davis at the *Davis Enterprise*, Max DeNike at the *San Francisco Examiner*, Sandy Dibbell, Tony DuShane, Andrew Ervin, Joe Fassler, Isabel Flower and Lidija Haas and Emmanuel Olunkwa at *Bookforum/Artforum*, Liz Fried, Lauren R. Fritz, Aaron Gilbreath, Dave Gilson and Mitch Grummon at *Mother Jones*, Michelle Goldberg, Ted Hamilton, Ted Hamm, Larry Hays, David Hershkovits at *Paper Magazine*, Stephen Heyman, Ron Hogan, Barney Hoskyns at *Rock's Backpages*, Nicholas Hune-Brown, Paul Hunter, Lisa Iacobellis and Eric Johnson and Geoffrey D. Smith and all the staff at the Rare Books and Manuscripts Library at Ohio State

University, Eric J. Iannelli, Hannah Jakobsen, Mary Heath and Katie Keene and Laura Strong at University Press of Mississippi for all their help and patience, Ewa Kern-Jedrychowska, Jillian Kestenbaum at *Salon*, Steve Kettmann, Karen Klaber at the *East Bay Monthly*, Alexander Laurence, Eric Lorberer at *Rain Taxi Review of Books*, Chris Maccini at *Willow Springs*, D.T. Max, Larry McCaffery for all his help and support, Max McClure, Brian McHale, David Myer at the *New Republic*, Timothy O'Grady, Paul Oldfield, Jill Owens at Powell's Books, Derek Peck, Laila Pedro at *Brooklyn Rail*, Allen Pierleoni at the *Sacramento Bee*, Steven Ross, Jordan Rothacker, Terri Saul, Donna Seaman, Lindley Sico at Vox Media, Michael Silverblatt at KCRW, Bardia Sinaee at *Literary Review of Canada*, David Streitfeld, Cary Tennis, Alex Thiltges, Matt Thorne, William T. Vollmann for his help with the chronology, Fredrik Wandrup at *Dagbladet*, Sam Whiting at the *San Francisco Chronicle*, Samantha Winkelman at the *Daily Beast*, and Paul Wilner.

Chronology

1959   William Tanner Vollmann is born in Santa Monica, California on July 28 to Tanis Carol Vollmann (*née* Kvaal) and Thomas Edward Vollmann, who is at University of California, Los Angeles completing a PhD in business management; they live in the Westwood area.

1962   Sister Julie is born.

1964   The family moves to New Hampshire, Dartmouth College, where Thomas takes a job as assistant professor.

1965   Vollmann begins writing at age six. His first works are science fiction space adventures.

1967   Sister Ann Louise is born.

1968   Julie drowns in New Hampshire pond, while nine-year-old Vollmann is meant to be watching her—an event which will profoundly mark his writing.

1969   Family spends time in Italy during father's sabbatical year.

1970   Sister Sarah Reed is born.

1971   Thomas accepts post at the University of Rhode Island. Vollmann attends Kingston Junior High.

1974   Thomas accepts post at Indiana University, family moves to Bloomington, Indiana. Vollmann attends Bloomington High School and at age sixteen audits classes at Indiana University and works at the Indiana Youth Service Bureau. In high school Vollmann joins the staff of the school newspaper and becomes reporter and literary editor. He is a SAT National Merit Finalist and receives his school's Founder's Day Award for academic excellence.

1977   Graduates high school and is accepted to Deep Springs College, where he discovers Ludwig Wittgenstein. Begins autobiographical work *Introduction to the Memoirs*.

1978   At Deep Springs Vollmann serves as student body president and chairman of the Deep Springs Committee to Institute Coeducation by Whatever Devious Means May Be Necessary. Is founder and editor of literary journal *The*.

1979   Reads Danilo Kiš's *A Tomb for Boris Davidovich*. Graduates from Deep Springs. Makes first trip to Alaska. Enrolls at Cornell University as a comparative literature major and begins living at the Telluride House, to which he presents the speech "Deep Springs: An Anti-Nunnian View."

1980   Takes part in an anti-nuclear protest in Seabrook, New Hampshire.

1981   Graduates BA summa cum laude from Cornell, with a thesis on Canto XIX of Dante's *Purgatorio*, Deconstruction, and the Seabrook anti-nuclear protests. Accepts a fellowship from the graduate program in comparative literature at the University of California, Berkeley. Moves to San Francisco and defers his fellowship. Works as a secretary at a reinsurance company for eight months, saving up money to go to Afghanistan.

1982   Starts writing the essay that will become *Rising Up and Rising Down*. In May departs for Afghanistan to help Mujahedeen rebels in their fight against the Soviets. After six weeks, returns to the US. Begins draft of what will become *You Bright and Risen Angels*. In the fall begins as a comparative literature PhD student at Berkeley.

1983   In the summer hitchhikes to Fairbanks, Alaska with a friend, and in the fall drops out of Berkeley. Begins job as door to door canvasser for about six months.

1984   Begins writing *Wordcraft*, a writing manual, buys his first gun, and meets photographer Ken Miller, with whom he begins to explore San Francisco. Takes a job as a computer programmer at NCA Corporation in Silicon Valley, where he writes the bulk of *You Bright and Risen Angels*.

1985   *You Bright and Risen Angels* acquired by Esther Whitby at André Deutsch (UK). Formulates concept for *Seven Dreams: A Book of North American Landscapes*. Begins *The Rainbow Stories*.

1987   Vollmann visits Iceland, Greenland, and Baffin Island. Debut novel *You Bright and Risen Angels* is published and gains critical attention. Receives Ludwig Volgenstein Foundation Inc. grant for *The Ice-Shirt*. Moves to Manhattan, living in a one-bedroom apartment near Memorial Sloan Kettering Hospital, while girlfriend Janice Kong-Ja Ryu does her residency in radiation oncology. Vollmann lives there for three years, and becomes friends with Jonathan Franzen.

1988   Is one of ten recipients of the fourth Whiting Writers' Award of $25,000. Travels to Cornwallis Island, Canada for *Fathers and Crows*.

1989   *The Rainbow Stories* published in UK by André Deutsch and in US by Atheneum. Receives Shiva Naipaul Memorial Prize for "Amortortak" (*The Ice-Shirt*). Travels to Baffin Island.

1990   *The Ice-Shirt* published by André Deutsch and Viking Penguin.

1991   Travels to Magnetic North Pole. *Whores for Gloria* published by Picador (UK). *Thirteen Stories and Thirteen Epitaphs* published by André Deutsch. Starts CoTangent Press to publish limited edition and book art objects. Travels to Cambodia on assignment for *Esquire*.

1992   *Fathers and Crows* published by Deutsch and Viking, *An Afghanistan Picture Show* published by Farrar, Strauss and Giroux. Produces "The Yugoslavian Notes" for BBC Radio 4, "a four-part series in which writer William T. Vollmann offers his views on the debacle in Yugoslavia."

1993   *Butterfly Stories* published by Deutsch and Grove Press. Vollmann is interviewed by Larry McCaffery for a "Younger Authors" special issue of *Review of Contemporary Fiction*. Travels to Somalia for *Esquire*, to Kenya and Madagascar, to Thailand and Burma for *Spin*, to Sarajevo for *Los Angeles Times*. Moves to Sacramento.

1994   *The Rifles* published by Viking. In Bosnia on assignment for *Spin*, Vollmann is involved in a roadside attack, which claims the lives of Bryan Brinton and Francis William Tomasic, who were accompanying him.

1996   *The Atlas* published by Viking. Marries Janice Ryu in St. Helena, California. Travels to Cambodia for *Spin*, and to Jamaica for *Gear*. First visit to Imperial County, California.

1997   Begins train-hopping as research for *The Royal Family*. Wins PEN/Hemingway Award for *The Atlas*.

1998   Finishes *Rising Up and Rising Down*. Travels to Iraq, Kosovo, Japan. Daughter Lisa Kirsten Vollmann born.

1999   Visits Columbine High School, Colorado, Nevada escorts, the Californian-Mexican border, and Colombia for *Gear*, Nunavut for *Outside*.

2000   *The Royal Family* published by Viking. Interviewed by Madison Smartt Bell for *Paris Review*'s "Art of Fiction."

2001   Returns to Afghanistan for the *New Yorker*. *Argall* published by Viking.

2003 *Rising Up and Rising Down* released by McSweeney's in a seven volume edition of 3,500 at $120. Is hit by a car cycling in Sacramento, breaks his pelvis, and is hospitalized. Spends a month in Berlin researching *Europe Central.*

2004 Suffers a stroke and a series of smaller strokes; later in the year HarperCollins/Ecco publishes condensed version of *Rising Up and Rising Down.*

2005 *Europe Central* published by Viking. It wins National Book Award for fiction.

2006 *Uncentering the Earth: Copernicus and the Revolutions of the Heavenly Spheres* published by Atlas Books.

2007 *Poor People* published by Ecco. In November 2007, the American Academy of Arts and Letters awards Vollmann the Harold and Maude Strauss Living Award of $250,000, in five yearly $50,000 installments.

2008 *Riding Toward Everywhere* published by Ecco.

2009 *Imperial* published by Viking. A companion book of photographs is published by powerHouse Books. Father Thomas dies.

2010 *Kissing the Mask* published by Ecco.

2011 Publishes his first ebook, *Into the Forbidden Zone: A Trip Through Hell and High Water in Post-Earthquake Japan* (Byliner).

2013 Publishes the article "Life as a Terrorist" in *Harper's Magazine* about his experience being suspected by the FBI of being the Unabomber. *The Book of Dolores* published by powerHouse Books.

2014 *Last Stories and Other Stories* published by Penguin.

2015 *The Dying Grass* published by Viking.

2017 French theatrical production of *The Royal Family—La Famille royale* by Thierry Jolivet.

2018 *Carbon Ideologies, No Immediate Danger: Volume One* and *No Good Alternative: Volume Two* published by Viking.

2019 Receives treatment for colon cancer. Visits Berlin for research. Publishes the article "Just Keep Going North" in *Harper's Magazine* about the US/Mexico border.

2020 *The Lucky Star* published by Viking.

Conversations with
William T. Vollmann

Under the Rainbow

Jonathan Coe/1989

From *The Guardian*, 3 February, 1989 © *The Guardian*. Reprinted by permission.

William Vollmann is a writer who likes to do his homework, even if it means being shot at. It's a dirty job, he tells Jonathan Coe.

Until now, William T. Vollmann, a charming, somewhat nervous twenty-nine-year-old American has been best known in this country for his enormous first novel *You Bright and Risen Angels*. It's been described as "a vast, mad, sprawling book," which is a literary critic's way of saying that you'll be lucky to finish it. In any case, it's well and truly eclipsed by his latest work, *The Rainbow Stories*—a collection largely made up of interviews with prostitutes, skinheads, derelicts, and drug addicts—which is not only a more accessible book but a far more daring and experimental one.

Vollmann himself describes it as "gloomy and in parts disgusting." His intention, he says, was to provide "some kind of an open window into a series of different worlds"—or, as his own blurb puts it, to write stories which will "forge a fragile link between people programmed to hate or ignore each other." And the only way it could be done, he decided, was by meticulous research: living with these people, befriending them, winning their trust. A daunting task, he agrees.

"What I do requires a sort of radical vulnerability. At first when I was doing the prostitute thing, since I was very nervous and really afraid of the pimps and drug dealers (in fact I got shot at by one of the pimps once) I would bring someone else with me. But then I found out that this might be more safe, but it completely defeated my object."

Vollmann found that with most of his subjects he could be perfectly honest about what he wanted: they believed him when he said that he was a writer, and they were usually prepared to talk. But when he started interviewing prostitutes in San Francisco, the enterprise became more problematic.

"With the prostitutes sometimes I couldn't be honest, because they were so used to making sure they didn't give away anything for free. So I sometimes had to act like a customer: like some kind of pervert that is aroused by stories. Otherwise they wouldn't trust me. So I'd make them take off their clothes, and maybe put a handcuff around their ankles or something, and then I'd sit there in the corner with my tape recorder and write everything down."

This explains the series of laconic footnotes which pepper Vollmann's text, in which he adds up the number of dollars which each of the prostitutes' stories have cost him. It's typical of the book's bleak, bitter humor, which tends to sharpen rather than dilute the prevailing tone of anger. Vollmann's narratives—pithy, fragmented, and often brutal—always elevate his subject matter.

"When you're writing you develop this video camera and you use it to invade other people's privacy—hopefully with their consent. It's a dirty job, just like being a prostitute. I'm no different. I try to exclude whatever would hurt other people or would hurt me, but I can't always exclude what's embarrassing to me, because I want to be honest."

In this respect he sees *The Rainbow Stories* as being an advance on his first novel: the narrator gives away more of himself in this book, whereas *You Bright and Risen Angels* "was a fiction. It's like some covert CIA operation—it's all ultimately very deniable."

At twenty-nine, Vollmann has two huge books to his name, plus a forthcoming travel volume about Afghanistan, plus another, unpublished novel, which carries the prostitution theme to such extremes ("It describes the worst and loneliest and most repugnant aspects") that neither his English nor American publishers will touch it. And that's not all. He's also at work on a sequence of seven novels which will tell the history of the relations between Native Americans and European colonists, starting in the eleventh century. He hopes to finish this project (which is called *Seven Dreams*) at the age of about forty or forty-five.

The first volume, *The Ice-Shirt*, will re-tell the story of the Norse landings in Newfoundland and Nova Scotia. The second, *Fathers and Crows*, is about French Jesuits in Canada in the seventeenth century. The sixth (which is already well-advanced) will describe what happened when repeating rifles were introduced into the Arctic. You will realize by now we're dealing with an extraordinary and ambitious writer, whose energy and commitment to his work seem boundless. I asked him whether he felt that other writers weren't a little lazy by comparison.

"I think there's too much easy writing, yes," he says gravely. "I see a lack of research and also a lack of balance. For instance, in a lot of narratives that are coming out now about Europeans and Indians, just as a hundred years ago such books would have portrayed the Indians as ignorant, bloodthirsty savages, now they're quick to idealize the Indians and say that Europeans are all imperialists and exploiters. But it's not that simple, and everyone deserves his chance to be portrayed as an individual as well as a member of a group. Everyone has some virtue as an individual."

This is the political creed which lies behind all Vollmann's writing and which gives it its undeniable integrity. Many of the skinheads he worked with were, he found, "very nice, warm, kind people," and such is his generosity of spirit that he's even prepared to believe the same of the rich.

"I'm attracted to anything extreme, because I believe that sometimes the extreme case will demonstrate the general case. I would love to write stories about millionaires too."

So what's stopping him?

"I just haven't met any."

Parallel Lives

Paul Oldfield/1989

From *Melody Maker*, February 11, 1989. © Paul Oldfield. Reprinted by permission.

William T. Vollmann is the author of The Rainbow Stories, *a startling new exposé of the blinkered way we live our lives. Paul Oldfield asks him what it was like to live with tramps, take his chances with skinheads, and liaise with whores.*

William T. Vollmann is the author of two fabulously compendious books. *You Bright and Risen Angels* was his alternative history of the world—a labyrinthine fable in "cartoon" idiom that describes a global struggle between "revolutionary" insects and the "reactionary" guardians of the national electricity grid, with the front-line action propelled by the old rivalries between members of a secondary school swimming team. It's all crazy ziggurats of conspiracy and terror, and sentences that switchback between different worlds, narrators, and eras. In fact, it's somewhere between *Gravity's Rainbow*, William Burroughs, *Tristram Shandy* and the Frank Chickens performing *The Decline and Fall of the Roman Empire*.

His new novel, *The Rainbow Stories*, is something else altogether. This time, there's just a succession of different, hard-edged texts that hardly meet up anywhere. There's an oral history of San Francisco's skinheads, an hour spent in the lobby of a large hospital, the hallucinatory tale of a fetishist's romance with a green dress, the true stories off prostitutes, pimps, murderers, vagrants, terrorists, and pathologists, a new version of a Bible story, a chapter on the Indian Assassins, and much more, all just coordinated according to the colors of the rainbow.

This is hardly fiction any longer. *The Rainbow Stories* plunges from one world straight into another, all of them equally real, without any story or Pynchonesque cryptic plots. All Vollmann claims for it is that, "Everything is TRUE."

"There are these different worlds out there. Every group of people thinks their world is the *whole* world: it's absolutely true for them. And all these groups are hermetically sealed. It didn't matter which kinds of people I wrote about. It could have been millionaires and accountants instead of prostitutes and tramps. In every case, it's as if the light's being bent by gravitation so that they can never get to see anything outside their own little circle. What I'd like more than anything would be if these little worlds could see each other. But there's not much hope of it."

There isn't much hope at all in *The Rainbow Stories*. The novel's full of characters who want to exclude, purge or exorcise something. Like the skinheads defending racial purity. Or the Nazis in the true account of the holocaust in Poland.

"People are repulsive, literally, when they're in the mass or group. And I've never met anybody without prejudice. Sartre once said, 'Two people form a community by excluding a third.' It's a shame, but that's how it is.

"In my book, though, you can see different lives. One thing books can do is to give people a window into other worlds without them being threatened with a punch in the face because they don't know the rules of that world. Sometimes I was threatened when I adventured into other people's lives.

"I was talking to a whore who couldn't understand what I was up to. She ran off with my money. Well, that's all right, it's a story in itself. But later she saw me, still in the same bar, writing my notes. She thought I must be a policeman, so her pimp ambushed me. I could have run away, but I'd have been disgusted with myself. I walked, and luckily he only shot at me once. Scary, though.

"The skinheads were fine. Tolerant. They mostly respected me when I let them see the story. I enjoyed my time with them. But it was hard living with the street alcoholics. You got fleas, and had to drink this awful booze, and shake hands with people whose hands are always covered in shit. They don't have toilet paper. But the ones with any of their brains left unrotted are interesting, screwed up in interesting ways.

"It's good that my readers can experience it without any of the fears. If I've made it possible for them to look at a stinking, foul-mouthed tramp and see a human being, perhaps give him a few pence, then I've achieved something."

But the novel doesn't seem to encourage greater understanding so much as the gratification of hearing and seeing true stories. It reminds me of J. G. Ballard's science fiction: just methodical permutations of accident and destruction, with no message unless it's that there's nothing to say or feel any longer.

"So you think that my book's just titillating, a pornography of atrocity? Hmmm. At the end I say that the bottom line is that something that comforts a newborn baby is more useful technology than a war machine. But reading about characters in a book is always voyeurism, I guess."

Is it possible to be anything but a forensic spectator with the world on the dissecting table?

"In *The Rainbow Stories*, there *is* a character who knows how to live. When the killer asks his tramp victims what they most want in the world, they all ask, in one way or another, for death: one man just wants his feet to stop itching forever, another one wants never to be hassled again. But there's a woman who says that she simply wants to go on living with all the good friends she's already got. The killer can't hurt her. He's the worst off of all the characters because he's schizophrenic, he can't even live properly in one world or one persona. But the woman can.

"If I had to sum up, I'd say that, although there are other worlds all around, you *have* to think your own is more important or true than the others. That's how you remain sane."

With William Vollmann, you can live in all worlds. But one at a time.

Night Writer: Leading Readers to the Darkness at the Edge of Town

Cary Tennis / 1992

From *The East Bay Monthly*, June 1992. Reprinted by permission.

In the novel *Whores for Gloria* a man named Jimmy wanders around San Francisco's Tenderloin district, trying to quilt the rags of his tattered past into a fabric he can call his life.

Jimmy is in a bad way. The Vietnam War wrecked him long ago. His only happiness is a girl named Gloria and she's gone. He pays prostitutes to talk to him. While they talk he hallucinates about Gloria. But it doesn't work. He buys hair from whores and pretends it's Gloria's. He drinks a lot. Nothing works. He just ends up a bad-smelling guy, a nuisance, a loud bore no bar wants.

At the end of the book Gloria blows Jimmy away with a .38 outside a Chinese restaurant. Jimmy's Vietnam buddy, Code Six, tells how it happens: "You know, gunfire has a distinct sound to it. Once you hear it in a combat situation, no, you'll never forgit it. And I look up, man I look around—I'm kinda jittery; only been back in the States about maybe ten or twenty years, still got that shit on my mind—I hear *gunfire*, and I know it. I turn around, man, and here comes Jimmy with his whore chasin' him. Usually were the other way around weren't it? Damn. And she *drilled* his motherfuckin' ass, *good* and *proper* . . . And that was how Jimmy died. Died like a hero."

"Writers are always selling somebody out," wrote Joan Didion in *Slouching Towards Bethlehem*. In *Whores for Gloria*, William Vollmann walks the narrow line between exploiting and being exploited. To research the novel, he spent much of the eighties befriending skinheads, prostitutes, and homeless people.

"It wasn't that I was studying them like bugs," he said recently. "It was that I didn't know what they were about. I sort of wanted to see what was going on. I didn't just want to understand them as phenomena; I wanted to know them as people."

While working on *Whores for Gloria*, Vollmann was living in San Francisco's Sunset district and commuting to the Tenderloin. "I used to just take MUNI down there all the time at night and just walk around. Sometimes I'd go down there in the daytime also. And it was actually very strange to be down there and come back to the Sunset. It was so totally different. It was almost a strain to do it."

In the beginning, Vollmann would formally introduce himself as a writer, but he found that approach was counterproductive. "It would intimidate people," he said. "When I was first trying to break into the prostitute scene in the Tenderloin, basically what I did was I'd go down and I'd give those ladies money to talk to me and tell me what it was all about for them. Looking back on it now, I'd say it was a good start, but I've come a long way since then. That kind of story, that sort of reportage, I don't think is really the right way to make something."

Over time, Vollmann evolved a more subtle method. "I think the best way is to go into a situation leaving yourself completely vulnerable. Don't expect to go in there and write about anything the first time. Go in there and try to become these people's friend. Try and figure out what they're all about and let them figure out what you're all about. Then when you know 'em, you can bring your notebook or your tape recorder or whatever you're going to do, and try to learn something from them. And then once you've finished, I think it's very important to show them what you've done, and then continue to spend time with them, so they don't feel that you were just down there exploiting them."

Vollmann showed his story "The Blue Wallet" (from his collection, *The Rainbow Stories*) to the skinheads. "Actually, it was very scary because it said some good things about them as people and it said some bad things about them as skinheads and I was kind of worried." Although some of the skinheads objected, none attacked him physically.

There is no laughing at the people in Vollmann's work, no cheap jokes, or making fun. We may laugh when a pimp named Spider cuts his own wife's hair off and sells it to Jimmy for $125 so he can have a wig to put on a whore—who later throws it down the sewer—but we don't sense that the author is laughing at them. In fact, *Whores for Gloria* veritably aches with compassion. In a complicated way, that steadfast compassion is the bedrock of Vollmann's dark art.

His first novel, *You Bright and Risen Angels* (1987), was characterized by the *New York Times Book Review* as a "large, sprawling, disorderly book—it even includes drawings by the author—that operates on many levels and suggests many interpretations." The book is about insects joining forces to battle humans—the inventors of electricity—for world domination. It follows Bug, a young man who joins the revolutionary insects, through his travels in South America, Alaska, the Midwest, and San Francisco. The book is a bewildering maze of diverse entertainments, but once you become accustomed to Vollmann's voice, things fall into place. But his voice—what is his voice? Many reviewers compared the book to Thomas Pynchon's *Gravity's Rainbow*.

"I hadn't read Gravity's Rainbow until after I'd written *You Bright and Risen Angels*," says Vollmann, "and I think that *You Bright and Risen Angels* is better than *Gravity's Rainbow*. In some ways I guess I can see the comparison because Pynchon writes long books, the syntax is often involved, but I think that my style is a bit darker than Pynchon's, I think my sentences are better, and I think my characters are better."

Vollmann was born in L.A. in 1959, but he grew up in New Hampshire, Rhode Island and Indiana. After graduating *summa cum laude* from Cornell in comparative literature, he went abroad, but not on vacation.

"I followed some Afghan mujahedin across the border into Afghanistan during the middle of the civil war," he said. (Nearly ten years in the making, an account of the experience, *An Afghanistan Picture Show*, will be published next month.) Vollmann recently returned from Thailand and Cambodia with a new set of experiences: "I found out that you're never supposed to touch the top of people's heads or point at them with your feet. Because the top of your head is a sacred place, the highest part of you, and your feet are the lowest part of you, so to pat a child's head would be a terrible insult. And all the beggars, the paralyzed ones that crawl around, have to make sure that their toes are pointing behind them as they drag themselves along, otherwise they'd be making people unclean. It was the same kind of thing with the Tenderloin. It's just a different world down in the TL."

Vollmann is also a painter, and with sculptor Matthew Heckert he produced *The Convict Bird: A Children's Poem*. Bound in a quarter-inch steel plate with padlock and hand-forged hasp, the book has a hatch cover that swings open to reveal a convict's face peering from the darkness of a cell window. The book also features a ribbon of barbed wire, brass, and light-gauge chain, tasseled with hair bought from a street prostitute. There are ten volumes, each one numbered by the author. Priced upwards of $750, a portion of the sales will benefit a woman in prison.

Vollmann may be obsessed with the dark side, but he said he just wants to do a good job as an artist: "I love seeing things and trying to write as beautifully as I can, and I enjoy learning from people. And I feel lucky that I can make a living doing it, and I'm happy that some people read my books and get something out of them. I wouldn't say I have any strong message that I'm trying to force down anyone's throat, but I do love to write about people my readers might not meet or might overlook or might be repulsed by or might be afraid of. That way I figure maybe they can learn something too."

William T. Vollmann: The Prolific Young Author Takes a Walk on the Wild Side—of Life and History

Michael Coffey / 1992

From *Publishers Weekly*, July 13, 1992. © PWxyz LLC, Publishers Weekly. Used by permission.

"I'd say the biggest hope that we have right now is the AIDS epidemic," offers William Vollmann, sipping from a glass of dark rum in his living room in a quiet section of Sacramento, California. "Maybe the best thing that could happen would be if it were to wipe out half or two-thirds of the people in the world. Then the ones who survived would just be so busy getting things together that they'd have to help each other, and in time maybe the world would recover ecologically, too."

Vollmann delivers this startling observation in a languid, deceptive drawl, like a pitcher with a slow, deliberate windup blazing a fastball by your eyes. You look closer to see just who this guy is, but his features recede in a haze of blandness. In person, the prolific young writer—at thirty-two he has published seven books of fiction and nonfiction, three of them in the last four months—is unprepossessing and somewhat odd. His bearing is distorted, or distorting: he seems wider in the hips than at the shoulders (perhaps an occupational hazard of the writing life) and looks taller for it, narrowing toward the top; behind glasses, his right eye has a bleary cast to it, and his complexion is that of a fifteen-year-old. He sports a moth-eaten mustache and his sandy-colored hair looks unwashed. In conversation, he is gentle and considerate, but one gathers that his informal uhmmms . . . and wells . . . are the ways his lightning intelligence brakes for pedestrians. In blue jeans, sneakers, and a madras shirt, this man who has written about everything from San Francisco's Tenderloin district to the impoverishments of Peshawar to the ravages of seventeenth-century Canada is an enigma dressed like a schlemiel.

Vollmann is ostensibly holding forth about his latest novel, *Fathers and Crows*, just out from Viking. But inevitably, his observations widen and address the larger historical themes of his *Seven Dreams* series, of which *Fathers and Crows* is the second installment. Having tracked the violent journeys of various Icelanders to Newfoundland in the first Dream, *The Ice-Shirt* (Viking, 1990), and then researched and reimagined the missionary efforts of Jesuit priests in Canada in *Fathers and Crows*, "the Young Man," as he sometimes refers to himself in his books, has seen enough of human foibles to call down the scourge of AIDS on all of mankind in hopes of setting something aright.

"The only times people really get along is if they're united against a common enemy," he calmly observes. "Perhaps that's what Sartre meant when he said, 'Two people can form a community by excluding a third.' The Huron," he says, referring to the Indian nation backed by the French in a war against the Mohawk, a conflict pitilessly described in *Fathers and Crows*, "were no better than we are. The reason they didn't have the equivalent of drive-by shootings and riots is because they had the luxury of this continuous blood feud that had gone on for as long as they could remember. So every summer they would go down and catch people who were not members of their particular nation. They'd bring 'em back and torture 'em to death and really make 'em suffer horribly, and everyone would just have the greatest time watching them die, and all the community hostility would be turned outward upon that one unfortunate person."

If Vollmann sounds a bit inured to violence, perhaps he is. He has surely made a study of it. He spent several months living among neo-Nazi "skinheads" in San Francisco, and gave a stirring account of the experience in his collection *The Rainbow Stories* (Atheneum, 1988). He maintains a "professional interest" in prostitution—visiting whores and brothels in the Far East, Mexico and many ports of call in the US, gleaning the tales of a streetwalker's life that inform his masterful novella *Whores for Gloria* (Pantheon), the first of his three books published this year (from three different publishers). And, just out of college, Vollmann "made a trip to a battlefield" after convincing Afghani rebels to take him behind the lines during the early months of the Russian occupation, which ordeal he turned into *An Afghanistan Picture Show*, published last month by Farrar, Straus & Giroux.

How did this young man—the product of a stable if peripatetic American family, an honors graduate of Cornell—come to be so widely published, all without benefit of an agent? From the outlines of his life's tale, the answer seems to lie in a mixture of genius, vaunted ambition and fierce self-reliance.

Vollmann was born in Los Angeles and lived there until the age of five, when his family moved to Hanover, N.H., where his father taught business at Dartmouth. The family later moved to Rhode Island and then to Indiana, where Vollmann went to high school. Vollmann supplies these details graciously but with disinterest, as if he were talking about a person he has only reluctantly taken aboard. But a query about a personal revelation dropped into *Picture Show* (in which he prefaces a chilling tale of fording a swift and icy stream with a reference to the accidental drowning of his sister) draws a tortured response. "She drowned, yeah. Well, I was nine and she was six and she didn't know how to swim and I was supposed to be paying attention to her and I sort of forgot. The floor of the pond started out very shallow and just dropped off."

Vollmann seems almost embarrassed by the cloud of discomfort that besets the room. He gallantly moves to disperse it. "I went to college first at Deep Springs in California, in Death Valley. It's a weird, private place, sort of a whole story in itself. It was set up by the guy who pioneered alternating current, L. L. Nunn, in 1917. His idea was to create 'trustees of the nation.' He wanted to turn out this little elite leadership to go and take over the world, basically. There are a few minor twists to it—he was gay, probably, and it was an all-male school . . ."

"It is a working cattle ranch and the students run the ranch," he continues. "There are usually ten or twelve students. They send brochures to the boys who have SAT scores in the top one half of one percent and if you are accepted, everything is paid for. Nunn's idea was to 'develop the foundations of character' in this isolated desert valley the size of Manhattan. You're not supposed to see anyone else during the school year. Once you develop the foundations of character punching cows, then you go on to places like Telluride [Nunn set up schools within larger universities, where Deep Springers finish their schooling] at Cornell, where you play around with stocks and ballroom dancing. I liked Deep Springs; I didn't like Telluride."

Vollmann's first book, *You Bright and Risen Angels* (published by Deutsch in the UK and Atheneum in the US, and now a Penguin paperback) was about a school and master vaguely suggestive of Deep Springs and Nunn. The novel drew comparisons to the work of Pynchon and Burroughs— remarkably, considering that it had been plucked from a slush pile. "I don't believe in agents, nah. I sent *Angels* in '87 to a bunch of places. I hadn't [ever] published anything. André Deutsch in England was the only one interested at that time. They took it and they were just great to me and they've been great ever since. My advance for *Angels*, I think, was 12,500 [pounds]."

Deutsch has published all of Vollmann's work in the UK except *Whores for Gloria*, which Picador issued, and *Picture Show*, which has not appeared there. In fact, Deutsch has really been Vollmann's first publisher, selling American rights to Viking for *Ice-Shirt* and *Fathers and Crows*. Esther Whitby is his editor at Deutsch, "Although she hated *Fathers and Crows*," Vollmann adds with a mischievous squint. "But they had to take it. I had a two-book contract. But they wised-up after that. Now it's book by book."

Vollmann likes hard truths. Just as he gamely recounted his role in his sister's death, just as he understands the imperfectability of society ("If men learned anything, sons would be smarter than their fathers," observes the narrator of *Fathers and Crows*), he is resignedly circumspect about his publishing future.

"I'm at a tough time in my career: I'll either make it or I'll be out of it fairly soon. On the one hand I seem to be getting better known all the time—I get fan mail all over the place. I'm getting great reviews, and that's a good sign. On the other hand, my books don't sell in huge numbers, and it seems to me that most publishers today, particularly American publishers, are more anxious to sell in large numbers than they were ten or twenty years ago. I don't know how long they'll keep being patient."

Vollmann is not exactly pausing to see if he should continue writing. Viking has already accepted the Sixth Dream, called *The Rifles*—about the ill-fated Franklin expedition to the North Pole in 1933—and will publish it next year. *Thirteen Stories*, which is in the *Whores for Gloria* vein, is being brought out in the US by Fred Jordan at Pantheon in January (Deutsch has already published it in the UK). Vollmann wants John Glusman at FSG to see a "book-length essay on firearms" (Glusman, while at Atheneum, published *Angels* and *The Rainbow Stories*), and he has just finished *Butterfly Stories*, which Deutsch has bought and Pantheon is pondering.

Nor is Vollmann letting the hard truths of literary publishing dampen his hopes for *Fathers and Crows*. "In many ways I think this book is comparable to *War and Peace*. I'd like to see these books taught in history classes." Through the book's mixture of exhaustive research (the seventy-three volumes of Jesuit Relations, the writings of Ignatius of Loyola and the diaries of Samuel de Champlain are just a sampling of the source material) and imaginary characters weaving in and out of the past and present, Vollmann has aimed to create a "symbolic history . . . an account of origins and metamorphoses which is often untrue based on the literal facts as we know them, but whose untruths further a deeper sense of truth" [from the end notes to *Fathers and Crows*].

Vollmann is not the first to suggest that a mingling of fact and fiction is at the heart of history and art. After all, Herodotus was no mean dissembler, and Shakespeare disfigured a king or two. But it isn't so easy to recall writers who have blended the sacred and the profane in the manner that Vollmann has in all his books. In *Fathers and Crows*, Kateri Tekakwitha, a Huron woman who converted to Catholicism after encountering the missionary Jesuits—and now a candidate for canonization as a saint by the Church— walks through the novel as if with a message to deliver. At book's end, her previously smallpox-scarred face clear and beautiful, Kateri strides through the red-light district in modern-day Montreal with a priest at her side. Seeing scantily clad women huddling in the cold, she approaches them with the call of "sisters," reaching across centuries and cultures to make a bond.

"I'm fond of prostitutes," admits Vollmann, when asked about their prevalence in his work. "I love watching them pick guys up. It's beautiful, the various ballerina-like movements that they perform on the corner. I think that we're all prostitutes. We all do things that we otherwise wouldn't choose to do, for the sake of getting somewhere else. And there is nothing wrong with being a prostitute. I like to remind myself of that by looking at prostitutes and talking to them."

Asked about the identification of the venerable and holy Kateri with Montreal's ladies of the night, Vollmann doesn't hesitate. "On the one hand Kateri has prostituted herself—to the Jesuits. She is trying to become a French girl, something she is not. On another level, prostitutes are despised people, and as an Indian she is despised also. Thirdly, most of these Catholic priests were very haughty and perhaps overly moralistic, ready to expel someone for being a fornicator, or if necessary having them executed for adultery. A true Christianity, if it existed, would insist on the equality of all the people who lived."

Soon Vollmann will be off on another research trip, this time to Mexico. It no doubt will be a refreshing break from his sixteen-hour days at the computer or in libraries. "I need to make $30,000 a year or so on these books, that's all. The trips I can write off, mostly. When I go away, I take my notebook, and when I come back I've got pages and pages of great stuff to put in my computer, and it's fun, it never seems like work. I'm always enjoying myself."

In Parkman's Footsteps

D. T. Max / 1992

From *New York Newsday*, 26 July, 1992. © D.T. Max. Reprinted by permission.

Through the white pillared doorway of a clapboard house in neat, conservative Sacramento, California, a man with the pale akin of a graduate student and the unwashed flaxen hair of a computer nerd emerges. Wearing a crimson crewneck sweater despite the heat, black jeans, and black boots with bike clips, he looks like a refugee from San Francisco.

"Jan went to the Price Club," novelist William Vollmann says. Jan is Janice, Vollmann's girlfriend. Her job as a doctor at the local hospital explains his domicile, far from the hipper parts of the world. It was also because of Janice that Vollmann lived for three years in an apartment above Sloan-Kettering Hospital in Manhattan. "It was pretty weird for my friends to come up in those elevators full of white coats late at night," he remembers.

When Vollmann takes off his glasses, he has startling, wandering eyes. "I can only use one eye at a time," he says in the genial adolescent voice of the computer hacker. "When I was a boy it always made me self-conscious. Balls would hit me in the nose."

Vollmann's living room is also neat, lacking the cluttered intimacy of most writers' homes. A matching tan-and-white couch and chair dominate, and there are no bookcases to be seen. A thirty-four-CD boxed set of Scarlatti sonatas, the gift of a literary-magazine editor who is one of Vollmann's many benefactors, graces a cabinet containing the entertainment center. The only discordant note in the pleasant decor is struck by a copy of a magazine called *Special Weapons* on the coffee table. "The problem with my eyes is called strabismus. It's a minor handicap that makes me feel empathy for other people with minor handicaps," Vollmann says, "like pimps, whores and murderers."

At thirty-two, William Vollmann is certainly the most unconventional—and possibly also the most exciting and imaginative—novelist at work today.

Born in Los Angeles in 1959, he grew up there and in New England, the son of a business professor. He started college at a working cattle ranch called Deep Springs College in Death Valley but graduated summa cum laude in comparative literature from Cornell. From there he held odd jobs—from working in a reinsurance company to door-to-door canvasser. Since his first novel, the science fiction-inspired *You Bright and Risen Angels*, was published in 1987, everything Vollmann has written—the realistic *The Rainbow Stories* and *Whores for Gloria*, and the first of his multivolume *Seven Dreams* historical series, *The Ice-Shirt*—has caught pigeonholing critics off guard.

Two more books of his are coming out this month: *Fathers and Crows* (Viking), a second installment of the massive *Seven Dreams* cycle, which he calls a symbolic history of the North American continent; and *An Afghanistan Picture Show: Or, How I Saved the World* (Farrar, Straus & Giroux), a nonfiction account of a one-month trip he took in aid of the Afghans who were fighting the Soviet Union.

This latter was a 1982 adventure that mostly consisted of sitting in the Pakistani gate city of Peshawar, battling dysentery, beggars, and exiled Afghanis who had the misconception that Vollmann could get Washington to intervene militarily. Vollmann remembers, "I was hoping to do all these Lawrence of Arabia antics. I was pretty young. *An Afghanistan Picture Show* is sort of a cautionary tale about how you have to be careful when you think you know how things are."

The *Seven Dreams* project is something else altogether: an impressionistic, exhaustively researched record of the North American continent from the invasion of the Vikings (narrated in *The Ice-Shirt*) to the seventh volume, which will be set in the 1980s. Vollmann works on all the installments simultaneously. *Fathers and Crows* takes up the winding thread with the competition among the French Jesuits, the fur trappers, the French nationalists and their Indian allies to shape the fate of Canada in the seventeenth century. "I spent a lot of time walking the Quebec woods looking at frozen waterfalls," Vollmann remembers, "until I started having the same oppressive feeling these men who came from French cities would have felt."

The only work the *Seven Dreams* even vaguely resembles is the highly colored, exhaustively visualized North American narratives of nineteenth-century Boston historian Francis Parkman. "One of the characters in the book I'm happiest with is [the explorer Samuel de] Champlain. But I could give myself more license than Parkman could. I would read Champlain's writings until I understood what his sentence structure and his preoccupations were. Then I would crib his sentences and put them in his [character's] mouth."

The resulting work owes as much to Werner Herzog's *Aguirre, the Wrath of God* as it does to Parkman. It is a brooding, frightened, pitch-perfect narrative: "I tried to write in the manner of the time, this time in florid French-style prose." The battle for North America turns history into a competition between superstition and pettiness.

"I have six more underway with four publishers," Vollmann says at first. But later he changes his mind. "I've got so many I'm not really sure."

It is upstairs in his study that Vollmann feels at home. The centerpiece is a 40-megabyte hard-drive computer. About computers Vollmann is always enthusiastic. On his return from Afghanistan he composed *You Bright and Risen Angels* at night, sleeping under his desk at a software company in Silicon Valley. "It's all right to be a little eccentric there," he remembers. Computers permeate his fiction: The world of *You Bright and Risen Angels* is generated by a computer, and the characters are computer data sets. "What's it about? I'll give you two choices: It's about bugs and electricity and it's a catalog of various modes of failed and perverted love."

Perverted love is also the theme of *Whores for Gloria*, a novel, and *The Rainbow Stories*. Both these books explore Vollmann's ongoing fascination with prostitutes. "Prostitutes encapsulate everything that's interesting about life: sex, money, freedom, bravery, adventure, and death. They're not the seamy ones. I find [ordinary] life seamy. I worked for six months in that reinsurance company saving money to go to Afghanistan. I can't bear to think of all those people still there spending all that time doing that. I can't help it. I love prostitutes. I love them more and more." Vollmann estimates that he has slept with thirty prostitutes, and says he continues his research both in life and in literature.

Like the poet / visionary William Blake, he is a visual artist too. His remarkable drawings festoon his novels and also find their way into the extraordinary publications of his CoTangent Press. CoTangent's books are physically and textually identical. For instance, to read a poem from a woman imprisoned for attempted murder the reader has to open a cold rolled-steel cover secured by a rough-hewn lock out of a Poe story. "Another book is a short story about prostitutes called *The Happy Girls*. The book is supposed to look like a massage parlor. There's a mirror on the front and a handle like a door. If you open the peephole, the buzzer and red light go off. The inner book is held in place by bra-straps you have to unhook."

CoTangent's books are beautifully constructed, each print handmade and all the type handset. Only a dozen or so copies of each book are manufactured. "Like Blake," Vollmann says, "I believe every step in a book's creation should be carried out by the author."

If there is an author Vollmann admires, it is Blake. "He has a religious sort of vision. I admire the way in Blake you feel he actually saw everything he wrote about." He mentions the image of the ghost of a flea that Blake described seeing in a letter.

Vollmann pauses to think. "Actually I could probably see that ghost of a flea if I tried too."

An American Aboriginal

David Streitfeld / 1992

From *Details*, August 1992. © David Streitfeld. Reprinted by permission.

Prostitutes have been good to William Vollmann in more ways than one. Many men wouldn't go out of their way to admit such a thing, but Vollmann has managed the trick of converting his passion into a profession. Two books, *The Rainbow Stories* (1989) and *Whores for Gloria* (published earlier this year), use a gritty, highly personal approach to the topic, earning the writer both rave reviews and raised eyebrows. Sympathetic portrayals of prostitutes in fiction have been out of vogue since Zola, and AIDS hasn't done much for their social standing, but Vollmann doesn't care. "They epitomize a lot of what I admire," he says. "They're brave, beautiful, often very graceful, and honest about doing what we all do—which is sell ourselves."

But then, the thirty-four-year-old author is sailing against the prevailing currents in many ways. He's been called the literary son of Thomas Pynchon and Kathy Acker (with Don DeLillo and T. C. Boyle as uncles). As opposed to the pale, self-referential stories favored by other writers of his generation, his recent novels are sprawling epics that retell the settling of North America. As a personality, he's obsessive and quiet, but hardly dull. One favorite jacket photo shows him with a gun pointed to his temple, and he's also been known to fire a starter's pistol during readings—he figures something bizarre is expected of him.

Long and lean and still wearing the scars of teenage acne, Vollmann lives with his girlfriend Janice, a radiation oncologist, in Sacramento of all places, where they share an opulent, mock-Southern mansion complete with pillars and antiques. These digs are a far cry from his life a decade ago, when he was working as a computer programmer in Silicon Valley. Back then, Vollmann didn't like to drive to work because of his poor eyesight (he was born with a serious astigmatism), so he started stowing a sleeping bag under his desk and coming in for a week at a time. After his shift, he would work on his first novel, the partly brilliant, partly unreadable *You Bright and Risen Angels*, a tale of a young man who renounces humanity to join the insect world.

"There was nothing to do but write," he recalls. "There were freeways on three sides. Sometimes around midnight I'd go out and walk around for a few minutes in this muggy air full of freeway exhaust with the office looking like a green luminescent aquarium. Creepy."

As often happens with bright young geeks, Vollmann has turned his liabilities into assets. He even has groupies, largely as a result of his writing about the dispossessed, which he does in a heartfelt, nonexploitative way. You could even call his tales about prostitutes love stories. "Love is a yearning, and sometimes people don't understand what they're yearning for, or why. All they know is that they're lonely. Some get married, others have friends, others get involved in their work." And some pay for sex, or watch it under the guise of participatory journalism. In one section of *The Rainbow Stories* that focuses on ladies of the night in San Francisco, Vollmann fetishistically footnotes how much each piece of information gleaned from prostitutes cost him. He once paid fifty cents to learn that one's favorite food was spaghetti.

You figure Janice must be a saint to put up with this, even if her boyfriend never brings his work home with him. But she's fairly certain that he is more talk than action. "People assume he fools around a lot, and he kind of encourages the notion, but I don't know if that's the accurate picture." She's more concerned about his other bad habits: "He's not very good at cooking, cleaning, taking care of the house."

There's another, less abstract urge behind Vollmann's interest in marginal types. The crucial event happened when he was nine, behind the family house in New Hampshire, when Bill was reading on the bank of a pond and his six-year-old sister Julie was playing in the shallows. "I sort of forgot that she was there," he says. "The bottom drops off sharply and she took a few steps too many. She couldn't swim."

Too young to be a lifeguard, yet old enough to suffer the guilt for Julie's drowning, the event warped his life. "I felt like an outcast," he says. "Like a murderer."

And then there's what he calls the matter of his "genetic or biochemical predisposition: I believed that I was an alien, an extraterrestrial." While the feeling is common among maladjusted teenagers, it's one that he never quite got over. "I never felt like I was a part of the people who were living ordinary, happy lives. I'm interested in failure. I'd like to write something positive, if there is such a thing." He'd also like to write speeches for politicians, which isn't really that farfetched—they're generally considered close cousins of prostitutes.

For his ongoing seven-novel North American series, *Seven Dreams*, Vollmann has spent time in Newfoundland, Greenland, and the magnetic North Pole. His newest installment is the 989-page *Fathers and Crows*, an opus set four hundred years ago during the wars between the Iroquois and Hurons. He got carpal tunnel syndrome writing it, and the sales won't likely provide much balm—bestseller heaven is improbable. "The books are difficult and depressing, so people don't really want to read them," he shrugs.

Typically, he is less eager to do battle in the publishing world than he was to literally go off to war. A decade ago, at age twenty-two, he tried to enlist on the side of the rebels in the Afghan civil war. "The idea was, join the Mujahedeen and help them attack airfields or whatever," he says. "But the truth was I had no training. I couldn't speak the language; I had scarcely shot a gun. All I could do was write something, and that didn't help them either since the book is just now coming out." As much as *An Afghanistan Picture Show: Or, How I Saved the World* is a chronicle of war, it is also a chronicle of frustration. Besides his obvious determination (he has three books out this year from three major publishers, a practically unprecedented feat), it's Vollmann's so-what attitude that is his most admirable quality. "The world doesn't owe me a living, so why should they do it my way? But I ought to be able to do it the way I want."

So far, he's been able to have it both ways. Nice work, if you can get it.

Pimps, Alcoholics, Crackheads, Pushers, Runaways, All the Forsaken . . .

Timothy O'Grady / 1992

From *Esquire*, October 1992. © Timothy O'Grady. Reprinted by permission.

William Vollmann is a novelist who works directly from life, and the life he works from tends to be life at its most desperate, whether he's running with the Mujahedeen in Afghanistan or auditioning prostitutes in San Francisco. William Vollmann could be mad or he could be a genius. Or he could be both.

In the Cinna Bar in the San Francisco Tenderloin I drank beer and watched a basketball game on television while Bill Vollmann conducted a research session for a new story in a hotel up the road. The walls and the light were red, the faces radiating a weird Hadean glow. Young men from Guatemala shot pool, three Koreans were playing a game of dice and a man walked in off the street and fell flat on his face, unconscious. Young women in miniskirts came and went, their voices gravelly and abrupt, like sudden bursts of radio static. Their hands shook a little as they drew on their cigarettes.

The story Vollmann was working up was to be called "The Queen of the Whores." "For a long time I've had a vision of a story," he told me. "It happens in an underground place in a city with trash piled up around the entrance and catacombs inside. You go down through there and come to a big central room with fires burning in trash cans and a Queen holding court over about a hundred street people, big orange flames lighting up their faces. There are pimps, alcoholics, crackheads, pushers, runaways, all the forsaken, and this Queen ruling them. She might be a beautiful runaway or a blind girl, but I think she's a prostitute. She certainly has a mysterious power over them."

Vollmann tends to work directly from life. While I was in the bar his friend Code Six (*nom de guerre* of the photographer Ken Miller) was trawling the Tenderloin for street prostitutes to bring to a room they had rented in a hotel. Vollmann would interview them there at $40 per session, placing them in hypothetical situations in his imaginary underground chamber, feeding the notion of the story. If they could get enough money together he and Code Six would run it for real in a night-long improvised session and film it. In the meantime, Vollmann would take notes and Noah Richler, a BBC producer, would make unobtrusive recordings from a position in the closet for a Radio Three series that we were making.

William Vollmann is thirty-two years old and inclining towards the pear-shaped. He has had eleven books published and is currently working on ten others. He knows several languages, teaches differential equations for fun and manufactures his own special editions of his books out of such substances as butterfly wings and hair purchased from prostitutes. He is currently taken up with a vast, seven-volume sequence of novels to be called *Seven Dreams*, an attempt to fathom the equations of power, cruelty and dispossession in the conflict between Native Americans and invading Europeans. The most recent is *Fathers and Crows*, over nine hundred pages of long cascading sentences, a lava flow of language made distinct by his coroner's eye for detail. He has been working sixteen-hour days for so long that, like a stripper he knows who is required to masturbate all day on stage, he has developed Repetitive Strain Syndrome.

From a distance, Vollmann is like one of those terrifying boy wonders you see walking along school corridors in their own worlds, playing in their minds with advanced calculus and crossword puzzles in Latin. When his high school exam results placed him in the top 0.5 percent of the American population, he was recruited by a tiny and hermetic college called Deep Springs, founded in 1912 by the inventor of the oscilloscope. Each year it takes in ten or twelve apparent geniuses and teaches them ballroom dancing, stockbroking, and the slaughtering of cattle and then sends them into the world as a kind of intellectual commando force. He still has something of the look of a schoolboy, his book bag on his back, his baseball cap, his look of adolescent innocence. He blinks at you slightly myopically like he's just landed in from the farm.

But within him there is this vast brain whirring and probing and hankering and a style of living that could be compared to stock car racing, with him as the car. The San Francisco photographer Jock Sturges said of him: "William's ideas come out of a furious engine informed by a monumental, out-of-control intellect in the grip of profane appetites. There's virtually nothing he won't find beautiful, though the closer he comes to the necrose edge, the more likely he is to be attracted to it. I'm amazed that he's survived. The way he lives, he should be dead six times over by now."

Literature has been stitched into his life in strange, sometimes disconcerting patterns. Like many children he inhabited what he read, though perhaps to excess. When he was nine years old and in charge of his younger sister, Julie, he was so trapped in a book he was reading that he could not hear her cries as she flailed about in the pond behind their home. She had drifted out of the shallows and then drowned. "I just kind of forgot she was there," he said. Nothing was ever the same for him again, and in many ways he is still playing out in his work the consequences of this grim coming together of life and death and words. "I felt like a murderer," he said. "An outcast. At times I felt that I was an extraterrestrial. I couldn't be like people who were leading ordinary, happy lives. I became interested in failure."

Writing became a means of comprehending the world, of making contact. "I realized that if I could not get out of my books I could at least bring other people in to visit me. I could do this only by writing books." He sought out people living at great distance from himself—hookers, skinheads, retarded people, transvestites, prisoners serving life—and made them his subjects. When he was twenty-two and had seen *Lawrence of Arabia* he flew to Pakistan, crossed the mountains of the Northwest Frontier and ran with the Mujahedeen in their war against the Soviets.

He has camped in the Arctic, been shot at by a suspicious pimp, and hung around with prostitutes on several continents. In Cambodia he married one, scars running down her back from wounds inflicted by the Khmer Rouge, and then lost her. "Whatever it is," he said, "this thing that people call love, it often seems to have a stifling or cloying feeling to it. Everyone always seems to be complaining about their relationships. But the prostitute/client relationship isn't like that. Each person is getting exactly what he or she wants—if they don't, then no hard feelings. I think that's beautiful. Anyway, we're all whores. Street prostitutes are just the most visible, brave, and vulnerable manifestation of us all."

When I last spoke to him he was having a bulletproof vest made for a trip to Yugoslavia. In the American manner, he charges to where he senses the work is and dives in, unprotected, returning the experience to the page without such analgesics as rhetorical flourish or interpretation. Because of this he has been compared to Céline, Genet, Henry Miller, and William Burroughs—the literary life as long, slow human sacrifice.

When the basketball game was over I left the Cinna Bar and walked over to the hotel to see what was happening. There were smells of cumin and chili peppers coming from the kitchens of the Indian owners, then of disinfectant and staleness as I ascended the stairs.

Up in his room on the fourth floor, Vollmann was lying on the bed wearing his baseball hat and fatigue jacket, taking notes. Stretched out beside him was a white-haired Chinese woman, murmuring like a nun at prayer. She was wearing blue pajamas and white workman's gloves and was resting her hand on Vollmann's crotch. Code Six told me later that her daughter had been raped and murdered several years ago and she had not spoken a word of sense since.

In the chair, a large, heavy-thighed black woman in a red miniskirt was finishing her testimony. "I be your Queen," she declared. "I be your Queen because no one in the Tenderloin gives pleasure like Angel. Baby, I give the best head this side of the East Coast." She swaggered out, her big, cannonball hips flattening me against the wall. A thin Midwestern girl wearing nightmarishly purple rouge was sitting on the floor, flicking a little absently through a box of Code Six's photographs. Her name was Cookie. She wasn't sure if she could be of any help. "I don't think I'd be such a good Queen. I'd be too nervous. But if I *was* the Queen I'd give everybody everything they wanted and make them all be nice to each other."

He came in a little later with a blonde named Domino. She was good-looking, with large eyes and an alert, angular face. Vollmann thought he and Code Six should be alone with her, so Richler and I went down to the 441 Club next door. We waited a long time.

The next day he showed me his notes about his encounter with Domino. "Belly wrinkles like sand bars. Long white lines of a motor-cycle accident. The white island of a bullet wound with granules of black hair. Round, round, bulging breasts—silicone. Lying naked on the bed, playing with a gold chain across her breasts, chewing gum. The two wounds near each other, the long white line and the white circle, like the two parts of an exclamation point not quite lining up. The orange glow of the pipe against her cheek. She exhales the crack into my mouth. Taste of bubblegum breath. Lips numb, tongue numb, the heart racing, the famous head rush . . ."

You sense that he writes from beyond society's defining edge in part to shock, to bring into close focus the unassimilable. When I first met him he was in the company of a black hermaphrodite named Marissa. He has given readings dressed in battle fatigues festooned with pictures of icebergs, in the midst of which he will fire a starter's pistol. He will give you his farm-boy smile, quote Pythagoras and then show you a picture of something so devastating that it will nearly knock you off your feet. "Sometimes," he told me, "people get a little hostile when I read and show slides of widely spread vulvas dripping with sores, things that I think people should be able to look at without any problem."

Vollmann is acute, formidable, and sardonically funny, but there is also in his manner a sadness and innocence, and in the work a corresponding tenderness and sense of wonder. An intellect such as his can seem almost brutal in its power, and the lifestyle a form of slumming or cheap thrills, but I sensed in it more a struggle for connection, for forgiveness, for a cure. When I suggested to him that his auditioning of prostitutes has the feel of a laboratory experiment, he replied: "Maybe. But I think that sounds too manipulative. I prefer to think of it as more like a painter with tubes of col-ored paint, something joyous like that."

Before I left, I asked him what made him happiest. "Walking through the Arctic with a big backpack on my back and it's getting heavy but all of a sudden I can climb off all this scree that's been hurting my feet and walk on ice for a while, and it's just so smooth and so cool and I can glide forward really fast. It's kind of dangerous because the ice might be rotten in places underneath and I won't know it but it's just so peaceful and beautiful and far away."

Young Novelist Undertakes
Bizarre Magazine Assignment

Elisabeth Sherwin / 1993

From *The Davis Enterprise*, August 22, 1993. Reprinted with permission from *The Davis Enterprise*.

Sacramento—When I met Bill Vollmann he was on his way to Burma to buy a sex slave.

You would never guess this to look at him. Vollmann, 34, looks like a well-groomed street person.

When I met him on the north steps of the Capitol on a hot afternoon, he was wearing a cammie cap, a long-sleeved shirt, long pants, and hiking boots. He was carrying a backpack. He looks young for his age. His shaggy haircut and glasses give him a vulnerable appearance.

He was en route to San Francisco for a series of readings in three Bay Area bookstores. He also was going to make sure there were no problems with his visa for Burma. I represented the first interview of his mini-book tour and I had to apologize. I hadn't finished reading *Thirteen Stories and Thirteen Epitaphs* (Pantheon) and I knew very little about the author.

I knew that one critic described him as "the only novelist capable of filling the seven-league boots of John Barth, William Gaddis, and Thomas Pynchon." I knew that others say he's a literary genius bound to make Hemingway look like a piker.

Vollmann has published eight books since 1987, including four in the past year. His reading, writing, and research are prodigious.

He has completed three volumes of a projected seven-volume history of the North American continent. *The Ice-Shirt* was the first followed by *Fathers and Crows* to be followed next year by *The Rifles*.

But the longer we talked, sitting on the Capitol lawn, the more my interest in him as a novelist diminished. He became a lot more fascinating as a journalist. I don't particularly care for his knotty literary style. It's brilliant, it's impressive, but I'd rather follow Vollmann the journalist.

In a little more than a year, in addition to publishing four different books by four different publishers, he has traveled to the North Pole, Cambodia, Mexico City, Sarajevo, Madagascar, and Somalia—and now he's in Burma. Several of his articles have been published in *Esquire.*

His next article is going to be about his trip to Burma to buy and set free a child sex-slave. *Spin* magazine advanced him $10,000 in expenses for the story. He thought a young girl might cost $2,000. He hadn't quite figured out all the details but was certain everything would fall into place once he got there.

"Do you want a daughter?" he asked me. I'm pretty sure he was kidding.

Vollmann does outrageous things and then talks about them as if they were commonplace. He knows no one in Burma and has no particular strings to pull. He will simply go to the district where sex slaves are procured and make his deal. We argued briefly about the ethics of playing God but I dropped my questions in the face of his implacable belief that any intercession he could provide would be positive.

"Involuntary prostitution should be crushed," he said. "Voluntary prostitution should be legalized, regulated, and taxed.

"You can't save another person but you can give them a chance," he added.

Vollmann's guardian angel must be busy working triple-time.

He doesn't appear to be motivated by anything more than curiosity and a desire to do good. He will tell you that his little sister drowned when they were children. He was supposed to be watching her but wasn't paying attention.

"I try to help people in my work and life. I guess to make up for my sister," he said.

He has a great interest in the seamy and dangerous side of life and has spent time living with the dispossessed—from prostitutes in San Francisco to rebels in Afghanistan—and writing about their lives. He isn't fazed by physical hardships.

Vollmann is attracted to losers, he says, because he has felt like a loser. He also is an idealist.

He now lives in Sacramento with a doctor—a woman—who works at the UCD Medical Center.

"He likes to put himself in extreme situations in life and on the page," said Paul Slovak of Penguin Books, publishers of the *Seven Dreams* series.

Vollmann's upbringing—except for the death of his sister—appears to be pleasant and typically middle-class. His father is a teacher. Vollmann went to Deep Springs College near Big Pine in California for two years—a school he describes as part college, part cattle ranch. The students studied in the morning and ran the ranch in the afternoon.

Deep Springs is affiliated with Cornell. So after two years he transferred to the university in New York state and graduated in 1981 summa cum laude. He then started and dropped a comparative literature PhD program at Berkeley, and lived in San Francisco for seven years before moving to Sacramento (that being where his girlfriend got a job).

In 1982 he became seriously interested in Afghanistan and began the first of a series of adventures that would take him away from his computer. He went to Afghanistan with all the naiveté of a young man who has discovered a cause. He laughs about it now. All his considerable efforts raised only $1,000 for the rebels.

The experience also resulted in a book, *An Afghanistan Picture Show* (Farrar, Straus & Giroux), which took ten years to publish.

And throughout the intervening years he kept writing. He has now reached the position where the money earned by his books provides him with the means to travel to places he has to go.

"I have a pretty good life now," he says. "I do what I want. I write all the time."

Except when he's in Burma, freeing sex slaves.

Vollmann's Vision

Tom McIntyre/1993

From *Image*, Sunday August 22, 1993. © *The San Francisco Examiner*. Reprinted by permission.

"Bill's got guns hidden all over his house," confides William T. Vollmann's close friend and personal photographer Ken Miller. "Careful, Tom. He's even got a flame thrower."

These reassuring tidbits of information, combined with the rumors about Vollmann's drinking, womanizing, and paranoia about letting people know where he lives, have me feeling in need of a drink myself as the city bus Vollmann has instructed me to take splashes its way through the labyrinthine streets of Sacramento.

Paranoiac fantasies drift through my brain. Is it possible that the author some critics consider one of the most gifted novelists of his generation has succumbed to madness at the tender age of thirty-three? He seemed like such a nice person over the phone. Will he pull a gun on me if I ask the wrong question?

The bus slows to a halt, delivering me just a few yards from Vollmann's house, a large two-story structure nestled comfortably, and for those who know Vollmann's work, incongruously, in the middle of the suburbs.

The bland suburban setting is especially surprising because Vollmann has built his literary reputation presenting characters and situations that often are riddled with uncertainty and danger. And, unlike most writers, he not only writes about life's extremes, he lives them—fighting with the mujahadeen in Afghanistan, hanging out with prostitutes and addicts, risking his life in the most terrifying war zones in the world. A few weeks earlier, Vollmann had returned from a two-way junket-to Hell, touring the ravaged landscapes of Bosnia and Somalia to research an upcoming nonfiction book about "the nature of force and when violence is (and isn't) justified." These are the kinds of subjects that fuel Vollmann's literary imagination.

Just a few years after graduating with honors from Cornell University and relocating to San Francisco, Vollmann exploded upon the literary scene in 1987 with the publication of his first book, *You Bright and Risen Angels*, an allegorical comic novel that is narrated by a computer and features a bizarre power struggle over electricity between a group of insects and human revolutionaries. Its frenzied, hallucinogenic imagery led many critics to declare it the most stylistically ambitious first novel since Thomas Pynchon's.

Vollmann's next work, *The Rainbow Stories*, a jarring collection of "journalistic fictions," was a complete departure. While *Angels* was an exaggerated, self-described "comic book" that provided a platform for the outer reaches of Vollmann's imagination, most of *The Rainbow Stories* focus on a motley group of "lost souls" who roam the streets of America's inner cities. Most of the action takes place in the depressed neighborhoods of San Francisco, exploring the harrowing, sometimes hilarious worlds of street alcoholics, prostitutes, Nazi skinheads, drug addicts, and electroshock patients. (There is also a portrait of the legendary San Francisco-based underground machine-art collective Survival Research Labs.) Vollmann's prose reflects the change of theme: the book is written in a gritty, direct style that has more in common with the blunt lyricism of Hemingway than Pynchon's pyrotechnics.

And the protean author wasn't through with his transformations. In 1992 alone, he published three new books: *Whores For Gloria*, a novel focusing on the subculture of Tenderloin prostitutes; *Fathers and Crows*, the second book of a proposed seven-volume cycle of novels tracing Western civilization's colonial relationship with the indigenous cultures of the Americas; and finally, *An Afghanistan Picture Show*, an autobiographical essay that reconstructs his political awakening in the early 1980s, when he reported on—and ultimately fought with—the Afghani rebels fighting the Soviet army.

Judged against this prodigious output, 1993 has been a slow year for Vollmann. He "only" has two new books coming out. The first, *Thirteen Stories and Thirteen Epitaphs*, a dazzlingly unclassifiable collection of lyrical and nightmarish tales, was recently published by Pantheon Books, while the upcoming *Butterfly Stories* is scheduled for release by Grove Press in October.

Vollmann appears very ordinary, the kind of person who could walk down a crowded street in virtually any part of the world without making himself conspicuous. Brown hair cut in uneven bangs frames his relatively nondescript features. The thick, watery lenses of his glasses make his eyes look a bit larger than they actually are.

His manner is friendly, although at times he's somewhat detached. After I entered his home, he offered me a beer and led me into his living room, where our conversation took place. He himself sipped a soft drink during the interview, thoughtfully pausing before answering my questions.

Our conversation, on literature, war, prostitution, and a variety of other matters, follows below:

TOM McINTYRE: What was your life like while writing *You Bright and Risen Angels*?

WILLIAM VOLLMANN: I was a computer programmer—not a very high-powered one. I don't drive, so I was commuting to Silicon Valley with this other guy who worked at Versatec. Sometimes he'd take a week off and he would drive down on a Monday with me and then I'd have to stay down there until Friday. And sometimes I'd drive down on a Friday with him and spend the weekend there so I could write. There was nothing to do, no place to go. You're completely helpless in Silicon Valley if you don't have a car. There were freeways three sides of me. The place I worked at was like this big square fishbowl; it just glowed very spookily at night; all full of computers. I would sleep under my desk. I had my sleeping bag there. I would put a wastebasket in front of my head so people couldn't see me sleeping there. The janitors got to know about it, and they were pretty nice. I lived on candy bars from candy machines. I used to get Three Musketeers because there was an extra half ounce for your money. (Laughter.) It was a pretty crummy life; nothing really to do except work on the computer.

TM: A brief statement you wrote at the time it was published says: "The kind of reading and writing that I value is a dying art. While it lasts and while I last, I intend to write sentences that are beautiful in their own right, to write paragraphs that respect those sentences while conveying thought: and to arrange those paragraphs in works that promote love and understanding for people whom others with my background may despise or fail to know." How do you "arrange (your) paragraphs" to achieve this aim?

WV: I try to describe people without sentimentalizing. Often they're ugly or they smell bad or they have mental problems or they're racist or they're full of other kinds of hate. Usually, those kinds of signals are enough for other people to say, "Okay, I don't want anything more to do with this person." My job is to say, "Okay, here it is; you have to see this; I'm going to rub your nose in it. But then, if you go beyond this a little bit, then here's what the rest of the person is like." And I believe that no person is completely bad.

Even Hitler must have had his good points. And if Jesus was a human being, if there was such a person, I'm sure he wasn't completely good either. That's just how life is.

TM: Many authors—Hemingway, for instance—developed a unique style that's instantly recognizable, but they rarely, if ever, strayed from it. You write many different kinds of novels. Is it a natural offshoot for you to write "journalistic fictions," as in *Rainbow Stories* and *Thirteen Stories and Thirteen Epitaphs*, as well as other, more allegorical novels, like *You Bright and Risen Angels*?

WV: I just want to understand what life is and what life is about. And that can't be done in just one way. You have to listen to all of the different people out there and hear how they speak and try to understand how they think. At the same time, you have to listen to what's inside you and try to understand how you think and the best way for you to speak to present those thoughts well.

TM: What do you think your limitations as a writer are, at this point?

WV: I'd like to continue to improve in my depiction of character. My ability to create plot has improved somewhat. I would like to create incidents better as opposed to having to go to real life. It would be nice if I could sit down and come up with a stream of coherent and interconnected incidents. It's something I do now but it takes a lot of work. It would nice if that got to be second nature.

TM: Describe your creative experience . . .

WV: What I have to do before anything else is massive doses of reading about the subject I'm concerned with. Then, if possible, visit the historic sites and take lots and lots of notes. I'm looking for connections, things that interest me.

Once I feel like have some understanding of my characters, then it's a great deal of labor coming up with the details. In *Fathers and Crows*, I wanted to imagine this Indian lady who's born underwater. I was trying to figure out how she got her magic power. In the first or second or third draft, I said, "Well, all right. Maybe she goes to a shaman and talks with him and makes friends with him or gives him some sort of present and finally, *he* helps her out." Well, an anthropologist who worked very closely with Mic Mac sources and knows quite a bit about the culture told me that was just preposterous. She would never do anything of the kind; she was a girl, the shaman was this old man. He would have nothing to do with her. They would never have anything to do with each other. So this whole scene was completely worthless, and I had to start over again.

After you figure out what's actually possible, according to the laws of fact, then, finally, you can start constructing. You have the building blocks of your world and you're free to arrange them the way you want. Finally, when the story starts to really build up, I can sort of close my eyes and I can walk around inside, in this case, seventeenth-century Canada. It may not, in fact, have been the *real* seventeenth-century Canada, but it's as close as I can make it.

TM: How about *You Bright and Risen Angels*?

WV: There, it's just a question of sitting in front of the computer screen and waiting for the feeling of excitement, the feeling of power in my fingertips from all the words that are coming out of my brain and flowing down my shoulders and into my arms and down my wrists into my fingers. All those words, just waiting to come out. The faster I type, the more words come out and the more beautiful they are. Then, after that's over, I can go back and edit the thing a little bit.

Something like *Thirteen Stories* is a little bit like *Rainbow Stories*. There are a number of stories there where I had to go out and gather the facts. Of course, that's what life is: a process of gathering the facts. That's why a newborn baby really can't write anything.

TM: Which of your books was most difficult?

WV: *Fathers and Crows*—the research was massive and I wasn't quite sure what I was looking for when I started. I knew basically what the subject was, but I didn't know what about the subject interested me. In the end, that proved to my benefit because I didn't have any particular axe to grind. I was able to describe an entire half-century in Canada—which I feel I did quite well—but the research was extremely difficult. I filled up notebooks with all *kinds* of things. I got very discouraged for a long time . . . It just seemed like it would be impossible for me to bring these people to life.

I was also in New York for much of the time, which was very good for research, because I was able to use the New York Public Library. The research facilities on the West Coast are really not that great. You can go to UC Berkeley and page books, but, unless you have a lot of money, you can't check the books out. And when you page the books, sometimes it's hard to get what you want. You have to wait and wait, and they don't have everything. So that was good, but I was working on that so much that I got carpal tunnel (syndrome) in my hands. Actually, they hurt right now: they hurt all the time. I was putting in many sixteen, seventeen, eighteen-hour days of typing on that book.

Once the book was finished, I was very excited about it. All of my editors *hated* it—they thought it was long-winded, sloppy. They just didn't get it. They were bored by it. They probably didn't finish it. They gave me ultimatums. They sat on it. They wanted me to cut it by half. I just refused to do it. It took a long time to get that book published; it sat around for a couple of years. When the book came out, I expected the thing to sink like a stone, and basically end my publishing career, because it was so expensive and they were all publishing it under duress with bitter, hard feelings, because they felt that I wouldn't listen. Fortunately, the book got very, very good reviews, and all of a sudden they changed their minds, as editors will do. Basically, most editors seem to be people who want the reputation of being independent thinkers, but, in fact, are very dependent on mob approval.

TM: In "The Handcuff Manual," in *Thirteen Stories and Thirteen Epitaphs*, the characters live in a city where guns, the military industry, etc., control all aspects of daily life. Eventually, Gun City collapses when the government stops pouring money into these programs. Do you think of Gun City as a slightly exaggerated depiction of America's inner cities?
WV: Yeah. And more broadly, it's kind of a metaphor for American society. We Americans glorify violence, whether we admit it or not. All you have to do is turn on the television and catch a Western or go to the movies, where someone is sure to kill somebody else—or turn on the news. That's what they zoom right in on. They expect you to go for the most sensational thing, which means going for the worst *possible* thing. That's what we're all about. I wouldn't even go so far as to say that it's bad. I don't know whether it's good or bad. It's just how we are.

TM: In "The Handcuff Manual," what's the significance of the imaginary handcuffs and the lucky dog tags? What do they represent for you?
WV: They represent people trying to find things to depend on: fetishes. That's one of the common motifs, I guess, in my work.

In "The Handcuff Manual," life would be a lot easier for the main character if he could just have these lucky dog tags, and they would make all of his luck. He wouldn't have to do anything anymore; everything would be taken care of. Of course, life doesn't work that way. It would be just a fairytale if it ever did.

This first pair of handcuffs is just a pair of handcuffs. He thinks it's the greatest thing to be able to do that. If you can't have some kind of a magical device, a fetish that works, then try and build one in your own mind. That's sort of what creation . . . what writing books is all about, too. But actually, it's like a neurosis for him and for Elaine Suicide. It ties in with the whole Gun City thing and it just gets uglier and uglier. The more these handcuffs disappear, the more they become internalized, the more ubiquitous and dangerous they become. That's finally what havens to Elaine.

TM: She seems to be the victim of this whole situation, right?
WV: Right. Of course, she is a *willing* victim. She is not a happy person. It's her fault just as much as his fault. There never was any time when he really forcibly involved her in the whole process.

TM: In *Whores for Gloria*, your protagonist, Jimmy, tries to create this safe world for himself and Gloria, an idealized, imaginary woman whom he tries to make real by weaving the memories of the prostitutes he sleeps with onto his vision of Gloria.
WV: Yeah, it's the same kind of thing as the imaginary handcuffs, really.

TM: Right. She drinks their memories, gradually becoming a real flesh-and-blood woman in Jimmy's mind. But the tragic irony is that the prostitutes' happy reminiscences often sour, sometimes becoming even violent, shattering this illusory world for Jimmy. Is Jimmy's quest for the ideal woman through the common prostitute symbolic of what many "johns" are looking for when they decide to seek out the services of a prostitute?
WV: Have you ever slept with a prostitute yourself, Tom?

TM: No.
WV: Are you at all interested in doing so?

TM: It's occurred to me. It's a fascination, but I've never plunged. I'm not sure how I feel about it. I got married recently so that would, for me, be an obstacle. Although for many of the "johns," I understand, it's not one at all.
WV: Right.

TM: It's almost a prerequisite.
WV: Guys go to prostitutes for several different reasons. Some guys who are married don't have satisfactory sex with their wives. Some guys think that novelty is the most important thing in sex. Therefore, after you've been with any one person a number of times, it's going to get old, and you've got

to find somebody else. That's especially true with guys our age. When you're in your thirties and then in your forties, no matter what you do, your sexual powers begin to decline just a little bit. You're not what you were at sixteen or eighteen, and that's very upsetting. That's a lot of their identity, and they want to try everything they can to keep death at bay. They'll have sex with as many women as they can.

Many guys go to prostitutes simply out of loneliness. You can be in a relationship that is otherwise very successful and still feel as lonely as hell. When you're with a prostitute, the rules are very clear. If she's at all decent and intelligent, she'll pay attention to you for as long as your money lasts. She'll make you feel good about yourself. She does the same kind of thing a psychiatrist would do, basically, except that you can go to a psychiatrist and talk and talk and talk, and have a slight catharsis. You can go to a prostitute, and she'll put her arms around you and comfort you and tell you you're the best she's ever had which, of course, is a lie. And you'll leave and feel like you're a real man and feel on top of the world. I think what prostitutes do is basically very, very good. They do a tremendous service for our society, and it sickens me the way they are picked on by our system.

TM: You've reported on and evidently become intimate with quite a few prostitutes, not only in this country but in places like Cambodia, Thailand, and Madagascar. What do your think would make the living/working conditions better in this country? Is legalization the answer?
WV: In the States, that would certainly make things better, yes. Maybe not necessarily the way that they've done it in Nevada. It seems like they're sequestered there in Esmeralda County, and so it really doesn't encourage society to respect them more. It would be nice if there were schools for courtesans and geishas and so forth, the way there used to be in the olden days, so that prostitutes who wanted to could learn all kinds of very sophisticated ways of pleasing the customer, with singing and musical instruments and dancing.

TM: There's a stigma to being a prostitute—and, not just in this country, where it's illegal. Even in the piece you wrote for *Esquire* about Thai and Cambodian prostitutes, you discuss how they have to play these games with their families about how exactly they're making their money. So in a way, they're still victims, even in places where it *is* legalized.
WV: Well, of course, conventional wisdom is that the prostitute is the victim and the "john" is a terrible, terrible exploiter . . .

TM: A lot of the problems that people have is how young so many of the prostitutes are when they get started.

WV: In my opinion, it's often the "john" who's exploited. It's often the case that the "john" and the prostitute are *both* victims. It's also often the case that the "john" and the prostitute help each other and make each other happy. I don't have any problem with prostitutes starting young if it's something that they want to do.

If they're being coerced into doing it, then, of course, that's bad. But it would be bad if they were being coerced into working in a factory at that age, too, and didn't want to do it. People like to sweep that under the rug—so it's clear that what they're really objecting to is the sex act. I don't really have too much patience with that. Where would those objectors be today if it wasn't for the sexual act?

TM: How did you get introduced into these exotic worlds you write about?

WV: Well, each one happened differently. Which one are you most interested in?

TM: How about the Nazi skinheads?

WV: That was entirely due to (photographer) Ken Miller. He shaved his head and became a skinhead. He just went right in there with his camera. Pretty soon, they liked him, they knew him, they liked his pictures. Then he was able to get me in a little bit. I was never into it as much as he was. They kind of tolerated me. They didn't know me as well as they knew Ken. He was giving them something; he was giving them pictures of themselves. Everyone always likes those. I was writing something; I was able to give them attention, buy them beers, which was nice. But the kind of stuff I write can be difficult for people who don't have a college education, which a lot of the skinheads don't. It was difficult for them to understand. But I try to always show what I write about people to those people, even if there's some kind of risk, so I showed it to the skinheads. I was a little worried about getting hurt, but I didn't. There was some bad stuff about the skinheads and some good stuff about the skinheads.

Sometimes people complain and say, "Bill, why don't you ever take sides?" I got one fellow really angry about my piece on Sarajevo. He said, "Why don't you come out and talk about all the awful things the Serbs have done?" I told him I did. I talked about the awful things the Serbs did, and I also talked about the awful things the Croatians did. I just don't think life is served by blaming people.

TM: When you're writing stories about "lost souls," what is it that you would like readers to understand about them?

WV: Basically, that the reader is a lost soul, too. We're all lost souls together.

TM: What kind of responsibility do you feel toward the people you write about?

WV: I do my best to make sure that whatever it is I write is not going to harm them. It would be a very unrealistic goal to say that writing itself is supposed to help them. I have made myself very unhappy in the past by believing that. I don't know if you've read my Afghanistan book, but that's what it's all about: doing your best to be good person and trying to be of service to others.

If you expect too much and try too hard, all you do is waste everybody's time. I think you have to be hardboiled about it and say, "Chances are, I can't do *anything* for all these people. On the other hand, maybe I'll make one or two friends. Maybe I can help those people a little bit." That's all you can really do, and that's all you really need to do.

TM: Do you ever worry that you might he exploiting your subjects?

WV: No, I'm not exploiting. What makes you think that?

TM: Many of the people you write about are in extremely vulnerable situations. As a photographer who takes pictures of what I see walking the streets of San Francisco, I'll come across a drunkard, for instance, who's passed out, lying in a puddle of his own vomit. This makes for a wonderful photograph, and yet at the same time, I know I am intruding into this person's life, and I worry, "Am I merely capitalizing upon his misfortunes?"

WV: I don't think that's a problem for me. I can understand how you would feel something like that, because a photograph could be recognizable. Maybe the person's family would see it in the newspaper and it could cause them grief and embarrassment. On the other hand, if I were to paint a watercolor of that person lying in his own vomit, or if I were to pull up a chair and sit there for half an hour and write a paragraph about that person . . . I can't see how that could possibly harm the person or offend the person. It would never be identified as that particular person. If I approached it with any sensitivity, it would be something that would make the reader say, "Gosh, it's a pretty tough world we live in," not make them say, "Gosh, how filthy or disgusting that guy is—he ought to be taken out and shot."

I think that whole notion of exploiting people is something that's been taken far too far. It really causes a lot of people to shoot themselves in the foot, to be filled with needless guilt, and to fail to do things they could otherwise do. You have to work out your own ethics on that—if you establish some kind of quick and easy litmus test and run that by in your mind every time, then it's going to be all right.

TM: What's yours?
WV: Is this person going to be hurt in any way by this? If the answer is no, then I feel that I'm *not* exploiting the person. The next question is, "Is the person going to get anything out of this?" If the answer is no, I'm still not doing any harm, and it's okay.

For instance, when I was writing *Whores for Gloria*, I paid most of the prostitutes for their time, for the interviews. They appreciated having a place to stay for the night or having the junk that they needed to be shot into their arms. I was helping them.

TM: The few times I've asked about your recent exploits abroad you've complained about the danger. In Bosnia, you got a piece of shrapnel in your hand, for instance. But you keep going back. Is it necessary for your creative impulses to put yourself in dangerous situations?
WV: Not in general—the things I'm interested in at the moment require that. I'm working on a book about the nature of force and when violence is justified and when it isn't. To research that, I have to see lots of violence. To write *You Bright and Risen Angels*, that obviously wasn't necessary. I could just get all pale and puffy and eat Three Musketeers bars and sleep under my desk.

But I've been very lucky—I've seen a lot in my life already. I feel like I've lived a lot more than many other people I know. If the price for that is an early death—which is always possible—then I'm certainly prepared to pay it. I'm not a suicidal person, I don't have any kind of death wish . . . On the other hand, we're all going to die eventually, no matter how safe we keep ourselves. But I don't enjoy it when people are shooting at me . . .

TM: This is a difficult question to ask but Ken Miller told me that you have many wives, scattered all across the globe. Is this true?
WV: I guess I'll have to neither confirm nor deny this rumor.

TM: Once I turn the recorder off, will you confirm or deny it for me?
WV: No. I figure, Tom, as you've said, you don't know me all that well, and I

don't know you all that well. Maybe in five or ten years you can tell me about your sex life, and I'll tell you about my sex life.

TM: Once the recorder is off I'll be glad to tell you about mine, if you'll do the same.

WV: Of course, it's also nice just to keep everyone guessing . . .

TM: Okay, so you'd prefer not to elaborate?

WV: You can ask me as many questions about it as you want . . .

TM: You just may not answer them.

WV: Yeah. (Laughter.)

TM: Okay. Are these legal marriages? Where do they live? Why do you have so many wives?

WV: Put it this way, Tom. If you were married to many, many different women all around the world, would it be in your interest to talk about it? Would it be in your interest to admit to it?

TM: Well, of course, it would. (Laughter.)

WV: If there was a rumor going around about that, and you said, "Yes, I am married to many different ladies all around the world," a lot of people would think you were a bad person. If you were to say, "No, it's just a rumor. I'm not married to anyone," a lot of people would be disappointed. So maybe the best thing is to not say one way or the other.

TM: I appreciate you protecting the feelings of the readers.

WV: Yeah, that's my main goal, as you know. (Laughter.)

TM: World mythology expert Joseph Campbell once said that each man chooses to become a king or pawn in his own life. You've already written so many novels at such a young age, plus you've put yourself in so many volatile situations all over the world. Where does your confidence come from?

WV: I guess I just don't care what happens to me, Tom. (Laughs.) That makes things a lot easier.

TM: Is that true?

WV: Yeah, it's true.

TM: In what sense do you mean you don't care? Obviously, you don't want to get killed, but you're just not going to worry about it, right?

WV: Yes. That's what I mean. Obviously, I wouldn't want to die in agony like some of those people I saw.

TM: What other groups of people or worlds would you be interested in exploring that you haven't already?

WV: Well, I know one billionaire. I'd like to know a lot more. (Laughter.) Let's see. I've always wanted to have a girlfriend who was a policewoman.

TM: A tough cop who could put you in handcuffs in the evening? (Laughter.)

WV: Yeah, and going to burger joints, with her, and sitting there with the sweaty holster on your hip, hearing about the day, hanging out with friends, driving around in the squad car . . . I would really like that.

TM: Salman Rushdie describes an imaginary sea where all stories come from in *Haroun and the Sea of Stories*. In "Grave of Lost Stories," in *Thirteen Stories and Thirteen Epitaphs*, you write about a place where the corpses of unrealized stories go. Do you think some of the stories you've written have come from somewhere else?

WV: Yeah, I think all of the stories have. I don't think people really *have* anything. I think people are given everything. When you sit down and create something, when you're doing your job, you're just some kind of a vehicle or a chain for that kind of energy to flow through you. Whether you want to call it God or electricity or whatever, doesn't really matter. All of the stories that you've written, or that got lost, or didn't turn out right, as well as the stories that you wrote and were successful, and the stories you never thought about, and the stories you *started* to write, and the stories you forgot about, they're all there in some particular place. Just like your first love from high school is somewhere in that place, as beautiful as she ever was. She's waiting for you, and she'll always wait for you. Whether it's true or not, why not believe it?

TM: Which of today's writers do you think are bringing new energy to the novel?

WV: Cormac McCarthy is pretty spectacular. There's a woman named Andrea Freud Loewenstein who wrote a book called *This Place* about a women's prison. But I don't think there are many good authors out there.

TM: Because of decreasing literacy?

WV: That's a lot of it. People are lazy. People have very low standards of reading and writing these days. It's the exception rather than the rule to pick up a book that isn't riddled with grammatical errors. If I see a book that's full of grammatical errors, that's a big turnoff for me. I'll think, "Well, if they can't even do *this* . . ." It's just plain sloppiness. I don't have any use for it.

TM: Your writing has been compared frequently with Pynchon and William S. Burroughs. Have they been important influences?

WV: No.

TM: Why do you think you get clumped with those guys?

WV: *You Bright and Risen Angels* was compared with *Gravity's Rainbow* because they're both kind of long books that sometimes have long sentences with dark comic episodes that kind of move around from one topic to the next. But I hadn't read *Gravity's Rainbow* until long after *Angels* was published. I bought it in high school, and it was $2.25—which was a lot of money for me. Then, I was coming home on my bike and the book fell into a mud puddle. I got off my bike, and it was swelled up like this (Gestures.) And I tried to read it but the ink had all run off the pages, and I would turn it and the pages would kind of pop and crack and fall off. So I said, "Forget this!" (Laughter.) I didn't have the heart to spend another $2.25 on it. So I didn't read it for a long time.

TM: What did you think of it?

WV: I thought it was very good. I thought *V.* wasn't quite as good. I was disappointed in *The Crying of Lot 49.*

TM: What about Burroughs?

WV: I like *The Ticket That Exploded.* I like *Naked Lunch. Junkie* is really good. I think I'm a better writer than Burroughs.

TM: You've expressed dissatisfaction with some of your work. Which of your books would you like to rework most?

WV: They could all use a little bit of work. I'd enjoy working on the last quarter of *You Bright and Risen Angels,* maybe trying to tighten up "Ladies and Red Lights" in *Rainbow Stories* and possibly shortening "The Handcuff Manual."

TM: I really like that story.

WV: Yeah, I like them all too, you know. It might be that if I sat down and read them again I'd say, "Well, I guess every word was needed." That was the impression I had many times with "Ladies and Red Lights." Each time I kept thinking, "There's something about this story I don't really like, it seems kind of long-winded." Then I'd read it again and say, "Well, all of these things here seem to have a place. So let's leave it."

TM: Yeah, maybe you're just extending the parameters of the short story, moving into a new area.

WV: Maybe. Some of what I do, since it's reaching out and trying to do new things, has the virtues and vices of any experiment. It might be that fifty or one hundred years from now, parts of my books will be unreadable.

I was re-reading *The Sun Also Rises* recently and thought, "So much of this book seems so *bad!*" And when it came out, it was probably this really amazing, brash kind of thing. But now, for instance, in the first couple of pages you get kind of stuck with the anti-Semitic references that just seem gratuitous now. These people seem like spoiled caricatures of rich coke-heads in a 1980s novel. It's just how it is—a lot of it isn't Hemingway's fault. Some of that stuff lasts, and some of it doesn't. *The Old Man and the Sea*, for instance—I think it's still just as perfect as when he wrote it. Everything has a life span. People have to read Shakespeare now with a gloss, because in Shakespeare, "to let" means "to hinder." Things like that. Sooner or later, the language will become so different that for it to survive it will have to be cast in a new form. Like *Beowulf* or the *Epic of Gilgamesh*. There just aren't very many people around who can read it in the original lines. Basically, those works are dead. That's just how it is. Nothing lasts.

TM: In some of your stories, I see stylistic similarities with Hemingway. Do you feel any particular kind of affinity with him?

WV: A little bit. I admire a lot of what Hemingway did. I think that the last generation of critics have really picked on him unfairly.

TM: Because of his attitudes towards women?

WV: Right. And that's totally unfair. People are riding the feminist band-wagon now—for which I have very little sympathy. It goes without saying that men and women should have equal rights. Well, fine. Let's leave it at that. Men and women are different. There's nothing wrong with that fact. It's like being worried about exploiting people. If we have to constantly bend over backwards to avoid offending somebody, because you might use one euphemism instead of another euphemism, then I don't call that femi-nism—I call it *1984.*

So Hemingway got sucked into that, too. A lot of the stuff he said about women was . . . it seems a little offensive now. A lot of the stuff he said about them seems both offensive and true. So he was kind of an a. . . . . . . Aren't we all? (Laughter.)

TM: People criticized him because he couldn't render female characters very well. There's Pilar (from *For Whom the Bell Tolls*) and there's Brett (from *The Sun Also Rises*), but I can't think of too many more beyond that.
WV: Right. The reason I don't think that criticism of Hemingway is valid is because if somebody were just to write about black lesbians and how great they were and not have any convincing men characters or white characters, or something like that, no one would have the guts to come out and say, "Well, this is flawed, this is unbalanced." And what's more, there'd be no reason why they should *have* to. If the world that person created with the black lesbians was interesting to read, book after book, then what's the big deal? The same with Hemingway. Yeah, his men characters are more convincing than his women characters, but I think he had some good ones like Catherine Barkley in *A Farewell to Arms*. A lot of women now might be offended by her, but I bet she was a very convincing type for the way a lot of women were then. And she reads very sympathetically to me now. He doesn't get inside her head, but gets inside the head of the guy who loves her and looks at her that way. That seems perfectly fine to me.
You can't hope to bring *everything* to life. I wish I could. My women characters in *You Bright and Risen Angels* weren't very convincing, either. I did my best but I just didn't know that much. Now I've learned a little bit; they're a little better. I think that Elaine Suicide is a good character.

TM: It's interesting that you used her in both "The Handcuff Manual" where she committed suicide in this allegorical story and yet, in other stories, she's like a personal friend of yours. You used the same name. Is it the same character?
WV: Yeah, it's the same character.

TM: Did Elaine Suicide commit suicide?
WV: Well, in one story she did and in another story she didn't.

TM: In real life?
WV: There's no such thing, Tom, as real life.

Conversation with William Vollmann

R. V. Branham / 1993

From *Paperback Jukebox*, October 15–31, 1993. © R.V. Branham. Reprinted by permission.

William Vollmann, born in L.A., in 1959. His life has forked and circled in interesting ways ever since. After graduating summa cum laude in comparative literature from Cornell, he did what any college graduate would do: He went to Afghanistan to help the mujahedin fight the Russian invaders, or at least document the plight of refugees and raise consciousness as well as money. Following some subset of the law of conservation of energy, he raised hundreds of dollars but spent thousands. Later, working as a programmer in the Silicon Valley—and not having a car, and frequently unable to get a ride home—he would stay overnight, stuffing a sleeping bag under his desk, shopping at the candy machine and writing his first novel. *You Bright and Risen Angels* was perhaps the most impressive novel debut since Thomas Pynchon's *V.* Vollmann is different from so many current American and European writers in that he is not a slave to style, or "voice"—he bends his style to the demands of the characters and their stories, rather than fitting them into a stylistic cookie-cutter. Also, the people he writes about separate him from most of his fellow novelists. He doesn't write about people who are having bad days—who've broken their coffee grinder. He writes about people having bad decades. He loves epigraphs and weaves them throughout his books—certainly he'd know the Auden line about whores and opera singers being the only ones likely to survive a revolution. His home-base of Sacramento is just that—expect to reach his answering machine, as he's usually out of town or in another hemisphere. He's as likely to be in the New York Public Library as in Thailand or Kampuchea, Somalia or Yugoslavia—where the shrapnel made him forget his carpal tunnel syndrome—or Powell's Purple Room on Saturday, October 30, at 7:30 P.M. Bring your flak jacket.

Paperback Jukebox: You recently went to Bosnia and Somalia. I heard you'd received a shrapnel wound.

William Vollmann: I got a small piece of shrapnel in my hand in Sarajevo, from an artillery shell. It wasn't really a big deal—it was scary, but it didn't really leave a scar. It was like a metal splinter.

PJ: Was the purpose the same as when you went to Afghanistan in 1982 to help with refugees, document their plight, or actually fight if necessary?

WV: When I went to Afghanistan I really thought that I could help large groups of people. Now I know better. Now when I help people I choose an individual and I go out and try and make that person's life a little better. I think that's all any individual can do. When I went to several of these other war zones—as you mentioned—I didn't really expect to be able to help anybody directly. I guess I've gotten a bit more cynical, or more realistic; but I'm working on a long essay—I've been working on it for ten years—it deals with the circumstances under which violence is justified. I've been always interested in war for just that reason. If some opportunity comes my way to solve somebody's problem or help somebody out I would do it.

PJ: I remember a passage in *An Afghanistan Picture Show* where you stated that you didn't begin to use firearms until two years after you'd returned from Afghanistan. I found it ironic, that you hadn't picked up a gun—except for your pen-pistol.

WV: I was just an idiot. I wanted to do some good, but I didn't have the first idea of how to do it. It's not that I was a bad person. Most people in my situation wouldn't have had any idea of what to do, and I don't fault myself too much; but my attempt to be of use and even really to understand the situation was a total failure.

PJ: So you were trying to, if not help, at least bear witness.

WV: What actually came of that experience was that they helped me. I learned some things about what to do, what not to do, how to be a little better prepared, what to expect. I certainly didn't help them. They were very, very kind and gracious people.

PJ: *An Afghanistan Picture Show* almost reads like a Bildungsroman—a young man's education.

WV: Except oftentimes at the end of a Bildungsroman the protagonist is more equipped to deal with things. At least in the immediate end of that experience I was less equipped. I was kind of demolished; I felt like a real jerk. In the long run it has certainly benefited me. I'm sorry that I couldn't have benefited them more.

PJ: When you were in Bosnia, did you hear about the mujahedin being in Bosnia?
WV: The Muslims over there are quite different from Muslims in the Middle East. The girls don't wear veils.

PJ: They're very secularized.
WV: Yeah. When I was in Croatia I did see some guys who had come from the Middle East—actually, quite a number of guys with attaché cases going about. And I sort of wondered what they were up to. When I was actually in Sarajevo I didn't see any evidence of that.

PJ: In your writings, there are always wars, conflicts, struggles, permeating them. Even in *Butterfly Stories*, your latest novel, I felt it was more about war and conflict than about the prostitutes and their plights because you have constant references to these Kampuchean killing field landscapes, to trees where Kampucheans were forced to watch their children get their skulls bashed against the trunks.
WV: I saw one of those trees very close to Phnom Penh. You can still see these hardened clots of blood on the trees. Just about every place you go you find these mass graves. Sometimes they're uncovered and they'll be full of rain water. And little kids will be fishing for frogs to eat, but you can see bits of bone and bits of clothing underneath the frogs.

PJ: Do you get much "PC"-motivated bullshit over your depictions of whores, junkies, and other "undesirables"?
WV: A little bit. Not too much. Oftentimes, when I read, I'll see people looking at me with somewhat hard faces. I find that as I read their faces dissolve as they see what I'm trying to do. They'll see that I don't have any ax to grind, and at the same time I'm not going to let myself be told what words I'm allowed to use, what words I'm not allowed to use. I see nothing wrong with calling a sixteen-or twenty-year-old human female a "girl." No doubt some people would find that offensive, but I really don't care. I was reading from *Whores for Gloria* in Portland, Oregon. I think that was the one time I was actually getting picked on a little bit. It was a sort of typical example of mob hypocrisy because these feminists were telling me how awful I was and how

I was exploiting these women. One girl was actually crying; she raised her hand; I thought, "Oh, no, I've really offended her." She just said, "Well, I used to be a prostitute, and a runaway, and I just wanted to say how moved I was by what Bill said." Then I was really sorry for these other ladies because since, obviously, she was the politically-correct one they had to all fall over themselves, to correct themselves, and agree with her. I really felt sorry for them.

PJ: I like how you try to fit your style to your subject matter. At one end's the rococo allegory of *You Bright and Risen Angels*, at the other's the straight-forward reportage of *Whores for Gloria* and *An Afghanistan Picture Show*. *Butterfly Stories*—your newest novel—seems to be an attempt to combine the realism and the dreamlike surreal allegory.
WV: That was sort of appropriate for that book.

PJ: Especially for the Butterfly Boy's fantasies and obsessions.
WV: He's sort of a sad character. I do think in every respect the form of a book should correspond to its content. That's one reason why I make my own handmade artist's editions of certain books. That's why the style, I think, has to be an appropriate vessel.

PJ: You've written two novels, *The Ice-Shirt* and *Fathers and Crows*, that are the first two volumes of a projected seven-part series, *Seven Dreams: A Book of North American Landscapes*. When is the third novel coming out?
WV: It's coming out in February. *The Rifles*. It deals with the Canadian Arctic, partly with the Franklin Expedition of 1845–48. Partly with Inuit—Eskimo—life in the 1880s and 1890s.

PJ: You're a very prolific writer. Do you actually schedule yourself a certain amount of time, a certain number of pages?
WV: I don't do that at all. I work on lots of different things. Whenever I get stuck on one thing I work on something else. I'm writing whenever I'm not doing anything else. Sort of like the difference between interactive and batch mode on the mainframe computer. I travel quite a bit; when I do that I'm always taking notes. When I get back I type the notes into the computer and start seeing how to use them. I'm usually just sitting at the computer unless I have something else to do. If I go on a trip, if I go out and see some-body, if I'm working on my art books, if my hands are hurting—and so I've got to do some reading instead of writing. I'm always occupied, and I think I've got a great life—I'm pretty lucky.

PJ: You got carpal tunnel syndrome while writing *Fathers and Crows*. Do you wear braces, or have you had surgery?
WV: I haven't had surgery; I'm reluctant to do it. Because, first of all, it would cost me about $10,000. Second of all, I'm concerned that cutting into the tendon sheathes of my wrists will weaken them, and maybe the next time I put on a heavy backpack or something I might tear my wrists. Sometimes I do have this one wrist-brace I use on one hand or the other. But, basically, what I try to do is let pain be my guide. When my wrists really start to hurt, then I just turn off the computer and do some other things.

PJ: You're outspoken about writers. Is there anyone else besides Cormac McCarthy you particularly care for?
WV: Jane Smiley. And there's a woman named Andrea Freud Loewenstein. She wrote a book called *This Place*, about a woman's prison, that I thought was very good. She has a new book out now, *The Worry Girl*, which I bought but I haven't read yet. I think a lot of American writing right now is not particularly good because most people can't write good sentences, and most people don't know how to read, anyway.

PJ: Regarding *Whores for Gloria*, how did the whole thing with Jimmy's obsession come about? He's this crazy Vietnam vet spending all his disability money on whores; he buys the memories of the prostitutes to make his fantasy dream-girl Gloria into some sort of Golem girlfriend. He's seriously delusional, I wasn't sure he was psychotic.
WV: Are you familiar with the theories of the Russian Formalists of the 1920s? Some of them had this interesting conception they developed from analyzing fairy tales. They noticed that fairy tales seem to have a finite number of motifs: The rescue of the princess. The discovery of the magical object. The wise old man who helps. What fairy tales were about, then, was not the invention of any new story, but it was the selection beads and the arrangement of beads and motifs on a given string. I thought this would be an interesting approach to take in writing something about prostitution. I tried with a story called "Ladies and Red Lights," in *The Rainbow Stories* to understand a little bit about prostitution. It was interesting, and for me it was a success *at the time*, it was the farthest I could go. The other stories, the ones about the skinheads, the street alcoholics, and so on so forth—I kind of felt I had failed. The prostitutes who tell their stories—it was difficult to get a sense of them as people. They would just tell the stories and I would pay them, and that was that, there were the stories. I knew that first

of all I would have to immerse myself more in that world. I had to just spend a lot of time in the Tenderloin and make friends with these ladies and do it better—which was what I did. And then I needed a way to present it.

So I said let's take these true stories the prostitutes have told and let's call those the beads. Then we're going to come up with some kind of a narrative—which is a fictional string—to put those beads up. I was trying to think of how to do that. Immediately there came into my head this notion of this guy who goes around buying stories. I have met a lot of people—a lot of customers—in Thailand, in the States, in other places, just very sad old men who are lonely, who need company, and who make up all kinds of things so that they can live in a happier world than everyone thinks they live in.

Lovesick

Liz Fried / 1993

From *Paper Magazine*, December 1993. © Liz Fried. Reprinted by permission.

William T. Vollmann loves women. We're at the Time Café, sharing a ginger-bread-and-ice-cream dessert. We've only been here for about ten minutes, and he's already asked me if I'm married. This comes as no surprise. I've been warned that he is a pathological womanizer (and to some extent, he works at cultivating this image). It is rumored that he has "wives" everywhere. But if you ask him, he won't admit to having even one. At the tender age of thirty-four, with eight books under his belt, Vollmann is possibly the most prolific young writer around. His "journalistic" fiction has been likened to Barth's, Burroughs's, Pynchon's—even Genet's—but if you ask him he'll say he's been more influenced by Faulkner. A slightly drunk Vollmann (from a lunch with his publicist) is telling me the story of how he and his friend Ken went to Thailand to free a fourteen-year-old sex slave. "Ken and I just went down and bought her for the night as if we were customers. And then we just kidnapped her." Vollmann speaks in a kind, soft, carefully measured way. His voice reminds me of a children's television show. He's dressed in a plum sweater, probably a gift from his mom or an aunt, and faded gray jeans. His thick glasses take up most of his face. It's hard to believe that this is the same guy in the stories who goes whoring around Southeast Asia. This is the same guy who smokes crack with the prostitutes and pimps of the Tenderloin District in San Francisco?

Vollmann is in New York to promote his new book, *Butterfly Stories*, just out from Grove Atlantic. Set in Thailand, it is a collection of interwoven stories about the adventures of a young journalist (Bill) and a young photographer (Ken) with the prostitutes that live there.

Liz Fried: What does *Butterfly Stories* mean?
William Vollmann: In Thailand, the girls are often looking for a husband

or a boyfriend. What they usually get is a butterfly—a guy who pollinates too many flowers.

LF: Is it true that you have wives all over the world?
WV: Why? Would you like to be one of my wives?

LF: Well, maybe someday, but in a lot of your stories, you refer to the prostitutes as "wives" . . .
WV: But what's a wife, after all, but a woman you love? A woman you want to be with, who will help you?

LF: You've been known to say that we're all prostitutes in some way. As a writer, how do you prostitute yourself?
WV: Well, this interview is an example of mutual prostitution, right?

LF: Sure.
WV: I'm doing it only because you're a nice person and I like you and I hope it'll sell some books. And you're doing it 'cause, hopefully, they'll pay you a little something—and there's nothing wrong with that. That fact that I like you and maybe you think I'm O.K. is totally immaterial. If we didn't like each other, we'd still be doing it.

LF: Your stories are about "saving" people—for example, the sex slave you just freed—or Vanna in *Butterfly Stories*. Where does this desire to help, against all odds, come from?
WV: Well, maybe you already know since you have some information on me. When I was a little boy, my small sister drowned. It was supposed to be my responsibility to keep an eye on her, and I didn't do it. And I always felt pretty bad about it . . . and I wanted to make it up to her, so I'm always trying to assist people who are in trouble, I guess. I'm especially attracted to women and girls who are in trouble, probably for that reason.

LF: Why do you so often write about social outcasts? Prostitutes, pimps, street alcoholics, skinheads.
WV: Well, I think by mainstream standards, they are losers, and I've often felt like a bit of a loser. I feel kind of miserable, inadequate, and bored when I'm around a lot of people.

LF: Why?

WV: Well, they talk about their lawns and the movies and the malls that they go to. And I don't really believe in that stuff. Because they care about all that stuff, and it's so harmless. When they start talking, I just can't listen. My eyes glaze over, and I feel really bad about it. I feel like an idiot, but I can't help it.

LF: In your stories, your characters often have fetishes. In "The Handcuff Manual," there are the handcuffs.

WV: I guess I don't think there's any real psychological difference between religious faith and sexual fetishization. People have a strong need to believe in something, whether it's God or a rabbit's foot. They can't quite bring themselves to rely on themselves in this random universe. How comforting it would be if handcuffs could solve all of your problems. Or if you could fall in love with somebody who'd take care of you. You wouldn't have to worry. We're always looking for easy answers.

LF: But Elaine Suicide didn't want the handcuffs?

WV: That's true. She wanted people who didn't want her, right? Oh, she wanted whatever she couldn't have, which is a very human thing. You know deep down inside that whatever it is you put your faith in is not actually gonna help you, so the best thing to put your faith in is something you can never have.

LF: Visuals seem to be important in your work. Your books have lots of drawings. Those beautiful CoTangent Press editions you collaborate on are like books-as-sculptures. Have any of your books been optioned for film?

WV: I wrote a screenplay of *Whores for Gloria* for Dennis Hopper.

LF: If he makes it, I guess he would play Jimmy, right?

WV: He'd make a great Jimmy . . . and you'd make a fine Gloria.

LF: Is *Butterfly Stories* the book that's going to break you out from the underground as a writer?

WV: No, I don't think so. I think I'll never be a mainstream sort of author. I think no one will give me too much attention, which is O.K. with me. I have enough money to live on. I can do what I want.

A Nerd in Action

Andy Beckett / 1994

From *The Independent on Sunday*, 26 June 1994. © *The Independent*. Reprinted by permission.

He looks like any computer-programming couch-potato. But William T. Voll-
mann is America's most celebrated literary action man, whose brushes with
danger are the raw material for millions of words of highly acclaimed jour-
nalism and fiction.

Around Sunday lunchtime a couple of months ago, the novelist and journalist William T. Vollmann was in a car with two friends, dozing in the back
seat, when they got lost in southern Bosnia and drove over a landmine. His
friends died quickly as the blast ripped up from under them. Vollmann was
slightly further away from the explosion and, unlike them, wore a flak jacket;
so he lived. He wasn't sure that he would do so for long.

"I heard the guys that did it laughing, and I waited for an hour for them to
come and finish me off . . . I was hoping that in seven or eight hours, when it
got dark, I could run away. Well, the soldiers came along. Their Kalashnikovs
were down-pointed. I knew they were gonna see me pretty quickly, and I
knew that the Yugoslavian admires a real macho type, so I just summoned
up my Serbo-Croatian and told them 'Good afternoon' with a big smile. The
Kalashnikovs all got erections. 'How many in the car?' they said.

"'Two dead. One alive. One probably about to be dead,' I said. They kinda
liked that. They said 'Croatian?' I said: 'No. American.' They said 'Aw, shit.'"
Vollmann laughs, loud and throaty, like the slab-featured Midwestern farm
boy he resembles, and settles deeper into plump candy-striped armchair.
After a short spell with minor wounds in a UN hospital, he is back home in
shady, heat-sleepy Sacramento, California, padding around in his socks, as
if he had actually spent the last few months watching the war on television.

He is opening beers at noon, scratching the back of his head with his
free hand, and letting his short, plain sentences sag with long country ahs,

I-guesses, and y'knows. He is affable, and volunteers a tour of the house twice, then lets me snoop around while he has his picture taken, grudgingly. His house is big, tidy and quiet, blocking out the suburb around it with net curtains, climbing plants and pretty wooden walls.

He fetches photographs of his dead friends that he took minutes after the explosion. "I don't wanna make a big deal out of this," he says, flatly. "Here's my friend who I've known for twenty years." He points to a thin man in spectacles and a T-shirt bloodstained at the heart, lying neatly on rough Tarmac. "I dragged him out of the car and put him there." The photos are calmly composed, level, and focused. "It was just an average sort of war murder," Vollmann says, lazy vowels still hiding any bitterness. "I was lucky that I was in the back." Then, his voice sharpening: "But I wasn't lucky that I was wearing the vest, because it was my choice. They chose not to wear theirs."

Vollmann, who is thirty-four, does dangerous journalism for a living: war reporting for the BBC and the *Los Angeles Times*, tracking down Asia's big heroin boss for *Spin* and spending two weeks at an abandoned Arctic weather station for *Esquire*. Vollmann gives shiny magazines a frisson of danger, of vicarious risk—and he increasingly gets their attention in return: a big profile in the *New York Times Magazine*, another in *GQ*, recommendations in *The Face*. They make him sound as dashing and fearless as a *Boy's Own* character—except that he gets hurt sometimes: hit by shrapnel, numbed by frostbite, tortured with cigarettes.

"I tracked him down after the explosion," says Bob Guccione Jr., publisher of *Spin*, in which the Bosnia story will appear, "and said 'Come home.' He said: 'The story's not finished.'" "If something were to happen," Vollmann had told the *Washington Post* a few weeks earlier, "provided there wasn't lingering pain . . . it wouldn't be the end of the world."

But Vollmann doesn't seem like a Hemingway, or even a Kate Adie. His eyes squint through thick oblong glasses from a chubby, scrappily shaved face, unflatteringly offset by a vicious crewcut. With a few spots, a backside as wide as his shoulders and an all-over indoor pudginess, he looks like a late-adolescent computer nerd. His shirt is vaguely khaki, but he hasn't buttoned it properly. It is hard to imagine him leaping from shellhole to shellhole.

He gets scared in dangerous places. ("The more scared you get, the longer you live," he says.) He is not "professional": he rarely speaks the local language, his eyesight prevents him from driving and he interviews by asking questions like, "What do you want America to do?" over and over again. He blunders his way to stories, relying on locals "to play big brother," being "continually embarrassed." He once wrote a whole book, *An Afghanistan*

Picture Show, about a year of failures trying to help the mujahedin, ending it with a letter from an Afghan general: "You have the brain—but you are not physically fit and you have no money—hence forget about the Afghans. Get down to a serious profession."

This gaucheness leaves him open to details and sensations—a rifle shot's "sharp, low snapping of the air"—that regular correspondents miss. His strange battery of images can give his observations life: the explosion of a shell, for example, is "a weighty, unpleasant sound of earth falling on earth, as if for a burial . . . fixing us in light for a forever second of terror, like some slice of tissue stained in eosin on the microscope slide of God."

And he does have the physical endurance to collect the raw material for his similes. The mujahedin may have laughed at his soft hands and feet, but he marched with them for days through high desert, and he remembered that "shade trees grew like miracles." His forward-leaning gait, you realize, as he shuffles round the house, is that of someone who is always carrying a backpack.

His journalism tends to be long and complicated, like drafts for a heavily researched novel. And that's exactly what it is: "I don't do anything for a magazine (or radio station) that I wouldn't be doing for a book." Since 1987 he has published eight novels using material from his reporting. "It's too easy to go on making things up," he says. "I want to experience . . . I want the things I write about to be real."

This isn't an unusual idea—American creative writing schools have long flooded the market with would-be Raymond Carvers eager to chronicle grimy real life—except that Vollmann uses his reportage as a jumping-off point for the kind of post-modern literary trickery usually found in Umberto Eco. Authorial interventions, arcane digressions and slippery chronologies chop up and toss Vollmann's slabs of reportage into an exotic Californian salad. Critics find it delicious: *USA Today* calls him "the reigning kid genius of American fiction"; the *Washington Post* thinks he's "the most prodigiously talented and historically important American novelist under thirty-five"; *Time Out* settles for "dazzling."

His new book, *The Rifles*, is typical. It weaves together the contemporary misadventures of a bumbling Vollmann-like narrator, variously called "I," "you," and "Captain Subzero," among the abused Inuit of northern Canada with a part-fictional, part-historical account of the explorer Sir John Franklin's doomed attempt to discover the Northwest Passage from the Atlantic to the Pacific during the 1840s. It needs a lot of stylistic horsepower to make it move: constant time-shifts back and forth, sometimes in the same sentence, authorial explanations of what's going on, and a glossary that takes up a third of the book. Sentences run on, typefaces change, and only Vollmann's sparsely vivid illustrations provide breathing space. Vollmann may have "a brain the size of Saskatchewan" (the *Financial Times*), but *The Rifles* can seem a cold book. Its subject, the cruelty and folly of explorers old and new, is as bleak as the grey tundra across which the characters struggle. Yet light and warmth come from its language, particularly in the many long prose-poem passages of minutely observed natural beauty: "The sea was emerald and the drift-ice bobbed in it and there were bubbles and tunnels in those floes, which were shaped like ships and rams' heads and camels, and they rode the waves in herds . . ." By the end, the exotic images, verbal pyrotechnics and double storyline are all clicking together, and Vollmann is beginning to read less like a trendy professor's idea of the perfect novelist and more like someone you might tell your friends to read.

Moreover, for all Vollmann's pessimism and dodging between perspectives, a distinct moral voice emerges. The plight of the Inuit—forcibly relocated to barren Arctic settlements by the Canadian government in the 1950s, and ruined by guns and drugs since—dominates the final sections of *The Rifles*. Vollmann includes letters he wrote to the government, transcripts of parliamentary debates and the addresses of relevant officials and academics.

"I'm real interested in doing good things and helping people," Vollmann says, still slumping in his chair but getting animated. "Writing is a way of creating something beautiful, and maybe inspiring people to do good, but if you wanna make the world a better place you have to go out and do something."

Last year he persuaded *Spin* to give him money to rescue a child prostitute from south Thailand and write about it. Blundering and creeping through a hot, squalid landscape of concrete-floored brothels, Vollmann snatched "the saddest little girl I have ever seen" from the pimps and spirited her away to a women's education center in Bangkok.

Of course, this raised a lot of questions. Was it just an exotic stunt? (*Spin* played it as one: "Vollmann travels through jungles and dungeons . . . to set her free.") How could he choose one particular girl to rescue? And what about his ambivalent view of prostitutes? ("In my opinion many did like it," he wrote.) *Spin*'s letters' pages fizzed with challenges and assents to Vollmann's conclusion that "the right thing had been done." Today the girl is still at the education center, he says, and he and Guccione have put up some money to help pay.

Rescuing people, specifically innocent young women is one theme (of many) blurring the line between Vollmann's fiction, his journalism, and his activism. Last year he sent the narrator of his novel *Butterfly Stories* on a frenzied search for a prostitute described in eerily similar, childlike terms to the one he rescued for *Spin*. He explains this fascination with his usual slightly detached directness, his eyes focused elsewhere, his expression blank: "My little sister drowned. I felt guilty about it, and I always wanted to make up for it, and so I'm really interested in being of service to other people somehow . . ." His legs splay out, long and slack in front of him; his right arm stays thrown back behind his head; only a slight mumble betrays much emotion.

The story of his sister's drowning is well-known—he talks about it in interviews and has just written about it for *Grand Street*, a New York literary quarterly. ("He publishes everything," says radio producer Noah Richler, for whom Vollmann once wrote ten thousand words on Yugoslavia in a single weekend, "and people will publish anything.") In 1968 his family were taking a break in New Hampshire from his father's job as a professor at Dartmouth College. The nine-year-old Vollmann was left in charge of his younger sister Julie, who was six, while she played in an apparently shallow pond. Lost in a book, he didn't notice her beginning to struggle—she couldn't swim—as its bottom suddenly dropped away beneath her. "Brawny ropes of water captured you," he writes in "Under the Grass," his agonizing nine-page attempt to deal with her death. "Until now I've scrubbed at the stain of your face on my brain's floor."

He had nightmares about his "executioneering" of Julie for years. But the guilt also drove him to write, "brazed to ferocity year by year by the memory of your blue face . . . No matter how many young girls I saved I could never undo or appease . . . your ghost."

Vollmann's writing is haunted by autobiography. He was not a happy child. Born in Los Angeles in 1959, he moved around the country with his father's teaching jobs. "I didn't have a lot of friends," he says, resigned. He started writing stories when he was six or seven. "I didn't have much else to do with my time." At high school he "had a hard time getting a girlfriend . . . I was shy and ugly and tongue-tied." (Now, he says "that stuff comes a little bit easier. I'm still ugly, but I can blab." He laughs. Later, his pretty girlfriend of nine years rushes in and out from her job at the local hospital, and he introduces her proudly. He lives in Sacramento to fit in with her work.)

Vollmann escaped lonely suburbia for the desert. He won a scholarship to Deep Springs College, a tiny all-male academy that solicits applications from high school students whose IQs are in the top half-a-percent. Its twenty-five students are forbidden to leave during term-time, and must run the ranch as well as devising and satisfying their own curriculum under elected professors. Students say it's "very demanding, very driven." "Deep Springs was a nice place," says Vollmann with a big smile, his first of the day. "You wanna eat, you gotta step in a little bit of pigshit . . . I enjoyed it a lot." Sharon Schuman, who taught him writing there, remembers a gentle, talented loner: "He was so unphysical. He lived inside his mind a lot. He was obviously driven to write and he had such unusual things on his mind that his writing wasn't like anyone else's. [It was] often sadistic, strange animals being dismembered . . . We tried to make his writing more normal."

From Deep Springs he went to Cornell University, to study comparative literature. "It was kind of a disgusting place," he says. "They taught people how to lead . . . They really didn't like me too much here. I guess I wasn't able to speak as eloquently as they could. Maybe my goals were a little bit different."

He left in 1982 to fight with the mujahedin, leaving behind a 135-page Honors thesis, linking up Dante, De Man's deconstructionist literary theory, and some reporting he had done on anti-nuclear protesters. "It was three times the required length," says the dean, Walter Cohen, who was on the thesis committee. "Not polished, but original, special. It was clear he wanted to be a writer and a witness."

When he got back from dodging helicopter gunships in Afghanistan, college seemed limited and he dropped out of a graduate course "reading other authors" at Berkeley: "It was just experience that I wanted." He took a job as a computer programmer in Silicon Valley, but he couldn't drive and it was hours away from his new home in San Francisco by public transport, so he had to live in his tiny programmer's cubicle during the week. "I'd bring my sleeping bag and as much food as I could, and I'd sleep under my desk, put a waste basket in front of my head so nobody could see me."

"Dreaming in front of the computer," Vollmann could only work, or write. He started to concoct a novel from his imagination, his education and the strange electronic tedium of his job. *You Bright and Risen Angels* was an obsessive 650-page account of a war for world domination between "revolutionary" insects and "reactionary" electricity. It jumped around like sped-up Pynchon, as Vollmann let a quarter of a century of thinking and watching pour out in paragraph-free pages. Some of it was just intellectual throat-clearing; much, American publishers agreed, was incomprehensible; but it dazzled Esther Whitby at André Deutsch in London ("At once I knew it was astonishing"), and so Vollmann got a publisher and, on the book's publication in 1987, a widening ripple of excited reviews.

But he was already bored with *You Bright and Risen Angels*, which he called "a kid's book." While critics salivated over its "electronic consciousness," he was writing about the skinheads, drunks, and prostitutes that he saw on San Francisco's street corners on weekends, establishing his *modus operandi* as a passive, but all-seeing "recording angel." (He even showed the skinheads a draft of what he was writing, and included their critique—"It should be cut, maybe to about half a page"—in the published version.)

The books that resulted—*The Rainbow Stories* (1989), *Whores for Gloria* (1991)—were an odd semi-fictional mixture of relentless, Charles Bukowski-style street brutality and lyrical epiphanies, usually inside the heads of the doomed characters. "Maybe you're a drunk or a pedophile," says Vollmann, "but inside you there's still something really special." He's not a relativist; he thinks that these marginal people are *better* than everyone else, because they're honest about their social transactions.

Vollmann likes to be literal. To learn about prostitutes he slept and smoked crack with them, then listed all the relevant prices at the back of *Whores for Gloria*. His life is mostly just material for his books because, by his intimidatingly direct logic, that's the obvious thing to do. There's not much else: "This year I've been home seven or eight days . . . This is really my girlfriend's house. I don't really know much about Sacramento." He talks about his work in simple sentences, without reference to literary theory or other authors. He goes into more detail about where we should order hamburgers for lunch.

"He doesn't frighten you," says Whitby, who has become a close friend. But, nice as he is—offering cold drinks for the road back, asking questions back that imply genuine interest—his gaze, made fiercer by his squint, focuses beyond you. "You're dealing with a higher intelligence," Richler says.

He reads ferociously: "Anything I can learn from or anyone who can write a beautiful sentence." He researches in libraries as well as brothels, mainly for *Seven Dreams*, a seven-volume "symbolic history" of North America he's writing. (He has published volumes one and two; *The Rifles* is volume six.) He once read all seventy-four books of French explorers' reports on seventeenth-century Canada. His writing voice in *Seven Dreams* constantly switches from child-like wonder at nature to formal period speech as if the idealistic Vollmann were fighting the erudite, streetwise Vollmann on the page.

The Vollmann fiction factory is a wide upstairs study: a fat, humming computer, a wall of books (William Burroughs, Elizabethan poetry, Eskimo history), a string of press cards and notebooks of large scrawl ready to be fed in, processed and published. Currently he's working (simultaneously) on a collection of prose poems, a book about an imaginary eastern European state, an essay about violence, a writer's guide and three more volumes of the *Seven Dreams*. Sometimes he types for sixteen hours a day. He also illustrates his books, with ethereal prints and watercolors of his dirty characters.

Vollmann makes people suspicious, makes other writers and critics feel insecure. Some say his mass of work, with its web of internal cross-references and repealed themes (truth in extremity, the beauty of nature, human weakness) looks impressive from a distance, but up close is thrown together, over-written, willfully difficult. Others think he's too good to be true: the *New York Times* got a letter claiming Vollmann was a hoax after it published a profile. What is clear is that he is still a cult writer, with a few critical champions, some obsessive fans (jailbirds and young girls, he says), much switching of publishers and relatively poor sales. His research can be expensive—his dangerous journalism has financial as well as artistic and philosophical motivations. And Sacramento's newspaper still spells his name wrong in its local literary round-ups.

Vollmann is disarmingly direct about his reputation, as he seems to be about everything: "Most people I don't think actually read the books . . . They look at 'em, and maybe flick through 'em a little bit. They see lotsa words, maybe not too many paragraph indentations, and they figure they're good doorstops . . ." He seems so pleasantly open as to be impenetrable, as if he never stopped being an egoless "recording angel," watching the world and creating his fat, visionary books, just because *that's what he does*.

But there are signs that his work affects him. He asks me not to use his girlfriend's name because "she's gotten death threats." And he bought a gun to protect himself when he was reporting for *The Rainbow Stories*. Now, up in his study a second time, he pulls out his squat black gun box to show me. "I like guns a lot," he says, cocking back a long and monstrous Desert Eagle pistol with the caliber of a heavy machine gun. "I was thinking of putting a laser scope on it . . . It'd be great if somebody ever broke into the house. I could just stand there at the top of the stairs, and they'd see a little red dot on their chest. It'd be so nice . . .

Has he ever killed anyone?

"That'd be illegal, if I had, wouldn't it?" says Vollmann, his grin suddenly more creepy than endearing.

Then he starts recording again: "How about you?"

Vollmann Ventures beyond the Edge

Sam Whiting / 2018

From *San Francisco Chronicle*, August 25, 1994. © *San Francisco Chronicle*. Reprinted by permission.

William T. Vollmann wears a haircut that looks self-inflicted, but there is a reason. In Bosnia-Herzegovina last May, the war reporter couldn't get the bloodstains out, so he had it all hacked off.

And how did the blood get into his hair? "Uh, well, uh," he begins, sinking into a soft chair in the living room of his Sacramento colonial home. The answer involves borders and civil war, but it takes a minute for his mind to find the file among the various novels, essays, and magazine pieces he shuffles like a general contractor.

Bosnia was two or three trips ago in a wanderer's life that since last September has filled sixteen pages of the third volume of his passport. Cuba, Peru, Madagascar, and Libya are still planned for this year.

"Well," he continues, slowly dragging Bosnia from its compartment, "how about a Calistoga? I'm drinking rum," and swirls the golden contents of a diminishing half-gallon at the ready by his chair.

Delivering Supplies

The details: On May 1, Vollmann, on assignment for *Spin* magazine; Francis Tomasic, his translator and high school pal from Indiana; and Bryan Brinton, a photographer, were driving from Split to Sarajevo to deliver food and supplies to some students Vollmann had befriended on a previous trip.

They took a wrong turn in Mostar, crossing from Croatian to Muslim territory, and were greeted by two loud pops.

"It's not clear to me whether it was mines or snipers," says Vollmann, 35, who was riding alone in the back seat. "But anyway my friends were killed, and that was that.

"One of my friends got a nice little hole in his head and the other one got a nice little hole in his heart, and there were two little holes in the windshield that looked like bullet holes to me."

He has pictures sitting in a box on the coffee table. They show both men slumped in their seat belts. That's the irony. A bullet-proof vest, like the one Vollmann was wearing, might have saved Tomasic, but a seat belt isn't much protection against a mine or rifle fire.

Waiting for Darkness

After the attack, Vollmann, who suffered only a few cuts, got down on the floor behind the front seat and beneath the protective weight of his thirty-pound Kevlar jacket and helmet—and the immeasurable weight of his fear. He planned to await darkness before making a run for it back to the Croatian side.

"Sometimes you feel kind of stupid and think you were a real idiot to get yourself into this situation," he says.

"Other times you think, 'Well, I was curious and I wanted to help somebody and I wanted to learn something, and maybe it's not going to work out for me, but in the meantime I'll try and enjoy life as long as I can.'"

Vollmann had an hour to enjoy life in this fashion, his head soaked with the blood of his buddies, before he heard two Muslims laughing as they approached with their guns.

"They were very surprised that somebody was alive, and they were very surprised to find out we were Americans," says Vollmann, who figures they had been mistaken for Croatians. Thus he was let go.

His editor at *Spin* offered to abort the mission, but Vollmann chose to stay in the war zone two more weeks to complete his assignment.

"I don't know exactly why people are making such a big deal out of it," he says. "It was unfortunate that my friends were killed, but we went there voluntarily and we were just doing our jobs."

As Vollmann sees it, his job is to get inside the minds of his subjects, who tend to be prostitutes and pimps, drug addicts and dealers, terrorists, skinheads, people who have taken wrong turns and landed where violence and trauma lurk.

"I enjoy seeing extremes of human behavior," says Vollmann, who has published nine books of fiction and journalism. He is now moving between a historical novel on Pocahontas (the fourth in a series of seven histories of North America) and a series of short stories based on his worldwide adventures, to be titled *The Atlas*.

Last month he visited Louisiana and Florida to research voodoo for a book on the legitimate uses of violence.

His fascination with death was molded by a childhood tragedy that he explains with the same matter-of-fact detachment with which he describes death in Bosnia. At age nine Vollmann was entrusted with watching his sister, 6, while she swam in a pond. But he was too busy dreaming to pay attention.

"My sister drowned. I was supposed to be watching her and I didn't."

It took him ten or fifteen years of nightmares to purge the guilt.

Untimely Death

"Probably the thing with my sister made me think about untimely death and what can be done about it," he says, "which is probably nothing."

Just in case, he took to carrying a concealed pistol while hanging around the Tenderloin gathering data for his books *The Rainbow Stories* and *Whores for Gloria*, published in 1989 and '91.

He smoked crack to prove he wasn't an undercover cop. He slept with prostitutes, and when he got to know them, paid them their hourly rate to tell him their life stories.

He got so deep into this grim urban blight that he took escape in the writings of nineteenth-century naturalist John James Audubon.

This in turn inspired Vollmann to launch his seven-novel treatise.

Three of the installments have been published—*The Ice-Shirt* (1990), *Fathers and Crows* (1992), and *The Rifles* (1994, Viking).

"I thought it would be nice to reimagine all these encounters between Native Americans and Europeans over the last thousand years," he says. "I've learned so much and had such a great time getting to know the landscape of our continent."

In the winter of 1991, while researching *The Rifles*, which examines the interactions between Eskimos, English explorers, and the repeating rifle, he decided to explore the magnetic North Pole by having a charter plane drop him off for two weeks at a deserted weather station 430 miles from the nearest settlement.

Vollmann wanted to empathize with explorer Sir John Franklin, whose party became icebound in the winters of 1846 and '47. One hundred thirty men died of sickness and starvation.

"I wasn't going to put myself in the situation of getting stuck for a couple of years and dying for this book," he concedes. "But what I could do was go up all alone in the middle of winter and get some sense of the fear and alienation, and it ended up being tougher than I thought."

His down bag failed against constant minus 40 temperatures.

"Eventually I couldn't sleep because it was all curled up like a frozen shrimp," he says now, laughing in the summer heat of Sacramento.

Sleeping in a Shed

His protective mask, covered in ice, ripped his face each time he removed it to eat, and was equally unpleasant to put back on. The abandoned weather station was too large to keep warm, so he ended up in a maintenance shed on the runway, waiting to be airlifted out.

"When it's pitch dark and it's cold and you know that you're your own best friend and worst enemy, then you really have to concentrate because if you panic, you're dead," he says. "It was great for my book."

Which seems to be all that counts, along with living long enough to write it.

Vollmann estimates that he has been home a total of about three weeks this year, and hopes to be home three more weeks before year's end, to complete *The Atlas*.

A Place for Books

He lives in a leafy part of Sacramento in a house he owns with his girlfriend, a doctor who declines to give her name. When Vollmann saw that a huge upstairs bedroom was already lined floor to ceiling with bookcases, he took the place. That's all the reason needed for a guy who leaves his study only to eat, sleep, and occasionally visit a firing range. Three or four handguns are scattered on a table in his office.

"This is a nice little one," he says, lifting a .50-caliber, ten-pound piece of overkill.

Because of astigmatism, Vollmann can see out of only one eye at a time. This is OK for aiming pistols, but he doesn't drive and hasn't seen much of

Sacramento. But he's enticed by a Davis freeway sign advertising Murder Burgers.

"It looks promising," he says.

A hall closet is filled with his survival gear, including the reinforced bulletproof vest with a dent in the front. Some Croatians wanted to test it with him inside, he explains, but they finally allowed him to remove his body before firing.

Another room has a wall covered with a world map. Colored pins and flags display the war zones and far-flung polar reaches he has visited.

When time allows, he plans to grab his bulletproof vest and helmet and get back to Sarajevo to finally deliver the aid to his student friends.

"I still would like to get those poor guys their vitamins," he says.

An Interview with
William T. Vollmann

Alexander Laurence / 1994

Portions of this interview appeared in *Cups* (October 1993), *The Bean* (August 1994), *Alt-X* (1994), and *Free Williamsburg* (May 2001). ©Alexander Laurence. Reprinted by permission.

I remember I first heard of William T. Vollmann in late 1989 or early 1990. There was some guy named Stuart who was couch-surfing at my place in North Beach in San Francisco. Stuart had a VW van and his girlfriend was my roommate. He lived there for free the whole time I was at that apartment in Spring 1990. I later saw him working at the library or at some bookstore. But the only conversation we had was about new writers. I think Thomas Pynchon's *Vineland* came out around that time. Stuart mentioned that Vollmann was good. I had only read one excerpt by him in *Conjunctions*, about skinheads. It was more documentary style writing with photos by Ken Miller. I used to read *Conjunctions* and *Paris Review* back then. Vollmann only had two books out at the time. I think that I read *The Rainbow Stories* first.

A year later the editor of *Conjunctions*, Bradford Morrow, hosted a reading in downtown SF, maybe fall 1991. The readers were Vollmann, plus Quincy Troupe, Kathy Acker, and the poet Norma Cole, who were all contributors. For such a spectacular lineup there was hardly anyone there: mostly other writers and people who I knew. It was the first time I met Vollmann. He came in the room in a camouflage jacket, looking that he just came back from a war zone. His latest book was the very difficult read *The Ice-Shirt*. As I recall Vollmann read mostly from *Thirteen Stories and Thirteen Epitaphs*, which hadn't been published yet in the USA. Back in those days Vollmann fired a starter pistol with blanks at certain points in the reading, as punctuation. He read for quite a long time, and left right after. Quincy Troupe also read for at least a half hour. By the time we got to

Norma Cole and Kathy Acker, many people had left. Kevin Killian told me later that he chased down Vollmann and got him to sign his books.

So there was a time around 1992, where it seemed like Vollmann came out with six books in less than two years. In 1993, there was an issue of the *Review of Contemporary Fiction*, by Larry McCaffery, that was about Vollmann, D. F. Wallace, and Susan Daitch. By this time I was writing for a few Bay Area publications. I was a writer at *Cups* magazine that was edited by Dave Eggers. Most publications at the time were not very interested in doing an interview with Vollmann. There was a bigger focus on gay writers or multiculturalism, I suppose. Eggers was more interested in this sort of interview. So the first interview was arranged in fall of 1993. I met Vollmann at Brainwash Café. I soon learned that Vollmann lived in Sacramento now, and he didn't drive a car. We spoke for about an hour or more. Some friends came by. It was a positive meeting. I didn't like the final result though. Very little of the interview was used, and Eggers didn't even use the picture that I gave him.

So during that time I ran into Vollmann often. He was at book readings, he was at book fairs, and he would be at City Lights. I ran into him at Book Expo in LA in 1994, not long after he saw his friend Francis Tomasic killed in Bosnia. I met other writers like Larry McCaffery, Michael Hemmingson, and Eurydice, who all came to San Francisco at that time, and knew Vollmann.

I met Ken Miller and Jerome Caja, and also Ben Pax who were Vollmann's friends from when he first lived in SF. Ken Miller ended up giving me some photos to use in *Cups* magazine. He was very down to earth and also larger than life. He did wedding photography. He lived in Richmond. Ken told me that he heckled D. F. Wallace at a reading in NYC one time. It was funny. Jerome Caja was a drag queen who I had taken photos of at Folsom Street Fair. Jerome had many art openings around town. His lipstick paintings are mentioned often in Vollmann's books. Both Ken Miller and Jerome Caja went to SF Art Institute when it was crazy in the early 1980s. Ben Pax lived around 24th and Sanchez, and Vollmann used to stay there a lot. I met him there once and we walked down to 24th Street BART. I was with Vollmann for an interview and a book reading in Berkeley.

Another coincidence was I knew Brandi the prostitute, who is mentioned in many of Vollmann's early books. I used to see her a lot when I lived in the Mission District. Around this time Vollmann made it clear that he was looking for nude models. I asked a few people and they weren't too interested. There was one person who was the managing editor of *Cups* magazine who ending up doing it. Around this time, Vollmann also hooked up with Dave Eggers and *Might* magazine. He ended up writing something for them or Eggers also found some nude models for him. I don't know exactly what happened. Vollmann also gave me a piece for *Cups* magazine about how we should eliminate cars, and go back to the horse.

Somehow another interview was set up with Vollmann towards the end of 1994. We had a longer interview and pictures by Ken Miller. We had an interview with Eurydice. Both Vollmann and Eurydice were writers at *Spin* magazine at the time. I sent a big stack of the magazine to the *Spin* offices and I heard it was very popular there. In a couple years in SF, it seemed like Vollmann was far more known in the Bay Area and all the readings were well attended.

One time I was with my girlfriend at City Lights Bookstore. It was around Christmas time. Vollmann was there with his family and his parents. He told me that they were staying at the Hyatt and I should come down and visit. I came with my girlfriend Laura. We were late. Vollmann left me a note. We went upstairs and we chatted with Bill and his sister. Vollmann's wife made him put on some dress slacks for some dinner they were going to later that night. So we watched Bill try to avoid the pants for almost an hour. It seemed weird so we left.

I moved to NYC in early 1996. *Infinite Jest* had just come out. D. F. Wallace did a few readings in NYC back then. I went to one with Susan Daitch, who was a friend by then. They were packed and uncomfortable, and one was in the middle of summer. I never really met Wallace, or ever interviewed him, although we talked about it and exchanged letters. I thought he was academic at the time. Vollmann was also in NYC a lot in 1996.

He was doing a reading at Books and Company, in the Upper East Side. Jonathan Franzen was there. My friend Gabor had wanted to translate *Whores for Gloria* into Hungarian. Not sure if that ever happened. Some other famous writers were there. Some others not so famous. My writer friends Joanna Rakoff and Robert Anasi were with me. They both have published books since then. A group of us headed over to some bar on 81st and York. Apparently this was some place that Vollmann and Franzen used to hang out five years previously. When they sat down they both ordered rosemary hamburgers. I was trying to seem different, so I ordered a French dip sandwich. I was sitting next to Franzen and across from Vollmann, so I was considered someone important. That didn't prevent Joanna Rakoff from calling Vollmann "ugly" and Franzen "some dork from Oberlin College." I doubt that they heard. At the end of the night publicist Paul Slovak, who I had met at Book Expo, pulled out a credit card, and paid for everyone's food and drinks. "This is for you, Bill!" he said.

Another time Bill came back to NYC for another reading. This must have been our tenth–twelfth time meeting. It was somewhere in Chelsea. I was with the writer Eurydice. It was a good reading. Afterwards we stopped by a bar nearby called Man Ray. There were about ten of us. We had some drinks and spoke about some crap. One good looking guy who I didn't know, who didn't say anything the whole time, stood up and said: "Man, I like your books, but in person you are disappointing." And then he walked away and left. Eurydice was a little pissed. Vollmann laughed it off. I only half heard what he said.

Another time Vollmann was staying at the Algonquin Hotel. I get the feeling he stayed there before. He invited me over. He was with his sister. His sister made me do some personality psychological test. I had to make some drawings and describe them. We had some more rosemary hamburgers. I think they cost close to $25 at the hotel. But he paid for it since I took the test.

I didn't see Vollmann much from 1998 to 2001. It was a very dark period for me. I went through a divorce. There were a lot of changes. As I remember, Vollmann was sick during this time as well.

I decided to do an interview over the phone for *Free Williamsburg*. It was 2000 and *The Royal Family* had just come out. It would be my third interview with Vollmann. After this I rarely did any literary interviews. I started writing about music. I saw him again at a reading in LA. I brought a friend with me who hadn't read any Vollmann books or anything at all. It was difficult to keep up with Vollmann post *Europe Central*. Everything the Greeks wrote can be collected into forty volumes. I have met only a few people who have read them all. With Vollmann, there is a lot, but you don't feel like you have to read everything.

AL: I want to talk about *The Rifles*. Alexander Theroux called this book "a travelogue"—how do you feel about that?

WTV: Well, there's been a fair amount of misunderstanding about the book. But people have the right to read a book any way they want; it doesn't hurt my feelings. The book is not about me and it's not about places I've been. It's about a specific area, the Canadian Arctic, and the way in which it has been changed by Europeans and by European technology over the past 130 years.

AL: There are many drawings in this book. What is your process in making images to go along with your text?

WTV: I bring paper and pens with me when it's warm. When it's cold I bring pencils, because otherwise the ink will freeze in the pens. Most of the time I've been in the Arctic in the summer, but I've been a couple times in the fall and once in the winter. I've been to lots of different places in the Arctic so maybe that's where people get the idea the book is a travelogue.

AL: Do the drawings complement the text? How do they function—are they illustrations? If they weren't there, what would be lacking, in your mind?

WTV: I'm a visual artist as well as a writer. I think that a good drawing, particularly by the guy who wrote the book, is bound to be an enhancement. It's bound to show something in a slightly different way and makes everything more three-dimensional for that reason. I think the book can function fine without the drawings, but it pleases me to have them in there. One section of the book deals with these scarlet mushrooms, and it's nice to have a picture of one, since most people will never get a chance to go there and see them. If the literal description in words of something is valuable, then I think a nice drawing of the same thing, with its freshness, is equally valuable.

AL: There's a part in the book about the Inuit, that "Inuit" is the proper term, while "Eskimo" (or Esquimau) is racist . . .

WTV: It depends on where you are. In Alaska, a lot of the native people call themselves Eskimos and there's nothing pejorative attached to it. In Greenland they call themselves Greenlanders or Eskimos; in Canada they call themselves Inuit. Inuit just means "the people," just like Sioux or Cheyenne, all those Native American names all mean "the people." As far as they're concerned, everybody else is not really "people"; we're not people . . . The Inuit are pretty racist, but that's the name they call themselves and a lot of them don't like being called Eskimos. That was a name applied to them by the Crees or Chippewa and it means "eater of raw meat," which they are, but some Canadian Inuit felt it was meant in a mean way, so some of them don't like it. If you're talking about the Canadian Northern people, you'd say Inuk for the singular, Inuuk for two people, and Inuit for three or more.

AL: This book deals with the introduction of the rifle, then the disappearance of certain animals and types of people, then it moves up to modern day Canada. What's the situation there now?

WTV: There's a political struggle going on over land claims. The Inuit have won a relative victory compared to other Native Americans on our continent. The Canadian government has agreed to give them a fairly large territory called "Nunavut," which means "Our Land." The syllabic alphabet was developed by Moravian missionaries—they didn't have a written language before the Moravians came. I think it's a neat thing, actually.

AL: How's your grasp of that language?
WTV: I can read it; I just don't know what anything means . . . But sometimes it's helpful; the signs might be in Inuktitut and every now and then I'll know a word. It makes people happy that I can read a little.

AL: Why is the introduction of the rifle so important?
WTV: The rifle is a metaphor for all kinds of things being introduced to Native (particularly Inuit) culture. In the old days, people hunted with spears. If you threw a spear at a caribou, there's a good chance you wouldn't hit it, or you'd wound it and it'd get away. So every time you saw a caribou you had to try to kill it (not every time—they had certain rules, like not killing does with young or pregnant does). The caribou would only come twice a year, so whenever you'd see them, you'd have to try to kill as many as you could so you wouldn't starve. Well, all of a sudden you get a single shot rifle, which increases your odds, and a little bit later you get a repeating rifle, which means that you don't have to load it between shots, so now you have incredibly good odds of hitting the caribou. If you go ahead and kill every caribou you can, just like in the old days, because you still had that insecurity and you don't really grasp the difference, you might end up wiping out a lot of caribou and then starving to death. So this tool which should really help you, which seems to make you so much more efficient, can be misused to really hurt you. And there's a lot of controversy over whether or not this actually happened. *The Encyclopedia Britannica* says various groups disappeared—just starved to death. But some anthropologists and biologists don't believe it. So it's not clear to what extent repeating rifles played a part in what happened. Maybe just the fact that caribou fluctuate in population caused a lot of people to starve. But the fact remains that the repeating rifle is a good example of tools that can be abused. Certainly the rifles have made some animals go extinct or nearly so, like the musk ox. Every time that happens, life for the Indians and Eskimos has got to change. If all of a sudden there isn't enough game, people have to live in settlements and pay mortgages and end up on welfare. Things become real different real fast.

AL: Guns have had an enormous impact on American society as well. How long have you been shooting guns?

WTV: Since I went to Afghanistan. How about you?

AL: I've shot a .44 a couple times—my brothers took me out to a range.

WTV: That's a nice gun. It's fun, huh? Making a big bang . . .

AL: It was a strange experience. In rap music there's a lot of stuff about big dicks and AKs—what do you think of guns as a metaphor for male sexuality and male orgasm?

WTV: I've got a friend from Minnesota who always used to say "the bigger the gun, the shorter the peter" and I think there's some truth to that, particularly with guys who get off from using guns to kill people, as a way of showing they are men. In my opinion, they're just despicable cowards and bullies, they aren't men at all, they're not even human. As far as I'm concerned they should be eliminated like some kind of dangerous animal. As far as the guns/male orgasm connection—sure! It's complicated, of course, but I do think sex has always been bound up with sadism. It always has been, and always will be. It's also definitely a male thing, because men tend to be more aggressive than women. I think this is due to hormone levels, and for the same reason men tend to risktakers and thrillseekers more than women. I don't mean every man vs. every woman, but as a general rule, that's been my experience. It has to do with testosterone, and certainly shooting off guns reflects that.

AL: More and more I see you writing in paragraphs, in an anecdotal style . . .

WTV: I don't know, *The Rifles* is based more on field research than *You Bright and Risen Angels* was. *Fathers and Crows* was equally divided between library research and trips to the woods in Canada. *The Rifles* is probably 25% research and 75% experience, so maybe that's why it seems more anecdotal to you.

AL: What kind of preparations did you make for *Fathers and Crows*? How much research and how much traveling?

WTV: I travelled some. I went to a lot of places in Canada. I got some Quebecois friends who talked to me a lot, and told me their point of view, and showed me a lot of things. Mainly I worked at the NY Public Library and read every primary source I could. There are maybe 250 or 300 volumes that deal with the first half of the seventeenth century of Canada, and I tried to read all of them I could.

AL: In *Butterfly Stories* and in *The Rifles* there's a structure you're falling into. There's usually a guy, an adventure and a love interest on the side. Why is that? Why do so many of your stories take that form?

WTV: Well, in my opinion there are only two or three stories in the whole world. One is: a person is born, grows up, gets old, and dies at some point. The other story is: two people meet each other and they love or hate each other and something happens. Every story falls into one or the other category, or both. The stories in the *Seven Dreams* all deal with the encounters of Europeans and Native Americans and most of the Europeans who arrived here as explorers were men. So you can have encounters between Caucasian men and Native American men, which there's quite a bit of in these books, and also, not to leave the women out, you may as well have encounters between people of the opposite sex. I think generally that two people who have some kind of love interest are going to have a more deep, profound, and interesting relationship than two people who are just friends, business partners, allies or enemies in war or something like that. Therefore it's inherently more interesting to write about.

AL: *The Rifles* is the sixth "Dream," so the seventh dream is more about American Indians?

WTV: The seventh one's about Hopi and Navaho, yes. The third one, which I'm about half done with, is about Pocahontas—it's a love story, sort of. The fifth one (but I'm not 100% sure yet) is about the Plains Indians, probably Chief Joseph of the Nez Percé. The fourth was going to be about King Philip and the Great Swamp War, and it may still be, but I love Canada so much that I'd like an excuse to go back there and do something else. Maybe I'll do another book about other Canadian Indians.

AL: What do you think about John Franklin? Is he a fascinating character to you?

WTV: I think what happened to him on these expeditions and what happened to him ultimately was fascinating and amazing and kind of horrifying. He was probably a pretty dull guy, in my opinion, probably a good person by the standpoint of his own culture, which is the only way you can fairly judge someone. It seems like he was a gentle, cheerful person, very brave and uncomplaining, but he was certainly unable to listen to the native people about where to go and how to go and when to go. That's why he got in trouble and his men starved on the second expedition. They narrowly missed trouble on the third expedition and they all perished on the fourth.

Sometimes I blame him for that, other times I think it's not fair, because he'd gone into the English navy when he was a young man and had been totally indoctrinated. People in the English navy at that time never had any other idea or thought that any way but the English navy way would work. Franklin didn't have the benefit of the education we have. We're all brought up under the assumption that everybody's equal and other cultures have the same rights and should be respected; he didn't know that, and you can't blame him, really, for thinking these people were inferior and knew less. And he wasn't bad to them, he was just stupid.

AL: Your male characters seem to really love women and are very empathetic toward them, so I'm never offended by these guys, but I wonder, have you had any problems with feminist critics?

WTV: Sometimes. There are always people who are angry and disappointed with me, especially since I freely admit I've had sex with prostitutes and I enjoyed it. As far as I'm concerned, I think, what's the big deal? I made the women happy, I paid them generously, they made me very, very happy; I was lonely, I felt good afterward. It seems to me nobody exploited anybody. But in this country especially, people are so prudish and so convinced that linking sex to economics is such a disgusting perversion. Both the right and left wing think it's wrong, and I feel sorry for people who think that.

AL: Anyway, I want to shift gears and ask about your story about Survival Research Laboratories ("The Indigo Engineers"—from *The Rainbow Stories*). I felt your ambivalence toward SRL, and wondered if you think they're fascinated by violence without really understanding it. I know you've been to several war zones . . .

WTV: I think Mark Pauline is a genius of sorts. The machines he makes are really amazing and he's a very intelligent, thoughtful guy. The things he says are very interesting. I don't like him, personally, I think he's a very tormented, kind of mean person. He was kind of mean to me when he dropped that beam on his finger.

AL: And you wrote about "the vampires" standing around with their attitudes, saying "Oh, the destruction!"

WTV: Well, it's a strange thing. More and more I believe that people are innately aggressive, just as they are innately sexual. And just as I think prostitution should be legalized, we have to legalize and give approval to some channel for people's aggressiveness and violence. Maybe what we need is some carnival for two weeks a year where everybody who wants to can get together with guns in some stadium and kill each other. Then maybe they wouldn't kill other people.

AL: Some ritual or ceremony . . .

WTV: Right. And it could be broadcast on television, people could tune in, it'd be more exciting than the Olympics. They could sell souvenirs, they could tax it and somehow control it, you know? And SRL is part of that. I think they're very nihilistic people and I found the stuff they did to be profoundly creepy. I think there's definitely a resonance between that stuff and the real things people like my friend Pawel are suffering. Obviously SRL fills a need, like prostitutes do. If people didn't need to be vicariously violent by watching the grim destruction those machines are about, then no one would go to their performances. But everybody loves them.

AL: How do you deal with your own aggression or innate violence? What do you do, personally, to sublimate that?

WTV: I go on these high-risk trips, which give me plenty of outlets for my aggression. I have to scheme to protect myself and accomplish whatever it is I've set out to do, like meeting the Opium King . . .

AL: When was that?

WTV: In Burma; I just did that. Those experiences are great for me, they keep me happy. I think a lot of people are unfulfilled and psychotic and so forth, because they have these impulses and there's no way they can legitimate them. Someone who wants to kill people can kill people—he can kill his neighbor and go to the gas chamber. Or if he's lucky, there'll be a war and he can kill somebody else's neighbors who are wearing a different uniform, and maybe he'll be a hero. So much of it is environment and luck. Regardless, both those people need or want to kill somebody. It's a phase of a person's life, particularly males from their early teens to twenty-five or thirty, when the hormone levels are at their highest, that's probably when they have the strongest need to prove themselves and be aggressive.

AL: In the *New York Times Magazine* you were compared to an empirical scientist, using your body as a field for research. Do you think that to create art, you need to "push the envelope"—physically, intellectually, and spiritually?

WTV: I think you do, not in reference to what other people have done, but with reference to what you've done and testing what your capabilities are. If you're not growing and doing something that's a complicated, tricky problem for you, that you don't know how to solve when you start, then there won't be any interest or accomplishment. Which isn't to say that once you've gotten to a certain point, you can't do very wonderful things that come without any seeming effort, because that's a part of it, too. Some of my best stories and drawings have just happened, and it's been this easy, delightful experience, but those are bonuses that come after a lot of hard work.

AL: What's your general feeling about war? You're working on a book about war and violence . . .

WTV: I'm still not sure. The book's not done yet. I'm trying to figure out when violence is ethical and when it isn't. It's too easy for people to say, no, you should never ever be violent. I think that's baloney. I think it was amazing what Gandhi was able to accomplish. I also think the Warsaw ghetto uprising was absolutely justified. Those people knew they were probably going to their deaths. If they'd wanted to go on a hunger strike, something Gandhi would've done, the Nazis would've said, "Great!" That makes them weaker, all the easier to haul them into the cattle car. By getting guns and killing Nazis, German soldiers, they didn't die for nothing and some of them actually did escape, a very small number succeeded in staying alive. So there's a clear example of violence being absolutely good. In general, I say any time you're aggressed upon, violence is necessary to defend yourself, the problem comes from determining what aggression is. For instance, if you're a radical Earth First person, do you say some factory with a big smoke stack in your neighborhood is an act of aggression and do you have to blow up the factory and kill the people in it? I used to wonder about stuff like that, and I'm still not sure what the answer is.

AL: What do you think of the recent movie, *Schindler's List*, about "the good Nazi?" What do you think of that general feeling of being an apologist for Nazism?

WTV: I think that Schindler was a great guy. I think he did a really good thing and maybe he didn't start off a great guy, and maybe at the end of the war he didn't stay a great guy, but without him all those people would not be alive, and results do count. I think words and good motives are not enough. A disastrous result with good intentions isn't as bad as a disastrous result with evil intentions. But a good result is the best thing of all, even a good result with bad intentions. I think you have to respect the guy. I'm always trying to figure out the best way to do good things and help people and sometimes I get involved with some fairly crummy people in the effort to try and do some good things, and that's just necessary. If you're going to do anything in the world, you have to get your hands dirty. That was Plato's problem: he wanted this ideal state and he couldn't bring himself to participate in politics because he could never find a situation that was perfect and theoretically perfect. I can respect the guy for wanting to be pure but I respect somebody more who jumped in and tried with all his imperfections to help other people.

AL: You've been writing for different magazines like *Spin*, the *New York Times Book Review*, and so on. Do you enjoy journalism?

WTV: I do a lot of writing about other places. Things like an essay on violence requires me to do high risk, high budget things all over the world. So what better than to say, "Well, the next chapter I write will be about Bosnia, so let's get *Spin* to send me to Bosnia." I'll write that chapter, give it to them, let them edit it and do what they want with it. I'll publish it my way in the book. So it seems like a pretty fair trade off to me. The sentences get a little trimmed in the editorial process of a magazine, but as long as I have the right to read it over and make sure the basic message isn't changed, I'm not concerned about it because in a few months that issue of the magazine will be obsolete. But if I put it in a book, the book will stay relatively perfect and germane for a long time.

AL: What's going on in Sarajevo? You're going back there soon, right?

WTV: I think it's getting better, in Sarajevo at least, but there are flare-ups in other places. I think there's a good chance that in another year, things will get better there. If they can play soccer now, it's got to be much safer than when I was there. My understanding is it's still a prison. People aren't getting shot at as much but they still can't go in or out. I think we were very foolish to have insisted on an embargo, because that meant the two sides that were the strongest were able to continue to get weapons in defiance of the embargo, and the weak side couldn't get any weapons. All we did was seal the fate of the Muslims. We could've at least sold them a bunch of weapons, so they'd be equal with the others.

AL: I wanted to talk about your article about the sex slave from Burma. How's she doing?

WTV: She's doing great. She's almost ready to graduate from the school.

AL: What about prostitutes in general? You've covered that area pretty well with your writings. Do they still currently interest you, or were those the good old days in the distance?

WTV: My interest will always be there. I think it's a fascinating time. Tolstoy didn't give up writing love stories till the very end. All prostitutes' stories are love stories. Why should I stop?

AL: In *Butterfly Stories*, you have an elaborate section about safe sex and using condoms. It goes: "Conscious pleasure, on the contrary, seems to require a steady and continual augmentation of the stimulus . . ." And so forth.

WTV: Is that what you have found? Well, first of all, I think condoms are a violation of human rights. It'll be great when there's a home AIDS test. You meet somebody at a bar and each take out your little needle and go "bink, bink." "Oh, negative! Oh, no problem."

AL: What do you say to the young people out there, about safe sex and condoms?

WTV: I say, "Safe sex is for wimps!" AIDS is a state of mind.

AL: Why do you write?

WTV: Because I enjoy beautiful things. I enjoy reading books that have beautiful sentences, and it makes me feel real good if I can try to create something that's beautiful, even if it's sad or on an ugly subject. If the thing is well put together, it makes me feel good.

William T. Vollmann

M. T. Kinney and Chan Marshall / 1996

From *Osmotic Tongue Pressure*, No 5. Reprinted by permission.

This interview was conducted at Mary's Place, Portland, OR, in April, 1996.

Osmotic Tongue Pressure: We were thinking of going to a bar or something. Maybe Mary's. A strip joint.
William T. Vollmann: I've been to three or four of the strip bars here, yeah, sure, I'll go there with you.

OTP: I don't know if they'll let me in.
WTV: Sure they will. A lotta girls like to look at girls.

OTP: I'm from Georgia and I don't know about my ID, they might think I'm an undercover weirdo.
WTV: You don't look like a weirdo, or undercover. We'll vouch for you.

OTP: It's a great book, *The Atlas*, one of my favorites. Did you work on the palindromic-layout thing for a while, or was that whimsical?
WTV: You know, halfway through I realized how it could be and I started writing some of the other stories with that in mind.

OTP: You are supposedly working on a long piece that's about humanity and violence?
WTV: It's called *Rising Up and Rising Down*. It's about the necessity of violence. In the beginning I have stuff about Alexander the Great; how his style in leading armies was to run ahead, and then the army had to follow.

OTP: What's your sign? How 'bout your girlfriend's?
WTV: Mine's Leo, and she's a Taurus.

OTP: What happened with that girl you somehow saved in Thailand?
WTV: She was a fourteen year-old in Thailand who I saved from a pretty brutal brothel. She thought it was a kidnapping, and actually missed the sex.

OTP: You also have another wife in Thailand, right? How often do you two talk?
WTV: Whenever I go there. She's got one thousand hubbies.

OTP: You spent some time in the highest place on earth, latitudinally-speaking, the magnetic North Pole. What did you eat there, and what kind of weird shit happened?
WTV: I ate cheese, my glasses froze, and I lost my eyebrows. I was up for eight or nine days straight, and my gas turned to jelly.

OTP: What's up with that seal story in *The Atlas*?
WTV: Walrus penises, the kids use them as baseball bats, and their pelts make great shoes.

OTP: When you're writing, do you stop and re-read what you've written?
WTV: Sure.

OTP: How many times do you do that within how many pages?
WTV: I'd say maybe five or six pages.

OTP: You have time to do that?
WTV: I try and do a good job if I can.

OTP: You get paid for readings?
WTV: No.

OTP: Your publishing company puts you up?
WTV: They pay for the hotel and stuff like that.

OTP: New shoes?
WTV: Oh yeah.

OTP: Pencil sharpeners?
WTV: Especially those.

Interview: William T. Vollmann

Dennis Cooper / 2000

From *Bookforum*, Vol. 7, Issue 4, Winter 2000. ©*Artforum*. Reprinted by permission.

Dennis Cooper was guest fiction editor for this issue of *Bookforum*.

Could there be a more appropriate interviewee for this "No New York" fiction section than West Coast author and meta-individualist William T. Vollmann? One of the most respected and well-published contemporary writers, he's also the great undomesticatible iconoclast of American fiction. From his mysterious and complex first novel, *You Bright and Risen Angels* (1987), to his ferociously direct and still complex new novel, *The Royal Family*, Vollmann's dozen novels and collections of short stories constitute as brave, unpredictable, and wholly original a body of work as the American literary establishment is capable of celebrating. Even so, his career has not been without controversy. Vollmann's 1993 journalistic piece for *Spin* about his efforts to kidnap an underage Thai prostitute caused some to question his morality, and his habit of firing a blank pistol during his readings has contributed to the mistaken impression that Vollmann is a man prone to the violent acts his work so frequently and brilliantly describes. A resident of California's obscure, all but uncultured capital city of Sacramento, the polite and surprisingly gentle Vollmann spoke with me by phone during a brief downtime between picking up his child from school and heading off on an East Coast book tour.

Dennis Cooper: Early on in your career, your novels and stories were compared to metafiction maestros like Pynchon, Gaddis, and Barth. But in reviews of *The Royal Family*, names like Steinbeck and Dos Passos keep popping up—a radical shift in the perception of your writing. Does it make sense?
William T. Vollmann: Sure. When I was first writing, I had this feeling of power in my fingers. There were all these words wanting to come out, and

it was an extremely exciting and pleasurable process, almost like automatic writing. I'd just sit there at the computer and start writing away, and I wouldn't know what I was going to write or what was going to happen. It was really thrilling. I'm forty-one now, but right when I turned thirty, I started getting carpal tunnel syndrome, which made it impossible for me to type quickly. With every keystroke, there was a certain amount of physical pain. So that changed the writing process for me. Instead of riffing and creating the most beautiful sentences that I could, I found that a lot more of the writing was going on in my conscious mind beforehand. So there was a shift to subject matter, I guess, whereas before I'd been interested in form. And I really, really do admire Steinbeck. I think he has such a fine heart. So much of writing doesn't have heart in it. I want to write about people with problems, and try to help them, or, if not help them, make other people understand them through my books. Certainly Steinbeck was interested in that, too.

DC: Don't you think Steinbeck's writing can get a little rigid? I sometimes think that even though his subject matter is emotionally explosive, his voice is so stiff that the war doesn't always break out.
WV: Everybody has faults, and, even with Steinbeck, there are a lot of failed experiments. But *The Grapes of Wrath* and *East of Eden* are really interesting and have a strong experimental quality as well.

DC: How is this change in the way you write fiction going to affect your novel cycle in progress, *Seven Dreams*? At least a couple of the novels predate your bout with carpal tunnel, and the series concerns itself a great deal with issues of form, structure, and style.
WV: Well, within that septology, there's a lot of room for variation, so it won't be a problem. I basically just want to tell the same story seven times in different ways: There's an indigenous culture, and a European culture comes in and destroys it. I just finished the next one, about Pocahontas. It's called *Argall*, and it will come out next year. Argall was the man who kidnapped Pocahontas, if you know your history. He was responsible for a lot of terrible things. He introduced black slavery to Europe, and was involved in a lot of violence. It's a pretty violent book.

DC: Books like *Whores for Gloria*, *The Rainbow Stories*, and *The Royal Family*, where you chart and reinvent your own personal experiences, have a rawness and immediacy that aren't in the historical novels like *Fathers and Crows* or *The Ice-Shirt*, for instance.

WV: I hope that's true. With the *Seven Dreams* books, I try to create a sentence structure that corresponds to the prose of the European protagonist of each volume. So *Fathers and Crows* has a glorious, pseudo-French style, and in *Argall*, the approach is sort of similar. That does create a certain amount of distance. With *The Royal Family* and the other books you mentioned, they're written in more or less current idiom, so the language seems to come more naturally to the people who are talking, and it comes fairly naturally to me. It will be interesting to see how readable those books are in a hundred years, though. Did you ever read Gide's novel *The Counterfeiters*?

DC: Sure. That was a major book for me.

WV: I remember reading it in French when I was in college, and I thought it was amazing, but I had a lot of trouble with it. My French teacher said that the slang has changed so much since it was written that a lot of French people have difficulties with it now. So I would think that some of the stuff in those particular novels of mine will be tough for people in the future. I think about that a great deal, so I give a lot of consideration to making the idioms seem hard-won and necessary.

DC: You're a forebear and something of a hero to younger, experimental writers like Mark Z. Danielewski, Dave Eggers, and Tristan Egon. Do you feel a kinship with these so-called postmetafiction guys?

WV: I'm really a loner. I live out here in Sacramento, where hardly anybody has a bookshelf. When I do get together with writers, I talk to them about their taxes or something like that. That's about it. I used to live in San Francisco, and wanted to live there again, but my wife got a job here. I don't drive, but it's only two hours by Greyhound bus to San Francisco, so I go down there a lot. But I don't know writers, even there. My best friend there is a housepainter, and my other friends are a stripper and a photography student and a sheet rocker. Do you have a lot of writer friends?

DC: Surprisingly not. Most of my friends are visual artists. One of the things I find inspiring about them, as a writer, is that they think and talk a lot about non-art things like physics, science, and math and try to apply those principles to their artworks. Whereas most writers don't seem to let their minds wander very far afield when they think about writing.

WV: I know what you mean. I'm working on a book of stories right now about Europe during World War II, and one of my characters is the composer Shostakovich, and the more I listen to his stuff, the more exciting it is to me. I'm trying to learn more about music, partly as a way to affect my writing. Take the way one of Shostakovich's symphonies is structured. I'll think, "How can I express that in words?" I'll study it, and figure out the fundamentals, and realize that I can repeat certain phrases and get a certain effect. And the way his music takes off from the chromatic scale and becomes abstract, I can try to create the same effect in my prose. I'm finding that it really works.

DC: It's strange that the conventions of the traditional novel remain so securely in place and that the worlds within the contemporary novel often end up seeming so lifeless and restricted. It's like fiction continues to move through time on this old train track, when there are so many modes of transportation available. But even at their most formal, your novels are almost overwhelmed with life. How do you do that, or does it come naturally?
WV: Well, one thing I kept thinking about when I was writing *The Royal Family* was that the social circumstances of the world I was describing—the world of prostitution, essentially—were very, very different from mine. People interacted more. They'd lived in the same tenement for most of their lives, and they knew their neighbors well. They didn't have television or video, and they weren't very mobile, so they were more focused on change over time. Most Americans aren't so close to their neighbors or family, and their lives are strangely more static than the lives of these people who do and see and experience a lot less. I consciously tried to represent that in the novel.

DC: What is it about prostitution that keeps pulling you back as a writer? It's the only chorus in your otherwise varied body of work.
WV: In the world of street prostitutes, there's a sense of community, and also an absence of community. There are a lot of dead-end relationships, which sometimes both parties want. And then there can be a certain amount of tenderness and trust involved over the long term, too. The wisdom of middle America is that the john has the power, and the prostitute is powerless, but it's a lot more fluid than that. The prostitute can give the john purpose. The prostitute can fall in love, or the john can fall in love. There are all kinds of things like that. The power really does go back and forth. It's very complicated, and that interests me.

DC: Your passionate treatment of subjects like prostitution seems to cause a lot of confusion amongst the literary establishment, as evidenced by your review coverage, at least. It's as though you're acknowledged as an important writer, but, at the same time, one gets the feeling that they wish you'd behave.

WV: Maybe so. I'm always really surprised by that. I don't set out to shock people. I'm not shocked by the stuff I write. It's just that what interests me is sometimes very depressing. But I think it's so important, and that's why I want to write about it. People think that writers can just write well about anything, and they don't understand that the force in the prose comes from the writer's personal fascination with what he's writing about. That makes it hard sometimes, and people misunderstand. But I don't know if it would be better or worse if it were otherwise. For me, the most important thing in terms of my career is if I can persuade my publisher to take the next book, and if I can somehow make ends meet. The reviews aren't so important. I really try to write books that will last and will interest people in the future— not just my writing, but the people I write about, whom most of the world doesn't know or care about. It would just make me so happy to think that in a hundred years from now someone could go read my books and know that the people in them were alive.

Creating "Many, Many Osamas"

Steve Kettmann / 2001

From *Salon*, September 28, 2001. © by *Salon*. This article first appeared in *Salon.com*.
An online version remains in the *Salon* archives. Reprinted with permission.

Novelist William T. Vollmann says if the US convinces Afghans of bin Laden's guilt, they'll support the move against him. If not, only "genocide" will defeat them.

Novelist William T. Vollmann, author of a dozen books including *The Rainbow Stories* and *An Afghanistan Picture Show*, has a different perspective on the Taliban than most of us. Not only has he read the Quran at least twice, as he explained last year in a *New Yorker* article about the Taliban, he has also interviewed Taliban leaders face to face and spoken with many ordinary Afghans about the regime. His experience with Afghanistan goes back to the early '80s, when as a young writer he joined the mujahedin in the mountains for several weeks. He did not actually fight, he said Wednesday in a phone interview with *Salon*—that is, he did not fire a gun "at anyone." But he was very much with the fighters in their struggle.

Vollmann offered this sobering warning in that *New Yorker* piece: "Americans worry that Afghanistan has become a petri dish in which the germs of Islamic fanaticism are replicating—soon Afghans will be hijacking American planes and bombing embassies everywhere. And their fears are not necessarily unfounded. The Taliban are unemployed war veterans, ready and even eager to return to the battlefield. 'In the nineteenth century, we beat the British more than once,' Afghans often told me. 'In the twentieth century, we beat the Russians. In the twenty-first, if we have to, we'll beat the Americans!'"

Kettmann: To start with the obvious question, where were you on September 11? And what was your reaction to the news?

Vollmann: I was in Bangkok. I don't watch television, so I saw the news in the *Bangkok Post* on the evening of the twelfth or the thirteenth. I felt very, very sad. I still feel extremely sad about it. In the Bangkok slum where I was conducting my research, I saw that a lot of the Thais were very, very happy, particularly some of the people I knew with ties to Muslims in southern Thailand. And I wasn't a bit surprised. But it's always painful and unpleasant. For the past few years, I've known better than the average American, I would say, how much we are hated around the world. Some of that hatred is justified, and a lot of it is just that we are the big kid on the block, and any time the big kid gets a punch, a lot of people are going to be happy about it. That's human nature. It's not even anything personal. But it's still a little sad and unpleasant.

Kettmann: Back in 1982, you spent several weeks in the mountains of Afghanistan with the mujahedin fighting against the Soviet army. What was your impression of them?

Vollmann: They were my heroes. I've never met anyone who was so serenely confident of doing the right thing, so willing to sacrifice his life for his homeland, so brave and so disciplined. The case of Afghanistan vs. the Soviet Union is the clearest case of good against evil that I've seen in my lifetime. I thought it was terrific the way they got their country back. I'm deeply saddened by the fact we stopped helping them once we got what we wanted, which was for them to be a thorn in the Russians' side. I feel like we sort of let them down.

At the same time, they obviously share some of the blame for their problems. They never could get it together to be unified, at least until the Taliban came along. They never have trusted each other. They are very quick to blame outsiders for all of their problems. Of course that's partly justified. Outsiders have done a lot of meddling in Afghanistan through the centuries. The average person in Afghanistan has become very used to thinking of themselves as playthings of foreign powers. That's what makes it so easy for them to think that our indictment of Osama bin Laden is some kind of great power strategy. That's why I think it's very important that we go the extra mile and explain to everyone what we're doing and why.

Kettmann: How would you assess the US approach so far in going after bin Laden?

Vollmann: The way I look at it, he's either guilty or he isn't. If he's not guilty, we're definitely doing the wrong thing. If he is guilty, we should be fighting one person instead of a lot of bystanders who are going to take his side if they think he's innocent. It just seems like very elementary logic to me. We have repeatedly failed to make our case to the common Muslim in the street in Pakistan or Afghanistan and probably elsewhere, too. Maybe it's not too late to make it. I don't know. I don't know what kind of proof we have. I was really disgusted when Condoleezza Rice said we have this proof but we didn't see any need to give it to Afghanistan because that country does not follow our standards of jurisprudence. I hope we do have proof, and our radio stations should be broadcasting that to the people of Afghanistan as often as they can.

I've never met Osama. He's probably a horrible person, and if those statements attributed to him are true, he's probably very, very happy with what happened. Did he take part in it? Very, very possibly. If nothing else, he's a poster boy. If there were lots of Latin American terrorists, say in the '60s, going around and attacking us and they had a lot of Che Guevara posters, does that mean we should drop a nuclear bomb on Cuba? I don't think so. I wouldn't feel sorry if Osama bin Laden were harmed, but that's as much as I can responsibly and fairly say.

I don't want to sound like I'm completely negative about everything the government is doing. I didn't vote for Bush, and I'm not particularly happy that he's president. But I will say I'm impressed that he didn't start bombing Afghanistan the day after September 11. The more time that passes without him bombing Afghanistan, the more I respect him.

Kettmann: Day by day, we hear more about likely US backing of the Northern Alliance in its Civil War with the Taliban. Do you think this is a good strategy?

Vollmann: I did interview Burhannudin Rabanni, years ago in 1982, and he seemed like as much of a fundamentalist as anyone. In terms of what they believe, compared to what the Taliban believes, it's probably apples and oranges. But I say just look at it pragmatically. The Taliban controls ninety percent of the country. The Northern Alliance controls ten percent. If you want to go and arm the ten percent against the ninety percent, you're going to cause untold misery. And who is to say the Northern Alliance won't turn on us? To me it seems like a fairly pointless strategy. All it will succeed in doing is to piss everyone off.

Kettmann: How do you see this playing out?

Vollmann: It really depends on how much knowledge of Afghanistan the Bush administration sees fit to pick up. If we want to launch a frontal assault on Afghanistan, then we'll have to be prepared for lots and lots of genocide. Maybe the only way to accomplish our aims is some kind of nuclear bomb, because everyone would fight, as they like to say, until the last drop of blood.

The Northern Alliance leader Ahmad Shah Massoud, the one assassinated recently, was a very brave fighter against the Soviets, like bin Laden. He was widely hated in the Taliban area and the northwest frontier with Pakistan, where I interviewed a lot of people. They said he was not only very corrupt but very cruel. I was often told that every potential Afghan leader was a war criminal.

The great thing about the Taliban was they took peoples' weapons away. They've done lots of terrible things themselves, but from an ordinary Afghan's point of view, it's probably better to stay with what they have. It seems to me the best thing to do is to really try to explain our case to the Taliban, and to do it in company with the Pakistanis, who they listen to. Presumably the government of Pakistan is somewhat convinced of our case or they wouldn't agree to do what they're doing.

If we try to take our time, and do it right, and involve Muslim intermediaries as much as we can, that seems like the least risky thing to do. We don't want them to declare a jihad and have everyone come to their aid like they did in their struggle against the Soviets. The ordinary Afghan is not guilty of anything, and is still grateful to us for all the assistance the CIA gave to the jihad against the Russians.

Kettmann: You quoted an Afghan rug merchant in your *New Yorker* article last year saying of the United States, "First you created one Osama. Now you are creating many, many Osamas." I imagine you see that as being more true than ever now.

Vollmann: Right. It would probably be millions. Put it this way—suppose there's someone you're predisposed to like or to feel kinship with, because he has something in common with you, maybe someone you went to school with, and then suddenly the big bully comes and starts punching him. You're probably going to take your friend's side, because that's all you know. That's how these people feel. All they are hearing there is that the Americans are threatening Afghanistan, calling on the people to topple the Taliban. They are not explaining to the average person why they think Osama did this.

So the Afghanistan people, considering their paranoia about outsiders and the things they do, and the fact we have been extremely stupid in not making our case, are probably going to get awfully pissed off when we start bombing them. If we target any cities, I imagine we will kill lots and lots of innocent people. One aspect of their culture that made them so effective against the Soviet Union is they believe in blood feuds. I think it's very, very easy by killing one Osama to make ten more, and by killing ten to make 100 more. Unless we lay out our case and let them know that justice is being done, we can expect a big blood feud.

Kettmann: Given all that you know about the Taliban, what's your assessment of the regime?

Vollmann: I wouldn't want to live in Afghanistan for the rest of my life. I'm an American, and I'm proud of the fact that I can keep guns in my house, I can listen to the radio, I can have whiskey and pork in the kitchen, I can have pornography, I can read *Mein Kampf.* I love the openness and relative freedom in my own country and the fact that I can have all these things. That being said, I respect the desire of Muslims who want to live under Islamic law. According to a lot of thinking, the Taliban government, for all its problems, is the most perfect manifestation of Islamic law. I know a lot of people are unhappy with the Taliban inside of Afghanistan. And a lot of people are unhappy with the Taliban outside of Afghanistan. It has done many stupid and brutal things. I talked to a doctor who was told he was not allowed to have anatomical diagrams to teach medical students.

When I was interviewing the Minister of the Interior, Mullah Abdul Razzaq, I asked him what should be done about the cases of widows with no family members, who therefore have to either work or beg on the street, both of which are illegal. He didn't really have any good response. It sounded like basically they would just get arrested. I think that sort of thing is wrong. On the other hand, the majority of Afghan women have always been uneducated and illiterate, and the fact that education for them has been curtailed is not such a terrible thing for them as we more educated people might think. That's not to be patronizing or condescending, you just have to look at it in perspective. From the Soviet invasion until the Taliban took over, women could be murdered, abducted and raped, and often were. Now the average woman is safe from being murdered and raped. People's possessions are safe. One reason that the Taliban is quite popular is they took everyone's weapons away. They said from now on we're not going to follow my law or your law, we're going to follow the law as laid down in the Quran.

Their interpretation of the Quran is very harsh. They are very, very strict. Maybe they are fanatics, but they are doing the best that they can. You have to remember that most of these people got their education in the religious schools, the madrasahs. That was the only education available. They would study in the schools in the winter and in the summer they would go and fight the jihad against the Russians, and a lot of them were killed. When you're a soldier, things have to be black and white. When basically all you've learned is how to fight and how to die, and all your legal, moral, religious and social education comes from one book and maybe you can't even read that well, then you're going to end up being the equivalent of a Talib. You're going to tend to see things in black-and-white terms. But the Taliban are very popular. I met so many people who said, "In 1979, I took up arms against the Russians for the Islamic jihad, and when the Taliban came to take away my arms, I was very, very happy, because the jihad had succeeded."

Kettmann: Last question: Have you been flying the American flag?
Vollmann: I don't own a flag. There are a lot of flags in the neighborhood. My little daughter, who is almost three, really enjoys counting them as I take her down the street to get ice cream. And the good Muslim girl from Algeria who takes care of my girl is a little bit afraid, and in the house where she lives with another Muslim couple, they are flying the American flag.

William T. Vollmann

Paul Hunter / 2001

Copyright © 2001 Paul Hunter. Reprinted by permission.

In the wake of the 9/11 attacks, *Literary Review of Canada* asked if I would interview William T. Vollmann for the upcoming issue (Volume 9, No. 8, October 2001). As the conversation was rambling, it was edited for the print edition. This is the full version of that conversation.

"Americans worry that Afghanistan has become a Petri dish in which the germs of Islamic fanaticism are replicating—soon Afghans will be hijacking planes and bombing embassies everywhere. And their fears are not necessarily unfounded."

William T. Vollmann, "Letters from Afghanistan: Across the Divide," *New Yorker*, May 15, 2000.

PH: You've gained a lot of insight into the minds of those in and under the Taliban as shown with your trips to Afghanistan in 1982—which you wrote about in *An Afghanistan Picture Show: Or, How I Saved the World*, and again in January 2000, which you wrote about in "Letters from Afghanistan: Across the Divide" for the *New Yorker*. Were you surprised by the attack that took place September 11 in New York?
WTV: No, I wasn't surprised. I was very sad, but I wasn't surprised.

PH: It is hard to relate to that breed of fanaticism. You talked about that before, that with *An Afghanistan Picture Show* the whole process of writing ended up "being about the unknowability of their experience," and what they've been through.
WTV: They have been through a heck of a lot and if we want to talk about unknowability—so much of that derives from our distance, from the people who are dropping bombs and kidnapping heads of state and doing all kinds of things like that around the world in our name. Americans, for instance,

periodically forget that we're still at war with Iraq, that we still have block-aded them. That thousands and thousands of kids have died there from diarrhea and other causes. When I was there it was really, really heartbreak-ing to see. The Iraqis obviously know that we are at war with them but we do not know. Most of us don't know. It is very peculiar that all these things are happening that most people do not read about or see on television, or if they do they immediately forget. But all of a sudden, somebody retaliates and people are stunned. I do not think that this attack is at all justified, no matter what we might have done. The only good thing I can see coming out of it is that maybe people will pay a little bit more attention to what is going on in rest of the world.

PH: Why did you return to Afghanistan?
WTV: Because the *New Yorker* was paying me and I love Afghanistan. I am always happy to go back there; I hope I can go again. I think the people are ter-rific. There was an old Pakistani general near the northwest frontier who took very good care of me when I was there before. He was still alive, and it was a big thrill to get to see him again. It was a wonderful trip. I am so happy that I got to go back, and it was very interesting for me to meet the Taliban as well.

PH: A country changing so drastically in such a short period of time must be intense. Right now it is definitely not the same place it was twenty years ago, or even a year ago. The stress on the people living there must be tremendous.
WTV: Some things have changed, but the people have not really changed. When I was there in 1982, they told me they were fighting a jihad against the Soviets. So when the Taliban came to power, very many people were happy because they thought, now we have accomplished our jihad and have an Islamic government that is more perfect than any other Islamic government on earth. We have to remember that the Taliban are really, in my opinion, the best and most practical of all the various alternatives for Afghanistan. They have protected women from being raped, men from being murdered, property from getting plundered. It's much better there than it was in the time of the invasion. So they enjoy a great deal of support. I do not say that I would want to live in Afghanistan under the Taliban, but then they probably wouldn't invite me.

PH: The ongoing theme of your books seems to be truth. You have talked about the slogan painted at the headquarters of Khun Sa, the Burmese-Shan "Opium King" that said: "The only obligation is to tell the truth."
WTV: I admire him for having that on his wall.

PH: It seems to be the ongoing theme in your books: about always striving for the truth. To a certain degree, it is a quixotic search for something, for love in some cases (certainly in the trilogy of the prostitute stories), along with the idea of "addiction as a form of enlightenment." Were you conscious of that connection?

WTV: Yes, of course. For me, almost anything can be redeemed in a sense, by love. If you are engaged in some sort of behavior or addiction, or whatever, that other people might consider disgusting or even reprehensible—if you can be steadfast enough, then somehow or other you are purifying what you do. You become more pure and you benefit, no matter how good or bad the activity is and no matter what happens to you. I would say that I have had so many deeply spiritual experiences involving sex with prostitutes, and illicit street drugs. For that matter I have learned so much from talking to terrorists and often very, very creepy people. If you can understand the extremes of the human continuum then you have a shot at understanding the whole continuum—which would be terrific and so amazing. But as long as we are here we might as well try to learn whatever we can and we might as well be faithful to something. Hopefully we can pick something good to be faithful to. If we cannot, we just have to do our best.

PH: It is true that spiritual enlightenment, or any sort of enlightenment, whether it is *satori* or something else, is an extreme state. To experience extreme states opens your mind. It is wanting to attain that thing just out of our reach, that is perhaps not even there. But if you could touch it, it would open you up. It would give you that burst of the unknown.

WTV: That is right, and it is so wonderful that in life there are so many things a person can do to go into darkness and discover something new. I remember in my twenties I was really depressed for a while. I thought well, the law of gravity is not going to change, all the human beings are going to look about the same and they'll have the same respiratory functions. Really, it is going to be a very boring life. Fortunately, I was so wrong. I think one of the great things about reading literature or, for that matter, writing it is that you can enter all kinds of new worlds. The more you read and the more you write, the more you discover and the more it becomes really possible to appreciate a lot of things.

PH: When you mention darkness, I think of the Comte de Lautréamont's *Maldoror*. I remember being so moved by that book when I read it.

WTV: What a beautiful book. I have my own little publishing company called CoTangent Press. I always wanted to do a new translation of *Maldoror* and I thought it would be nice to have it on titanium pages that were rainbow anodized. I would like the edges of the pages to be razor sharp and dipped in some kind of poison.

PH: The "poison-filled pages" (*Maldoror*, First Canto).
WTV: Exactly! So, you would have to have a special pair of steel gauntlets or something.

PH: Like butcher's gloves. A lot of the stuff you've done through CoTangent is just brilliant.
WTV: As a matter of fact I was working a little bit on one of my CoTangent bindings when you called. They're four platinum prints. They are fairly expensive.

PH: What are the platinum prints of?
WTV: They're nudes. The women involved are in an overgrown backyard in Oregon, and they're holding a papier-mâché mask that I made. It's got bones for teeth, a bunch of crow feathers, and the hair of a woman who is a good friend of mine. As well as the platinum prints there are some watercolor drawings of that mask and of some of the women. It's an attempt to mix photography and fairly representational drawings. I'm hoping to finish it up by Friday; I probably can because the weather is nice and warm. Probably close to 40° C today so the glue dries very quickly.

PH: How are your hands holding up, by the way? You have had problems with carpal tunnel syndrome in the past.
WTV: They are a little bit better. I have a little daughter—she is going to be three tomorrow—and I play with her a lot, put in several hours a day with her. I carry her around on my shoulders too, so I am less productive, which is probably good.

PH: In discussing *Seven Dreams: A Book of North American Landscapes*, you talked about the barrier between myth and history. The early *Dreams* dealt with a period in which the subjects are not definitely known. A lot of it is myth—wonderfully rich stories, as opposed to the history and where the actual fact lies. Did you find that same sort of problem with *Argall*, but in a different way, with, say the effect of the Disneyfication of history on the Pocahontas story?

WTV: With Pocahontas, there is so much to talk about. There is what really happened, and then there is what everybody pretends happened for so long. And after a while both of those things are equally important. Just like when you read the Norse sagas or the Norse myths, you are looking back at an outlook, and any outlook is truth, in a sense. These things that we desire to believe about Pocahontas, because we desire to believe them and try to convince ourselves that they are this way for so long, reveal something about us, and therefore they are true. Where they deviate from literal fact becomes very interesting and if we find out how they deviate from literal fact, we are likely to learn even more about ourselves—why we want to lie in this particular way, why we decide to make these particular lies true. That is one of the things that I try to do in each one of the *Dreams*: not only to look at the conflict between the two belief systems—in this case, European and Native American—but also between what, as far as we can tell, actually happened, and what each side claims happened.

PH: You used the Vinland Sagas as reference for *The Ice-Shirt*. I read them years ago, wonderful series, which included the *Grœnlendinga Saga* and *Eirik's Saga*.
WTV: Yeah, I love the Icelandic sagas so much. I'm German, Swedish, Norwegian, so I figure that's my ancestors they're talking about . . .

PH: I'm sort of the same way, but mine is Scottish, so it's the Celts and the *Orkneyinga Saga*.
WTV: That's right, yeah! There might have been some Scots that settled on Iceland, it's unclear, there was definitely some Irish.

PH: The earlier books in that series have a more dreamlike quality, maybe because they are closer to myth than history, and you are able to create a truth. In this latest one, *Argall* you are more straightforward in your narrative. Was this a conscious decision?
WTV: I would say that that it is true. It is very important to me that these *Seven Dreams* do not end up degenerating into seven copies of one formula. I try to make each book very different than the others. The interesting thing, in a way, about the Pocahontas legend is that it is kind of a dream, but both sides, the Powhatan Indians and the English colonists, were exceedingly practical; you can only get a hint of the weirdness in the belief systems from the language itself. Some of the conceptions of hierarchy and faithfulness,

and faith, that are embedded in Elizabethan language are fascinating, and it was fun, for a change, to bring those out more subtly through the language. Also, there are very few Powhatan myths surviving. In fact, the sources and the landscape and everything else is so impoverished, compared to the sources for, say, *The Ice-Shirt*, where you can go to Iceland and see the ruins of Eirik the Red's house. Out of respect for what is there, I don't want to make anything up. I do not mind elaborating on myths, but when so little is known about a whole people, it seems disrespectful to just make things up.

If You Really Want Radical

Michael Hemmingson / 2004

From *San Diego Reader*, March 11, 2004. © by *San Diego Reader*. Reprinted by permission.

. . . . . he felt. . . . . as if he were supposed to be doing something else, something grander, higher, more difficult, more dangerous, more daring.
Steven Millhauser, *Martin Dressler*

It's a warm winter day in Ocean Beach, and I'm rushing from my apartment on Muir toward Newport Avenue for a meeting with William T. Vollmann and Larry McCaffery, who teaches at SDSU. I find them in the back of the Black—past the bongs, lava lamps, and guitars; they're looking at books.

Vollmann has written much about prostitutes—so much that he's attracted legions of degenerate fans and has been blasted by stuffy critics for being "too obsessed" with the oldest profession on earth.

The writer and the professor have returned from two days in Calexico, where Vollmann has been doing research on a book in progress about the Imperial Valley.

Larry McCaffery is wearing his usual attire of an old Hawaiian shirt, faded jeans, and tennis shoes; Vollmann wears a flannel shirt, baggy jeans, hiking shoes, and a baseball hat.

Vollmann spots me before I recognize him. "Mike," he says, "good to see you."

McCaffery glances around the Black and says, "I've always loved this place."

"They don't carry your books," I tell Vollmann, like this is a small crime. "They should," I say. "But the used bookstore on Bacon Street does . . ."

The main reason for this meet is to iron out a misunderstanding—a miscommunication—between Vollmann and me. It has to do with a book McCaffery and I are working on called *Expelled from Eden: A William T. Vollmann Reader*. It's really a casebook, but the publisher,

Thunder's Mouth Press, felt "casebook" was too academic and "reader" was more general, in commercial terms.

The problem? One, there are some song lyrics, poems, and letters that I want to use which Vollmann isn't comfortable with, and because I tend not to be able to curb my enthusiasm, I failed to take Vollmann's wishes and feelings into account—treating him more like a subject than a human being. Two, the publisher had wanted to rush this book for a spring 2003 publication, but Vollmann prefers that we take our time, two or three years, and get the thing right.

I feel bad about this, so I'm a little nervous as I stand there with him inside the Black, the smell of incense all around like the stench of dead fish at the edge of the Salton Sea.

A William T. Vollmann primer in 500 words: Novelist, essayist, photojournalist, war correspondent, poet, and painter—he's been praised in every major newspaper and magazine for his vast artistic output. His first published novel, *You Bright and Risen Angels*, dubbed "a cartoon" that's really an alternate universe science-fiction yarn, was written during late hours at his computer programming job in San Francisco. He lived off candy bars and slept under his desk. The novel was eventually published in England in 1987. No US publisher would look at his work because he didn't have an agent and didn't prepare his manuscripts "right"—so several of his subsequent books were first issued in the UK and later in the States: *The Rainbow Stories, The Ice-Shirt, Thirteen Stories and Thirteen Epitaphs*. American editors started to notice him, and he began to acquire assignments from *Esquire, Spin, Gear*, the *New Yorker*; Viking, Pantheon, and Farrar, Straus & Giroux picked up his books. His early memoir of going to Afghanistan was published to much critical but scant commercial success, yet remains a dear favorite with fans. He journeyed to the magnetic North Pole and almost froze to death, which he wrote about in *The Rifles*. He traveled throughout Cambodia and Burma, exploring the underworld of prostitution and drugs, which he wrote about in *Butterfly Stories*, and he interviewed Pol Pot's brother. Much controversy surrounded his *Esquire* piece about purchasing a preteen prostitute from a brothel in Thailand, enrolling the girl in a school, and helping her to set up a small business. He was a foreign correspondent in Somalia, Kosovo, and Belgrade. He attended Saddam Hussein's birthday bash in Iraq, searched for terrorists in Yemen, and turned down an assignment from the *Los Angeles Times* to return to Afghanistan during the 2002 air strikes because the newspaper wouldn't put up the cash for a bodyguard. In the summer of 1994, while in Bosnia, the jeep he was in ran over a landmine; he was the sole survivor—a long-time friend, a photographer, and his translator died instantly; he was shot at and later rescued by Spanish soldiers from the U.N. He took pictures of his dead friends and shows these images during slide shows while on the lecture and book-signing circuit. People ask him how he can, in good conscience, do this; his reply: "It is my job." He has documented his travels around the world in the PEN/Hemingway Award-winning collection *The Atlas* and, more extensively, in *Rising Up and Rising Down* (which he dedicates to his two friends who died in Bosnia). He has published a 300,000-word opus on San Francisco's Tenderloin, *The Royal Family*, for which he agreed to a one-third cut in his advance in order to have the book published in its voluminous state. Speaking of which, this "essay on violence" that he has worked on for seventeen years, *Rising Up and Rising Down*, is a 3400-page, 7-volume work that few publishers braved to even look at in theory; some did but knew better than to pitch such an expensive project to their sales and editorial boards. He shopped it around from 1997 to 2001, and it was eventually published by Dave Eggers's McSweeney's Books in late 2003: a $120 boxed set, bound in cloth, and printed in China (an 800-page abridged paperback edition will be released by Ecco Press). One of Vollmann's current (major) projects is *Imperial*, a book-length essay about the Imperial Valley, the Salton Sea, and the US-Mexican border in Calexico. For this, Vollmann, a resident of Sacramento, has been coming down to San Diego almost every other month since 1999.

We go to a bar and grill across the street from the O.B. Motel (where both Vollmann and McCaffery stayed the night before).

"Bill was looking through the Yellow Pages for escort services last night," McCaffery says.

"Did you call any?" I ask.

"I decided to read a book of collected Raymond Chandler stories," Vollmann says.

McCaffery gets a drink, I get a beer, and Vollmann has a soda water with a lime twist. It's noon.

We discuss writing, women, and war—three of Vollmann's favorite topics, which also happen to be section headings in *Expelled from Eden*.

"Let's talk about this book," Vollmann says. "I think we started off on the wrong foot, Mike. I would like if we could get that behind us, no hard feelings."

"I'd like that as well," I say.

"I want you two to know that whatever you include in the casebook are your choices. I won't interfere."

"But you'll have complete veto power of what finally goes in or doesn't," McCaffery says.

"And you'll see the manuscript and galleys," I say. "I'll make sure of that."

"However you two want to present me, I'll live with it," he says. "If you choose to make me out as a monster, so be it . . ."

I'm a little surprised by this remark, and so is McCaffery.

McCaffery says, "Not at all . . ."

"Well, the title," Vollmann says.

"I lifted it from *The Rifles*," I say.

"Do you see me as expelled from the *Garden of Eden*?" he asks rather softly. "Because I don't."

"The sales and marketing team think it's a great title," I say, feeling foolish; surely I can come up with a better response than that, goddammit, but I can't. C'mon—I do feel he's been expelled because I have, we all have, in that old Judeo-Christian sense . . .

But I'm glad we've put our differences aside and can continue with the project.

"We need to get to the airport," Vollmann tells McCaffery, and they hurry into the prof's white SUV, drive off, leaving me by the O.B. Pier.

William T. Vollmann does not drive. Because of his eyesight (he refers to himself as "William the Blind" in his *Seven Dreams* series), he has never been able to obtain a driver's license. "Abolish the automobile," he once wrote, "because it has no reverence for space." Incidentally, he has often relied on hired hands, friends, fans, and escorts to help him move about on his travels.

In his latest excursions to Southern California, his guide, ride, and platonic assistant has been San Diego State University student, poet, ghostwriter, and devout Mormon Terrie Petree.

I ask Terrie how she wound up becoming Vollmann's chauffeur throughout San Diego, Imperial, the Salton Sea, and beyond.

"As with all good things, I ended up tooling around with Bill by chance," she says. "I owed McCaffery some indentured servitude as part of an independent study class. He asked if I was willing to spend a couple of days helping William T. Vollmann. I gave Bill a call, he found out I spoke Spanish fluently, and the next thing you know we were planning week-long blocks of travel time."

"He is known for being a man who likes to put himself in danger," I say. "Has he gotten you into some dangerous situations? I'm curious about this since he wouldn't let my girlfriend accompany him a few years ago to an outing on the border to interview illegal aliens because he said it might be too perilous for her."

"Bill has never gotten me into a dangerous situation. He has led me to the edge of several and then let me decide if I wanted to take the leap, but he's not the type of man who would willingly endanger anyone. Except himself."

"Care to elaborate?"

"Well," she says, "an aborted carjacking, being abandoned in a dark alley by a bilingual pimp, betting on cockfights, having the passenger's-side handle of my car door ripped off by a crowbar, tunneling underground, and driving around the Salton Sea on a 115-degree afternoon with no air conditioning . . . how could I choose the most salient one?"

"My first involvement with Bill Vollmann was in early 1990 while I was completing work on a collection of literary interviews with 'radically innovative American fiction writers,'" says McCaffery as we wade in the Jacuzzi at the Roadrunner Club in Borrego Springs. "Sensing I needed a final interview that could sum up the features I was ascribing to, I wrote my colleague Tom LeClair for suggestions. Tom responded with a note suggesting several possibilities that concluded with this: 'But if you really want radical, you should check out a new guy named William T. Vollmann.' I checked *You Bright and Risen Angels* and *The Rainbow Stories* out of the library and was only a few pages into *Angels* before I sat down and wrote Vollmann a letter asking if he would be willing to be interviewed for my book. He agreed, sent me a package of goodies including the galleys of *The Ice-Shirt* and a description of his *Dream Series*, and I interviewed him at his apartment in Manhattan in May."

I ask, "What were your initial impressions of Bill?"

"I came away from that first meeting convinced I had seen the future of American fiction. Over the next few years I met with Bill a half dozen or so times—eagerly read all his work, reviewed most of his books, published several interviews with him and critical essays, and guest-edited a 'Younger Authors' issue of the *Review of Contemporary Fiction* featuring the first extended discussion of his writing."

"When did your relationship with him change from that of author-critic to personal friends?"

"In the mid-'90s, when Bill moved from Manhattan to California," McCaffery says. "My motives in nurturing this friendship are surely self-evident—who wouldn't want to be able to hang out with somebody who was not only 'the most dangerous man in America,' but also, as I once put it in a review, 'a rough-edged beast who has been slouching towards some Millennial Bethlehem with a kind of monstrous elegance, utter fearlessness, and voracious appetite that one associates with Melville, Whitman, and Pynchon'?"

McCaffery submerges his head into the water, comes back up, and rubs his eyes. "At any rate, the regular visits I started making to see Bill at his home in Sacramento allowed me to peek into his bookshelves; look through his huge archive of photographs, watercolors, and ink drawings; watch him constructing his book-object assemblages; and gaze in amazement at the large map he has on his studio wall onto which he had carefully pinned innumerable markers indicating places he had visited while conducting research.

"But the real change in our relationship began in July 1997 when Bill accepted my invitation to visit me here in Borrego. On this first visit, we spent several days hiking and touring the area in my SUV and made several extended side trips to the Salton Sea and the Imperial Mexicali Valleys to the southeast. Given his fascination with travel, danger, and extremity, I had hoped Bill would find this region to be irresistible, and sure enough, he took the bait. Since that first visit he has revisited the Imperial area dozens of times to conduct research that he used in *The Royal Family*, in various magazine articles, and for a nonfiction book about Imperial Valley that has, in typical Vollmann fashion, expanded and mutated unpredictably in a manner comparable to *Moby Dick*'s evolution during the latter part of its composition.

"During this period, I've become Bill's part-time chauffeur, father confessor, tour guide, hiking buddy, literary confidant, and partner in crime."

"Any weird stories from these trips? Dangerous adventures and anecdotes?"

"It's not so much that Bill necessarily wants to place himself and his friends in strange and dangerous situations, but somehow that's usually what happens. In my own case, what's happened has been that I've done a lot of things, met a lot of people, and wound up in a lot of places and situations that I wouldn't normally have encountered. I've gone to strip joints and whorehouses, for example, slept in flophouses, donned a flak jacket, fired off rounds of the world's largest handgun, been to cockfights, and descended into dark, watery Chinese tunnels beneath Mexicali. I've lugged a view camera and tripod into the Anza-Borrego badlands, glided along the most polluted river in North America in a rickety boat. I've met homeless people, drug dealers, migrant workers, pimps, prostitutes, coyotes, sipped sake across the table from a Yakuza member, and followed the trail of illegal aliens' empty water bottles and discarded clothing to the top of Mt. Signal in Mexico."

Of course, I, too, am eager to join Vollmann on his adventures, experience a bit of danger, hang out with questionable women, and foray into the unknown—all the things in his books that have made him a literary cult hero. I'm sure there are many who'd like to be in his company, who pester him about it like groupies to a rock star, so I'm hesitant to bother him. I know that writers need to be alone for their research and work. Jack Kerouac, Charles Bukowski, and Henry Miller (to name just three) were constantly hounded by fans who camped outside their homes thinking they could party with their idols and become part of their lives. I also know the pitfalls of great expectations; there have been incidents where I discovered that the authors I admired on the page were not what I envisioned in real life.

Nevertheless, over the next year various plans were made for me to join Vollmann and McCaffery on these excursions into Imperial and beyond, all of which fell through for one reason or another—conflicting schedules, illnesses, mix-ups on dates, inopportune delays, looming book deadlines.

I had hoped to hook up with him during his February 2004 trip to Indio, during the Festival of Dates.

"I'm not sure where we'll be; I have a lot of things to do and people to see," Vollmann says on the phone, "but let's try to meet up somewhere. Have dinner. Why don't you give Terrie your information, and I have your number."

The day he's due to come in, Friday, I call Terrie and ask what the plans are. "This is what I know," she says as she packs her suitcase. "Bill called and said, 'Pick me up at the airport at 10:00 A.M.' From there, I have no idea."

She doesn't know what hotel they'll be at, where and when they'll be out and about in Indio.

My girlfriend and I make plans to go to Borrego on Saturday and Indio on Sunday, but unforeseen events stop that.

On the phone, Bill says, "Monday and Tuesday won't work; we have to go down to Calexico. Terrie's bringing me into San Diego on Friday. Why don't you, McCaffery, and me head down to Tijuana and check out some strip clubs? That should help you with your article."

"McCaffery's never been down to Tijuana," I say. "It's about time he goes," Vollmann says.

That doesn't work out either. Vollmann has to meet someone in Mexicali he can only see Friday afternoon; he checks in late into the O.B. Motel. McCaffery and his wife Sinda also have a room there.

I settle for a get-together in the morning.

"When's the first time you visited San Diego?" I ask during breakfast at Shade's, an eatery along the beach. McCaffery, Sinda, Terrie and her boyfriend, and my girlfriend are with us, several small tables pushed together.

"I was three," Vollmann says. "My mother took me to the zoo. We came down from L.A., where we were living on Wilshire. My father was getting his graduate degree at UCLA."

"Now, you've been down to Tijuana before?"

He nods.

"He's seen the donkey show," McCaffery says. "Bill has a story set in San Diego that I published in *Fiction for a Daydream Nation*," McCaffery says. "It's also in *The Atlas*, right?"

"It is," I say. It's a surreal section (the narrator talks with a lizard) of a longer piece called "Houses" that starts off: *Down in the golden grass near San Diego where houses and new houses terrified me, families lived the California life, saying to one another: if you can't feel it, never mind it.*

"It almost got cut, but I fought to keep it in," Vollmann says.

"Do you have any San Diego sections in *Imperial*?" McCaffery says.

"There are a couple parts."

"Hmm. Don't think I read them."

"When did you start *Imperial*?" I ask.

"Oh, around 1997."

"I thought you began it in 1999," but I know that his 780-page (1400+ pages in manuscript) novel, *The Royal Family*, has parts set in Imperial and a place outside the Salton Sea called Slab City, inspired by his trips down here in 1996–97, so this makes sense. "When do you think it'll be finished?"

"Another two or three years," Vollmann says. He smiles. "Have to make sure the book is really big."

"Another seven-volume set," McCaffery laughs. "Or maybe just three."

"I could write a chapter about every grain of sand in Imperial. Wouldn't that be something, McCaffery? Write 100 pages for every grain of sand, that grain's history, and every-thing it has seen."

Bill stops a Shade's employee who is refilling water glasses and asks the young man where he's from. He's Hispanic, dark-brown skin, and smiles with confusion, like, *Why does this man with thick glasses and a crew cut want to know?* "Yucatán," he says.

"I've been there," Vollmann says, and talks a while with the employee about the region.

Breakfast arrives and we eat.

"I've been praising you to Bill, how great you are at karaoke, Mike," McCaffery says. "How your 'Copacabana' is legendary in Borrego."

"I haven't done that one in a while," I say. "Lately it's been 'Ring of Fire.' McCaffery does a good Elvis."

"I bet he does," says Vollmann.

McCaffery sings a verse from "Ring of Fire."

"We need to get you out there for karaoke," McCaffery tells Vollmann. "How does that sound? Doable?"

"Sounds good, McCaffery."

"You know, Mike has just published his 27th book."

"It's in the stores," I say, "but I don't have copies yet. There was a mixup at the publisher's warehouse."

"Which one of your books is your favorite?" Vollmann asks.

"That's hard to answer," I say. "The one I'm currently working on."

"*Expelled from Eden*, of course," McCaffery says.

"How long have you and your girlfriend been together?" Vollmann asks.

"Two and a half years."

"Oh. For some reason I thought you two had been together longer."

"Well, I knew her a year or two before—"

"Before you knew her biblically," he says.

"It's apocryphal," McCaffery says. "Bill, she does book art objects, too."

"She does? I'd like to see them."

"Maybe you can go to their place after breakfast," McCaffery says.

"I'd like that."

"Are you going to the National Critics Book Circle ceremony in two weeks?" I ask Vollmann. (*Rising Up and Rising Down* has been nominated best nonfiction book of 2003.)

"No, I don't care about those things," he says. "I'll be in Japan then, anyway."

I don't believe him. Many writers can feign indifference about being nominated and not winning, but all are secretly pleased if they win—a nod to the talent, the effort, and the work.

Vollmann suggested that Tara bring some of her book objects by his room and we could kick back until checkout time. Friends of his from Encinitas were coming by to pick him up. My girlfriend was reluctant to get her book objects, but we went back to the apartment and gathered three.

I pick up my samurai sword. "You think Bill would like to see this?"

My girlfriend shrugs. "Do you really want to bring it?"

"He likes weapons; I think he'll appreciate it."

Walking down Newport with the sword, people step out of my way and give me strange looks.

A man pushing a shopping cart is yelling at anyone who crosses his path: "DON'T EAT MEAT! YOUR PARENTS TOLD YOU MEAT WAS GOOD BUT THEY LIED TO YOU! MEAT IS EVIL AND BAD FOR YOUR BODY!"

It starts to sprinkle.

"That storm's coming in," I say.

Vollmann is waiting in his room at the O.B. Motel. It's getting windy and starting to rain harder. He has a view of the pier. There are surfers out in the water, and they look like seals.

He's in Room 206. This is the same room my girlfriend's parents stayed in when they visited for Christmas. I mention this, and Vollmann says, "I hope I slept in the same bed as they did."

The room has two beds. "They slept in the other one," I say.

"I think they over-charged me. McCaffery and Sinda had a room just like this one and they paid $69. They charged me $110."

His Macintosh Titanium laptop sits on the bed stand, playing Japanese music. My girlfriend says it sounds nice. "Had to get my money's worth," Vollmann tells her.

He doesn't have e-mail and never logs onto the Internet. McCaffery has told me he doesn't trust the Net.

I show him my samurai sword. "Got it at an antique store down the street." He doesn't seem very interested. I say, "Not sure if it's a real antique. It's not even sharpened."

"You can always blunt someone to death," he says.

My girlfriend shows him her book objects, and I sit in a chair. They talk about glues and the smell of glue. "Smells like postage stamps," he says. I mumble something about the apartment smelling like glue for days when she works on her art. They talk about binding and paper and printing methods. He seems genuinely interested in the books, and my girlfriend is acting timid, losing her voice. She sits on the floor, and Vollmann lies back on his bed, holding one of the pillows.

"So, Mike," he says, "what are you working on? Any new books?"

"There are always books and deadlines," I reply. "Some more for Blue Moon, a crime novel set here in San Diego, a Western. My agent has my new novel out."

"So why do you need an agent? You do all these books for publishers; seems you do okay for yourself." He closes his eyes. "I didn't have an agent for years. Then I got one with *The Royal Family*; she turned it into a two-book deal. Why give fifteen percent of your money to an agent?"

"I sometimes wonder about that. But I need him, he gets me past doors I can't; my stuff's read by the top brass rather than going up the ladder—not that it means much, that it gets me a sale. He knows everyone. He used to be an editor at St. Martin's Press, where he did all the pop culture and music books, discovered Douglas Coupland . . ."

"Mike has an antagonistic relationship with him," my girlfriend says.

"I do," I say. "He's a cranky old bastard, at least on the phone. In person, though, he'd give you the shirt off his back."

"That's why you have to meet them, get to know them," Vollmann says. "They have to be aggressive, and I guess you want that."

"I haven't been to New York since 9/11," I say, remembering how, on September 11, my agent was in L.A., couldn't get a flight back, so he and two other people rented a car, drove to Chicago; from Chicago he took the train into Manhattan, where he wrote me an e-mail: *We think differently of the dead now.*

"I'll be writing a book that's 50,000 words," Vollmann says. "It's about Copernicus. This is for Norton. They're doing science books by literary writers. They just did one by David Foster Wallace—"

"On infinity," I say. "Yeah, I've heard about that series." (It's called Great Discoveries, from Norton's Atlas Books imprint.)

"I signed a contract and got half the advance last December, and it's due this December. I figure it'll take me a month to write."

"So what are you going to Japan for? For a magazine?"

"I'm writing a book about Noh theater. I'm going to Kyoto, where I've never been before."

We talk about classical Noh—the masks, the movements. "Some critics believe the masks are more important, others believe it's the music," Vollmann says. He explains how the performances are often different each time, even though the actors may have presented the same piece for years. "They'll work with musicians they never have before, and there's no rehearsal." He opens his eyes. "So, do you two have any travel plans soon?"

"Not really," my girlfriend says. "We go to Borrego Springs a lot," I say. "Hang out with McCaffery. If he's not there, we find things to do."

"Do you like Borrego?" Vollmann asks my girlfriend.

"Sure," she says.

"She likes the pools," I say.

"Pools are nice," she says. "I like the Salton Sea, too. Smells bad, but it's great out there."

"Maybe you could swim in it. See what's on the bottom."

"Oh," she says, her voice cracking, and laughs.

"I've taken a boat trip on the Salton Sea, with this guy Ray, the only professional guide left."

From *Imperial*, in a chapter called "The Water of Life," this is how the guide is described:

> *Ray Garnett, yes, oh, yes, proprietor of Ray's Salton Sea Guide Service, was a duck hunter, but he preferred to take his birds in Nebraska. He knew quite a few men who hunted the wetlands around the Salton Sea, and he used to do that himself, but about their prizes he remarked: I don't like 'em, 'cause they taste like the water smells.*

Why can't I write huge books like Bill Vollmann? Then again, he has problems with his publishers about such tomes: too expensive to produce. McCaffery and I have run into this obstacle with *Expelled from Eden: A William T. Vollmann Reader*—it has three announced publication dates; contract problems, life, and a jigsaw puzzle of a manuscript have caused delays. After three rounds of cuts—a once-300,000-word manuscript has now become 165,000 words—the book should be a 500-page trade paperback when it comes out as scheduled in the summer of 2004. We have a real cover and should go into production—galleys and blue lines—soon. How will Vollmann feel about the final product, as well his readers, fans, and scholars? My hope is that all the bright and risen angels will shine upon us and the calculus will be: we did the man justice.

L'Américain Tranquille
(The Quiet American)

David Boratav / 2004

Portions of this interview were published in French in *Chronic'art* #15, summer 2004; interview conducted in May 2004. © David Boratav/Chronic'art. Reprinted by permission.

It was a bright, hot day when I visited William Vollmann at his home in Sacramento. I had come to interview him about *The Royal Family*. His wife was there, as was his daughter, a lively child around five at the time, who was running around the house and occasionally peeping from behind the living room sofa. I came alone and unlike other interviews had to do a photo shoot myself, with an old digital camera. That was the thing I liked least, but Bill was very nice about it. In one of the shots we used, he posed in that huge sofa of his, folded his arms on his chest and stared. I was in the opposing seat myself, and the effect is that in the photograph he looks like a benevolent giant, with a hint of melancholy, although his eyes are blurred by the reflection on his glasses. There is another photo that I like, where he is seated on that sofa and where, to his right, stands a dollhouse. Again the giant: his hands, I recall, are big with a strong grip, the hands of a farm worker almost—even though on closer look they were well-kept and even delicate. He was working at his great European masterpiece *Europe Central* at the time, and while we were discussing Russian writers, he rose and put some Shostakovich on, one of the string quartets I think. Re-reading this interview I realize that there was also an Algerian nanny in the house, whom Vollmann somehow turns to at one point to ask, with his usual candor, about the Quran.

You will notice that we start the interview with the question of style against content: Vollmann is definitely a stylist, not for the sake of it as he says, but a writer clearly inhabited and haunted by the beauty of language and indebted to other great writers. Being a prolific reader, and astute researcher of such powerful topics, be they prostitutes, war, violence, radiation, or tramps, I think some people who like his writing perhaps tend to forget that he writes on all these topics with a greatness and what one may call a malleability that is simply amazing. I remember preparing an article on *Imperial*, reading stuff from this mammoth document and discussing it with a fellow journalist with whom I was writing the review: the style was multi-layered—sometimes it read like an investigation, sometimes like a Western, and sometimes like some of the best science fiction you could read . . .

Now that I am writing this, I realize that I visited Bill not once, but twice during my three-week or so stay in California. Guns were the topic of a reasonable chunk of the interview, but he did not show me his guns that first day, because we had drunk some whiskey during the interview and he said that with guns you needed a clear mind, not just for shooting them, but for handling them as well. So we made an appointment and upon my return from Los Angeles I visited his home again. That is when he showed me his gun collection. No need to say I was completely ignorant of gun culture and looked at all this gun business with a certain European irony. Bill was the only person during my stay in the United States who seriously challenged and informed some of my preconceptions on guns. We spent some time looking at his collection in the garden where a pool was under construction. He had fetched the weapons from his garage, at the back of the house. His wife was in the kitchen and it was the only time when I sensed her nervousness about my presence, as if Bill and I had become too close to her liking, two complicit children playing with matches in a dry backyard. There was a strange drawing on the table or somewhere nearby, the simplified face of a smiling boy on a piece of paper—maybe a picture he'd made for his daughter. At that moment, with the guns spread on the table, it looked odd, as if that drawing was out of place, a potential target. Bill showed me quite a few guns, a dozen or so, and I recall two in particular: one was an Israeli army automatic weapon, possibly an Uzi ("very powerful, it can kill a lot of people," Vollmann said in his slightly trailing, matter-of-fact voice), and the SIG Sauer P226, a gun of world renown, which he made me hold and handle, and which later inspired a short story and a chapter of my second novel, *Portrait du fugitif* (though in my novel the scene happens not in a back garden but on the seat of a car). At some point though, the tension coming from the kitchen became too loud and Bill said we would get out of the house and visit his workshop.

He showed me a lot of his artwork there, and I forget how the afternoon ended. It was a marvelous day. He never showed any boredom, and I felt completely at ease, and even if I had prepared the interview I was baffled by the range of his numerous talents. He had opened a door, literally, onto his remarkable life. I discovered a true artist, a sensitive, humble man with exceptional gifts that enabled him to see the world in all its beauties and imperfections. I had met an attentive and loyal friend.

In retrospect, my interview with William Vollmann was much more than an interview. Bill opened up to me as much as I myself was ready to open up to him. Between 2003 and 2008, the years of my stay in the United States, I did numerous interviews with writers: Nick Cohn, Richard Powers, Bret Easton Ellis, Nick Tosches, among others. But this was more than an interview, and Bill Vollmann is the only one with whom I developed what can certainly be called a friendship—however distant geographically that friendship became. We met twice in Sacramento, and once again in NY and then mostly kept in touch by postal mail, exchanging short notes on his travels, the publication of my novels, his aging, the birth of my children, etc. I have cherished all his correspondence, because as with the interview, it is never a formal Vollmann writing, but Bill himself, as if we had only recently seen each other and carried our conversation over the years. When he says in the interview: "I want to be your friend, not just you and me, but as an American I want to be friends with Europeans, I want to learn from them," he really means it and does it even though he is at his busiest, painting his watercolors, taking those amazing photographic portraits of anonymous people, writing his novels and reportage—he does not compromise and he is ready to accept the commitment that his words involve. As a writer as well as a human being, he is an extraordinarily dedicated and generous person.

DB: There are many different facets to your work. There is fiction, nonfiction, autobiography. You are a novelist and a journalist. You are interested in people who are experiencing hardships here in the United States and abroad. Give us an idea of who you are and what makes you write.

WTV: I am interested in furthering beauty and truth, as I see it. So when I write something like *Rising Up and Rising Down*, I try to get at some kind of truth, wherever the truth is. I want to be fair. I don't want to judge other people except when it's absolutely necessary, and sometimes it's necessary. But to me style is very important, and I try to make my sentences as beautiful as I can. When I write my fiction, I might be less interested in literal truth, but I try to create something that I think is still true. And so it's very rare that I try to create something that is just beautiful.

DB: When and how did you come to writing the way you just defined it—in the search of truth and beauty, but not for the sake of it?

WTV: When I was very small, I did not have very many friends, but I always used to read, and when I did, the books would seem to come alive for me, and I would really believe that I was in the world that those books created. There was a coherence to it, a kind of truth. There was some kind of belief . . . People sometimes talk about "suspension of disbelief," but it was beyond that. I believed in the world that was created and I wanted to do the same. I wanted to live in that kind of world and create it. And for me the most satisfying part of writing is when I am about three quarters finished with a book and the world that I built is mostly constructed. And I can walk around inside that world and enjoy it and try to figure out what should go here and there and I just know what's right. That's really a wonderful feeling. And when the book is finished, it's pretty much over. I wouldn't really pick it up again, but I have happy memories of writing the book.

DB: You are a writer whose writing often seems triggered by experience. Yet you have just talked about these books that you were so much into when you were a kid. Are there any authors that influenced you early on and made you want to write?

WTV: One of them for certain was Lautréamont. He is one of the world's great stylists. I remember being so impressed by the beauty of his sentences when I first started writing in the early '70s when I went to high school and I wanted to do something like that.

DB: Your essay *Rising up and Rising Down* has not been translated in France yet. It's huge. I did not really read it myself yet . . .

WTV: It's OK I still like you. [*Laughs.*]

DB: . . . what made you at this point of your literary career write this massive piece of work on violence?

WTV: Well, I started it about twenty-four years ago, and I finished it last year. So it took me twenty-three years to write, which was a lot . . . And it changed. Originally I was interested in extreme environmentalism, eco-terrorism, i.e. under what circumstances is it appropriate to destroy property or perhaps take human life for the sake of the biosphere. So I wanted to come up with some kind of moral calculus for that and once I started thinking about the principles of proportionality and discrimination which they use in warfare, I thought: "Well, maybe there are other principles as well . . ." And I got more and more interested in trying to come up with a universal moral calculus. There isn't any such thing, but I think it's possible to pigeonhole most acts of violence. I came up with five finite categories. Then I just tried to be systematic and determine whether an action could fall into one of them.

DB: By writing this essay on violence, did you want to reach out to other kinds of readers, people that would not necessarily read novels, academics and politicians for example?

WTV: I wanted to answer the question to my own satisfaction. You know, when I write my books, I never really care that much whether other people read them. It gives me pleasure to write them. What I do care about is that I can sell my books. And if I can get enough money to live, and write another book and do what I want to do, then I'm happy. But I really don't care who reads them. My wife doesn't read my books. That's fine with me. But as *Rising Up and Rising Down* took so much work, eventually I started thinking that it would be nice if terrorists could read it, and also politicians, soldiers, executioners, magistrates . . . And eventually I thought that perhaps any citizen anywhere in the world might have an interest in this topic. I don't think that the world owes me a living or that anyone is obligated to read it, but I think that if someone is interested, it may be helpful.

DB: The United States seems a great place to study violence. There is a lot of violence in the country, it's all over the media . . .

WTV: Absolutely . . . It's in the culture, it's in the foreign policy . . . I often take European visitors through parts of Sacramento that Americans would call "a bad neighborhood." Europeans who haven't spent any time in America don't have any sense of danger in those places. It's very interesting. Just as I can go to certain places, say in Africa or Bosnia or wherever, and I won't pick up the cues to know that this particular place is more dangerous than some other place a block away.

DB: How does the violence that you see here in this country fit into the five categories you've just mentioned? What kind of definition could you give it?

WTV: I would say that most violence, most of the time in most part of the world is unjustified. Violence can be justified where there is imminent danger, for self-defense, or some sort of retaliation to restore social symmetry, if everyone kind of agrees that this is the right way to do it. But a lot of the violence in the United States—and in our borders I mean violent

crime—is violence on a very low level. Usually it's the violence of poor people against other poor people, who have been brutalized themselves and
have been brutalized by the culture and have never really thought about
anything but themselves and it's unjustified and sad. You know, there is
bound to be sequels to September 11, here and in your country. And as
those things happen and claim their victims—and obviously it's a terrible
thing—the one good thing that might come out of it is that people might
get more conscious of violence and where it comes from. I remember that
right after September 11 many of my friends whom I never heard speak of
politics at all and had no interest in our foreign policy or anything else suddenly started calling me up and asking me why I thought this had happened
or reading a little bit about the Middle East and so forth . . . And I thought:
that's really good that's some good can come out of that. Europeans think
that they know Americans. Europeans know Americans better than Americans know Europeans, because Americans are a little bit narcissistic, very
comfortable and so forth . . . But one thing I would say is that most Americans are not monsters, they're not arrogant, nasty, brutal people. They're
just people who are ignorant. And much more ignorant than most Europeans really know. And if you try to remember that most Americans really
don't understand and it's not their fault, that they're bewildered, that is a
very important message. I went to Iraq in 1998 for Saddam Hussein's birthday. Because I was American, everybody I met was sure that I was a Jewish
spy for Mossad. And that was the level on which they operated. And they
weren't angry! They weren't mean to me: that's just really what they thought!
And so many people here are sure that Iraqis were behind September 11
because the President implied it and they think the President must know.
It's very important to remember that the mass media here operates on a
very primitive level, and most people never have a chance their entire lives
to understand that there is more to it than that.

The other thing I would say is that September 11 did happen, and that
was unjustified, and it's our duty to find out who it was who caused that and
to hunt down these people and kill them. That having been said I think our
President is a war criminal and I would be very pleased if he was indicted
as war criminal by the Hague. I think that everybody in the world needs to
take responsibility, not only for Iraq but also for September 11. I went to
Yemen in September 11, 2002, just to see, you know, how that was. Most
people were very happy on that day. They were celebrating the death of the
Americans at the WTC, and so on and so forth, but they were nice to me
personally. The people who were not nice to me over there were the handful

of European tourists who were very hostile and said I had no right to be there. I didn't get angry at the Yemenis, mostly. I would get angry at these stupid tourists who were telling me that they were insulted that I was in Yemen and that I was a bad person: they did not know me. I am not saying that Americans are better than Europeans or that they are worse! Right now because the US has more bullets, it is doing bad things. I suspect that anyone who had the most bullets would do bad things, that's what human history is all about.

DB: Considering the context you've just presented, what is your opinion on the forthcoming election and what do you think will come out of it?
WTV: Of course I hope Bush is defeated. I think he is a very dangerous, stupid, evil person and he caused a lot of harm all around the world. I think though that there is an excellent chance that he'll win. For instance, if he succeeds in catching Osama, say a month before the election, that's some trivial thing like that which could make all the difference. I don't think that Kerry would necessarily be a very good President, but I would rather try somebody else, for sure!

DB: You are also a journalist, you covered a number of wars, including Bosnia, you went to Afghanistan in another era, when the Soviets were there . . . What is the relationship between your journalism and your fiction? Is there one?
WTV: It's all on a continuum. I remember once when I was writing *Fathers and Crows*, one of my *Seven Dreams*, I had written what I thought was a very nice chapter about a female protagonist of mine, an Indian woman, who was being taught something by a male shaman. And then I read a little bit more and then found out that it could only have been a female shaman, or an old woman that wasn't a shaman. So I had to throw that chapter in the garbage. I really liked that chapter. I liked the way the sexual dynamics worked between the two, I was sorry to lose it. But something like *Seven Dreams* is written on the foundation of fact, and every deviation from the fact is for some very important reason in the service of a larger truth, whereas a book like *You Bright and Risen Angels*, my first book, is more a book of imagination. There is no particular reason to follow literal truth. When it comes to my journalism, I am on the other side of the continuum, and I think it is very important to make everything literally true. And I am sure that most journalists have been tempted at times to make up some little detail, because no one's ever going to know or whatever . . . I've never

done it and I never will and I am very proud of that. Whereas if I were writing a novel, I would make up anything I wanted to make up. All the same, I feel that it's of a piece with the rest of my writing. If I write about somebody in Serbia who has suffered during the war at the hands of Croats and might have committed some war crimes herself, I'll try to use my skills as a novelist to describe her as a full living, three-dimensional character. So instead of someone just finding out she's done these bad things, she's a bad person, period, the reader's going to be forced to say: OK, this happened to her. And also: she's very loyal, she's very intelligent, she tries hard, she's a mixture of good and bad. You can't just say: this is what it is, in two sentences. So this is what I try to bring to my journalism and really to all my writing. Whatever I think, and whatever you think, I always think my first job is: let's think what the other side might be.

If you had been an American journalist when we were talking about September 11, international politics and so on and so forth, I probably would have saved all my criticism for America, because most Americans still haven't heard enough criticism, they still don't realize how much in the wrong we are. But since you're a European and that's fairly obvious to you, I'm sure, that we're doing some very evil, wicked things, then I figure that it's my duty to tell you that there's always another side.

DB: On the jacket of *You Bright and Risen Angels*, there is that quote: "William Vollmann prefers a Sig-Sauer P226 for dispatching giant beetles, and a Browning BDA-380 for close work." You have first been in close contact with firearms when you first went to Afghanistan. Can you explain your relationship and fascination to firearms and how do you reconcile this with your own position on and knowledge of violence?

WTV: I respect guns. I love guns very much. I own quite a few firearms. If you wanted to see them or handle them if that's something that you haven't done, I would be happy to show you some! There's a lot to say about guns. In many ways, maybe in most ways, European culture is superior to American culture, but I feel very proud of the fact that unlike most citizens in the world I am trusted by my government to dispose of the means of lethal force, and that I can keep that in my house, and that I have the right to make decisions about this. And it may mean that I could make a bad decision. There could be some tragedy. I could be a selfish person, or confused, or evil and use the gun to kill someone else. I could be careless, in which case maybe my little girl could be killed or kill somebody else, and if so I would have to live with that for the rest of my life. On the other hand—Thoreau talked a little bit about this—one of the things that one gains from firearms ownership is a sense of personal responsibility and a sense of freedom, a sense of self-reliance. I feel that I don't have to worry and wait for the police to protect me necessarily, that if some bad things happen, I'm there and I can save my life and I can save someone else's life. And it goes with a habit of mine: because I know that I can do that, it means that I don't need authority to guide me or instruct as much as I might otherwise do. I can be a little bit more distant towards authority, a little bit more critical. I am not a member of the NRA and I don't agree with everything they do. But one NRA member said something nice once. He said that the purpose of the Second Amendment (the right to keep firearms) is to keep the US government honest.

DB: You mean in the sense that you could rebel against authority?
WTV: Exactly. And Jefferson said so. He said that if necessary people will exercise their revolutionary right to amend the government. I think that in most part of the country the capability for that, the understanding of that is long since gone. But there are the vestiges of that and I think it's a glorious thing, really. And then there are some demographic things to say about attitudes to firearms in the US. Most of the large media in the States tends to operate in urban areas. And if you grow up in an urban area, you're going to have less exposure to firearms. There is a real split between urban and rural in the US. It's not necessarily obvious. People in Montana, or Nevada, or Eastern California often feel very bitter towards the government for not recognizing their right to be pioneer-like, in certain ways. I guess summing up I would say that a gun is a tool. The fact that so many Americans have done terrible things with guns is not an indictment of gun-ownership, or of guns, it's an indictment of American culture. It might well be that at some point we will lose the right to possess firearms as a result of these people who have been abusing this right. And that would be very, very sad.

DB: Let's move on to your novel, *The Royal Family*. It is a huge novel that is set mostly in San Francisco; however, you live in Sacramento. How would you say is your relationship to that city, San Francisco?
WTV: *The Royal Family* is sort of a long love letter to San Francisco. I love San Francisco so much. I love the fog, I love the vice. I love the different neighborhoods, the different worlds. When I graduated from college, I moved out to San Francisco and I lived there for a year when I was working in insurance as a secretary to save up the money to go to Afghanistan. And the instant I came there, I felt like it was my home. There are three

or four places in the world in the world that I feel that are my home. Sacramento is not one of them. I used to really hate it here, it's horrible in a lot of ways: it's like being in the belly of the beast. But it has some good qualities. People are very friendly. There is a lot of space here. It's a very quiet, dull place, which means it's a good place to raise a child. Maybe I should bring down some of my sketches from upstairs . . . [*Brings down a portfolio with dozens of drawings and watercolors of prostitutes, front doors and objects from various San Francisco hotel rooms.*] Some day I intend to publish them. And since it wasn't going to happen any time soon, I thought I might as well do my own stuff. [*Shows the watercolors, smiles and gets animated. Points at a drawing of paint tubes and brushes.*] Those are my watercolors. Sometimes I would let the prostitutes stay in my hotel room with me overnight and then oftentimes they would steal my red watercolors and use them for lipstick. There was one prostitute, she was a grandmother, she was still working and she always would steal my cadmium red. And I'd say you know this is like lead, this very bad for you! And she'd say: I'm not worried, something else is gonna happen to me—and it's true, she got strangled. So she was right. The cadmium red did not do her any harm. I love those women so much, you know. Possibly for the same reasons that I love firearms. They are . . . We all live a mixture of freedom and desperation, and to the extent that they're addicted to various drugs, they're desperate . . . But one of the points that I make in *The Royal Family* is that addiction is kind of loyalty. And so in a way, it might even be not so far from enlightenment, if you're focused on something—maybe your drug, or your sex—as your God. Anyway they have that, but they're also very free in a way. It's up to them.

DB: Free in their language? Or with their body?
WTV: All those things . . . A prostitute is in my opinion one of the best artist models. She's very relaxed with her body, she's not gonna be shocked, she's very matter of fact, and she sort of lets her body speak. She knows so much about life. She's seen so much, and of course all sort of terrible things have happened to her, usually, if she is a street prostitute—but in a way, that's almost like a badge of honor.

DB: Part of the experience of reading the book is the feeling of being drawn into the life of prostitutes, tramps, drop-outs, people with whom it is rare to interact in such great depth. What can readers get from this experience?
WTV: One thing that I think is so beneficial to all of us as human beings is

that we can set ourselves the mission of trying to identify with and appreciate as many different people and things in this universe as we can. We're gonna be happier, we're gonna know more, we're going to live more fully. And if we do that for others, and others do that for us, I think we are all going to benefit. In *The Brothers Karamazov*, Dostoevsky said that when somebody commits a murder in Africa, in Timbuktu, we should all feel guilty, because we are all brothers and sisters. And if we do, if we really try and feel guilty about it, maybe the world can become a little bit better. One of the reasons I think that Bush is a war criminal and that Americans are so far in the wrong about this war, is that it's so difficult for us to see the other. I am always sickened when I read in the newspaper that people are starting to worry about how much money the war is costing and how many American soldiers are being killed, but it was only this latest thing with the torture—which to me is really quite trivial—that suddenly made anyone express any concern about the Iraqis . . .

DB: Isn't it precisely what comes up, the guilt? Don't we all feel guilty, American and European alike, about the torture of the Iraqis at the Abu Ghraib prison?

WTV: I hope, I hope . . . And when I see a street prostitute suffering, I feel guilty. And sometimes I give her some money so she can at least get a hotel or a place to fix, sometimes I don't. And whether I do or whether I don't, it's not really that important. And whether I feel guilty or not is not really that important to her. It's just important to me. I am going to be coming to France again this fall. I am going to spend an extra week or so in Paris and I would like to write some kind of poem and illustrate it about somebody in Paris, I don't know who . . . Because Americans need to see the other! And for me, what could be more fun, and more exciting and thrilling, like maybe I could find some amazing Parisian girl, and she could be my muse, or I can hang out with some *clochard*, whatever . . . I can speak a little French, I can get by . . . I want to be your friend, not just you and me, but as an American I want to be friends with Europeans, I want to learn from them and I want to help other Americans do the same.

DB: In *The Royal Family*, there is a moment when the narrator says: "I ask you, where have all the interlocutors gone. There are more people than ever and yet Tyler cogitates alone." Tyler, the main character in the book has an eye and a compassion for the people he meets, everyone has an echo in himself and in his body. At the same time though, there is this sense that people don't really relate to each other anymore in Western societies, they don't really want to see the other . . .

WTV: I think that's true. Part of it I am sure is due to technology . . . If you just look at the way Dostoevsky's *The Idiot* begins, with people talking to each other in a train: very few people here take trains. They're in their cars, with people that they already know. I was in Germany last September—I just finished some short stories about Europe during World War II. I was in Berlin and I felt that on the U-Bahn or S-Bahn in Berlin it wasn't really better. People also weren't talking to each other. But in a place like Madagascar where you take a taxi bus and everyone is just crammed together and you're stuck there for hours and hours, and someone who wants to go to the bathroom has to climb over ten people . . . You have to get to know each other a little bit. And maybe it takes some kind of emergency, or some necessity, to make people do that.

Maybe they wouldn't naturally do that, I don't know. I also always find that everywhere I go in the Muslim world, I can always get to know people as much as I want to and that's a tremendous gift. There was a Pakistani guy I met once who came to the US and where he was from it was very common, if you stand in line, to buy lunch for the person behind you. And the person ahead of you buys lunch for you, and everyone does that and it's just nice. It took him about a year to stop. No one would ever buy his lunch, and he would buy lunch for the person behind him whom he'd never see again . . . This poor guy, every time I think about that, I find it so sad. [*Laughs.*]

DB: You have written a lot about marginalized communities in your books. The United States is a country of immigrants, who are often marginalized. How would you say people abroad relate to you as an American journalist, and how do you feel people in the countries you've visited relate to America?

WTV: I think until probably about 2000 maybe mostly, especially in the Third World, they idealized America. I thought that was very good for them. It's always nice if we have illusions in life. It makes us happier. I'm always sure that someday, I will make a lot of money and I will meet the perfect muse, and I will be able to really become a better than adequate platinum printer, and of course I'm getting closer and closer to the grave! And so, these people in Afghanistan or Mexico, who used to tell me how much they wanted to come to America and how easy things would be for them, how happy they would be—I always thought the best thing was to just let them continue to be happy, unless I thought they had a real chance to come. Then I would tell them that it was going to be a lot harder than they thought, everything is expensive and people are not necessarily so friendly. America used to be a kind of myth and at the moment America is a myth of Hubris, and arrogance and evil, and I am sure that that will shift again soon. There are going to be a lot more terrorist attacks on European soil. And possibly one virtue of that is that Europeans and Americans can become a little bit reunited again and also realistic. Sartre used to say that two people form a community by excluding the third, and I think that's true.

DB: In *The Royal Family*, it is pretty clear that there is not an obvious separation between fiction and experience. And it is difficult to relate to most of your books as works of fiction only. Can you explain this need to mix fiction and experience?

WTV: Partly, it's a matter of respect for the ones who are real, and for what they do. *The Royal Family* has a predecessor: *Whores for Gloria*. It's a very short book, also set in San Francisco. It's about Jimmy, an alcoholic Vietnam veteran, who pays prostitutes to tell him stories and he imagines that there is a woman who really loves him named Gloria, and he's paying these prostitutes to tell him happy stories that he can use as memories of things that happened to Gloria, and to himself and so forth . . . And unfortunately most of the time these prostitutes who try their best with happy stories end up with sad endings. The stories in that book were all real, and the prostitutes were all real, and I would pay them to tell me happy stories and they would always end up being sad. I was very interested with the Russian Formalists at one time. They started with fairy tales. They said that all fairy tales have a finite number of motifs: the trickster, the wise old man bringing the king to the rescue of the princess. It is like a necklace, really. You take these things and put them like beads on the string. So I thought: let's try these with *Whores for Gloria*. Take these stories and use them as beads on a narrative string. Jimmy never existed. He's the string. By the time I wrote *The Royal Family*, I felt that I'd spent enough time in that world that I could make composite characters and I could even create characters. So a lot of the people in this book are fictional. But if I had tried to do that at the very beginning, I couldn't have. I am writing a book now about the California-Mexico border, and originally I wanted it to be a novel. After having spent five of six years there, I realized that I don't know enough, so it's gonna have to be a work of non-fiction. And if I keep spending enough time there, maybe some day I could write a novel about one of these illegal aliens, but I definitely can't do it yet . . .

DB: Do you feel you need more experience to write fiction than you need to write books of non-fiction?

WTV: For certain kinds of fiction, yes. If you're Nabokov or Faulkner, not necessarily. If you are Zola, probably. In a way something like *The Royal Family* has a lot of naturalistic elements. Frankly, one of the serious defects in American popular culture that I see is that people want shortcuts. They take some crude stereotype of the prostitute, and create a dumb movie. And everyone sees that and they say: "Oh, OK! So that's how a prostitute is," and "How nice!" or "How terrible!" and they don't have to think about it. And I think if I did something like that, that would be an insult to the prostitutes.

DB: Another huge project of yours are the *Seven Dreams* novels. None of them has been published in France yet. What was the genesis of this project?

WTV: For *Seven Dreams*, I thought how wonderful it would be to imagine all the various changes that the continent of North America has gone through since the indigenous times and how great it would be to use Indianness and Christian theology and all kinds of things and give them all the same weight to try to show one kind of thing changing into another kind of thing. Originally it was going to be one volume, seven chapters. And then I started to get more and more interested in the history for its own sake. And I started thinking why not use a different sort of narrative and prose structure for each volume.

DB: Do you apply the same type of method, drawing from experience like in *The Royal Family*?

WTV: I decided to entertain the hypothesis that people's experience is determined by the landscape that they live in to some extent. Therefore, if I went to these landscapes, and looked at them very carefully and walked in the same places as these historical people have, the same seasons and try to see the same things, the change of the foliage, the shape of the mountains, that would be one point in common I would have with those people. And then if I did all the archival research that I could and try to get anthropologists and archeologists to help me as well, I can get a little bit closer to the way they used to see these things. And finally, where there was a gap, I would feel free to use my imagination. Increasingly though, I wanted to subordinate my imagination to what it was that I saw. It would make me happy if these books could be taught in classes about history, or anthropology or something. Part of the place where I get to exercise my own individuality I suppose is in the prose structure. When I wrote *Fathers and Crows*, it was about French Jesuits in Canada, and I read a lot about the Jesuit relations and I had a lot of fun in trying to recreate the florid but elegant style of the Jesuits. I tried to come up with a kind of French. [*Laughs.*] In *The Ice-Shirt* on the other end, I tried to use Norse-English, which in a way was easier than with the French, because English is probably closer to Norse.

DB: The *Seven Dreams* novels involved a lot of traveling, particularly to Canada sometimes in extreme conditions. What draws you up North?
WTV: Well, I was born there, so like a good Croat, or a good Serb or a good Bosnian I am loyal to my birth place. The farther you go up North, the more beautiful it is. I love the fact that when you're up in the North there's nothing extraneous. There's just you and the sky. You're very close to it. In the summer, when the sun doesn't set you can watch it as it goes round and round in the sky. The animals are beautiful. Again, it's some of the same thing that I guess I like about firearms: this feeling of being free, of being totally responsible for my own life. If I freeze to death or I am uncomfortable, that's my fault. If I see some beautiful thing, it's a victory! I have watercolor books that I make and bring up there. What could make me happier than seating in front of a waterfall and try to do a quick watercolor sketch of the waterfall? If I'm in a town maybe I'll go on a walrus hunt with the Inuit and do some watercolor sketches of them bringing in the walrus . . . I could do that for the rest of my life, I just love it.

DB: You are also a visual artist. In several books of yours there are pictures, drawings, maps . . . Why is the visual so important to you?
WTV: There are two inspirations for me in that regard. One is Gauguin. I really like *Noa Noa*. Even though the text is not particularly good. He wasn't a very good writer. Because of his insecurity he was a little bit too pugnacious. But when you see the words mixed in with the watercolors, it looks really beautiful. I guess the other one that I like is Blake. The form of a book should correspond to its content. That's why I started making the CoTangent books. My first one was a poem called *The Convict Bird*, it's about a friend of mine, a woman who's serving a life sentence in prison for attempted murder. And so the book is its own prison: it's steel, and it has a lock and a little window and you have to unlock it to take out the book. Also I really like some of the things that Matisse does, especially the studies—the quick studies he would do seem to me very calligraphic, and the idea of combining text and pictures all in one person's hand to me is very exciting. I would like to have the time to try to figure out a way to come up with a new alphabet. The

alphabet would still be legible, but it would be more graphic and pictorial the way that the Arabic alphabet is in those illuminated Qurans. It would be so exciting to draw a letter A that would still be legible as such but maybe it would resemble a tree, or a beach. Or maybe it would just be something abstract and beautiful, with different weights on the pen strokes but still, that would be wonderful.

DB: You seem to be writing with no limits, no inhibitions. You seem to be hitting at absolutely everything within your reach . . . Your books are very long . . . Is there a limit? Have you got a big goal, something that is dragging you somewhere?
WTV: There are lots of things that I would like to do. I have lots of potential projects. About three or four years ago I started thinking I wanted to become more politically engaged. I started writing some ballads. I have a friend who is a singer and I'd like her to sing some of the songs about the drug war and Iraq and so on but, that's not really enough. I don't know whether I need to take it as far as Mishima did, but I would like to act somehow in this world and I am not sure how I want to do it. You never know.

DB: Are there writers that you communicate with? What is your opinion of people you have been compared to, like William Gaddis or Thomas Pynchon?
WTV: I try to exist in as much isolation as possible, which is one of the reasons why I don't have email or a fax machine or anything like that. American culture for a long time has been narcissistic, self-congratulatory, self-referential. And so when I have the time I would rather read a book by someone who is not American so I could learn something, which isn't to say that I want to say anything disparaging about American writers. Probably my favorite American writer at the moment is Cormac McCarthy. I think he's wonderful. On the other hand who can beat a writer like Danilo Kiš . . . *A Tomb for Boris Davidovich* is one of my all-time favourite books. I love that book. I was very happy that Dalkey Archive reissued that book. I am sorry that he died. I would have liked to meet him. Eastern European writers have always been fascinating to me. I guess in a way it's like the street prostitutes. They've had a very hard time and they've had to go inward a little bit, so there's something kind of mystic about them in a way. I like the Polish writer Tadeusz Konvicki, especially *A Dream Book for Our Time*. Kundera's short stories are very good. I don't think his novels are as good as his short stories . . . Hrabal's *Closely Watched Trains* and *I Served the King of England*. I really wish that I could read some of those languages.

DB: How do you feel about Afghanistan? It has been the focus of attention in many ways, since the days when you went there to fight with the Islamist militias . . .

WTV: I feel so lucky that I went to Afghanistan in 1982. There was an old Pakistani general there, and President Zia had been his subordinate in the army, so this guy had a lot of power and he essentially adopted me as his son. He gave me clothes, like a *pathan*, he let me stay in his house for a long time, he gave me meals for nothing and of course he gave me a gun, because without a gun I would not be a man in that culture. And he also arranged for me to go to Afghanistan with the mujahideen. When I went back in 2000 to visit the Taliban, I visited him and it was just a wonderful experience to see him again. He still remembered me. I'd kept his business card and it now had a couple of more digits on his telephone . . . He was in his eighties. He was happy to see me. I love the Afghans. I love Afghanistan. I am very proud that the CIA helped them against the Russians. Of course we did it for the wrong reasons, not to be nice but because we wanted to create problems for the Russians, but so what? It was still a good thing. I am very happy that we helped them to regain their freedom. And it's too bad that at that point the various mujahideen groups became bandits and fought against each other. But that's something I don't blame the United States for. I don't think that it's our obligation to take care of everybody for ever and ever. We gave them a chance . . . But I was very much against our invasion of Afghanistan after September 11 and I think that's another disaster which no one is paying attention to, it's much quieter now but I think it's going to be a long-time disaster. For us, for Afghanistan and for the world. The Taliban was bad. But I think they were better than any alternative. So it made me very sad that the Taliban was destabilized.

DB: At the beginning of *The Royal Family*, there is that quote by Francis Bacon: "It would be madness and inconsistency to suppose that things that have not yet been performed can be performed without employing some hitherto untried means." What are these "untried means"?

WTV: Henry Tyler is not very good private detective. But he is a great human being. And the reason he is great is because he is a loser. And he doesn't know that that's why he is great. And it takes him a long time to understand that the reason the Queen of the prostitutes is so great and a lot of these other people are so great is because they are losers. John, Henry's brother, is not a bad person. I actually have a lot of sympathy for him. He is trying to help his brother. He was supporting Irene. I make him out to be a very smug, annoying person and at first that's what you see of him. And then later on if you start thinking about it, from any real point of view John is the one who is trying to help and save everybody. He is more effective than Tyler in a lot of ways! All the same: it's once Tyler understands that you have to let everything go, that you have to be a loser, that you're trying these "hitherto untried means" that you might actually get somewhere. You might actually have a chance . . . In the end, *The Royal Family* is a book about failure. Tyler doesn't succeed in keeping the Queen whom he really loves, just as he didn't succeed in keeping Irene. And it's because he's ultimately not willing to let himself go and be a complete loser, until the very end when it's too late. I think that when we're stuck in life in some kind of situation that blocks us it's important, instead of making the same mistake that we made, to try to make a different mistake!

DB: You have said somewhere about this book that prostitutes and undertakers are the only eternal optimists . . . What did you mean by that?
WTV: Well . . . They always know that they're going to get business. There's always going to be sex and there's always going to be death. And so they really don't have to worry too much . . . Everything is OK: if you're an undertaker, someone is going to die. If you're a prostitute you can be pretty sure that very soon someone is gonna come and give you enough money for your hotel room. And so what a great world!

DB: *Open All Night*, the book you made with the photograph Ken Miller about the San Francisco underworld looks at times like a family album. Reading it I had a sense that these were people you could always go back to . . .
WTV: Oh yeah! Ken was the one who introduced me to the neo-Nazi skinheads and a lot of those people on Haight Street in the mid-1980s. He was a street photographer in the '80s. He was very good to me. Extremely charismatic guy at that time. He was really interested in the street alcoholics and the derelicts and so forth, and once I started meeting those people, I started pursuing the prostitutes and he and I did some of that for a while and then I kept doing it. And now, he is sort of burned out. He had some sad experiences and now he is a wedding photographer, that's all he does. It's all over for him.

DB: So you started to get interested in these aspects of San Francisco through photography, right?

WTV: I think so. I used to love going out with Ken. He had a big camera. He was taking 5 × 7s. And now I have several big cameras, I take 8×10s. It was really wonderful being with Ken in those days.

DB: In the introduction to *Open All Night*, you wrote that when these people Ken Miller used to meet clutched his images in their hands everyone could see that they were not as lost as one might think or want to think. Do you think that you can achieve the same thing with words?

WTV: I think you achieve a different thing . . . I've never gotten too excited about good or bad reviews but for about six years I did an 8 × 10 project on street prostitutes here in Sacramento, and what used to really make me happy was when I would give them a copy of some picture I made for them and they would say: "I'm gonna give this to my children for Christmas" or something like that, and I would feel very proud and happy as I never did with a review. But most of them, and a lot of the people that I've interviewed and worked with, could never read one of my books, it's too difficult. I think that a photograph gives instantaneous context. It's not bad or worse. I think the nice thing about something like *The Royal Family* is that it can offer a portrait which people can read long after all of us are dead. They can read that and get some feeling about what those people were like. Whereas even if the photographs survive, when you're looking at photographs of those people, they might not know what a tattoo signifies, or what the person's dress signifies, or—if a person dresses in a provocative way—whether that person is a prostitute or something else . . . Context is always needed, so it's just different.

DB: Is that why you also draw, and take pictures?

WTV: You know, my big project right now is this California-Mexico border project. I've taken hundreds and hundreds of 8 × 10 and 35 millimeter pictures. What would make me happy is to put this in some archive, so that three, five hundred years from now people could look and say oh, so that's what they looked like, that's who they were . . . And there would be words with that, so they could really know something, as opposed to just looking into someone's eyes and say: I wonder who that person was, what was that person like, and a photograph can't tell you that.

DB: So the written word is still important. It's a good complement . . .

WTV: Right. And everything is mortal. Words are mortal, images are mortal. All you can do is try to make things as immortal as you can. And if no one reads the words, at least the words still exist in some way, and if your words are destroyed and every copy of your book is destroyed, maybe the fact that you created this means that it is still somewhere. That's my comfort.

[*He turns to the Algerian nanny and asks her: "If some bad people found every copy of the Quran on Earth and they destroyed them all, would the words to the Quran still exist somewhere?"*]

Long-Term Visitor: An Interview with William T. Vollmann

Daniel Lukes / 2004

From *While You Were Sleeping*, August/September, 2004. © Daniel Lukes.
Reprinted by permission.

Some writers you read; others *speak* to you. My first encounter with William T. Vollmann was a brief and enigmatic one, a quotation inside the CD sleeve of the self-titled debut album by long-forgotten sleaze-industrial rock band Nature (BMG/Zoo Entertainment, 1995): "So fear repetition not; there remain many seas of blood and cream to be traversed." The words danced in my head until I acquired *Butterfly Stories*, and one cold and wet British winter, I took my first, tentative steps into his chaotic, exotic, and often uncomfortable world.

Now living in Sacramento with his wife and daughter, Vollmann's voice down the phone line is friendly and his words carefully considered, periodically interrupted by the sounds of his daughter playing and banging things together. He's just back from a trip to the California/Mexico border on which, among other projects, he is writing a book, providing the perfect opportunity for a reflection on the mind-expanding benefits of seeing beyond one's corner of the world.

DL: What do you find traveling gives you as a human being? What kind of benefits?
WTV: Well, Daniel, I think it gives you two seemingly contradictory benefits. The first is that you realize that people and places are profoundly different and there are acts, points of view that you never would have considered or imagine that someone would accept as normative. For instance, my experience in Madagascar is often that many of these tribal people believe in lying and backstabbing to an incredible degree, and it's sort of like

the Dobu described in Ruth Benedict's *Patterns of Culture*: if they can pretend to be each other's best friends and then stab each other in the back, it's like a triumph, and it's really, really interesting. Or, let's say up in the Canadian Arctic: You see five-year-old boys being left alone with firearms, and handling them safely and making sure their three-year-old brothers don't hurt themselves or anyone else, and then you realize what they say here about how children should never be near guns and how inherently dangerous guns are, is very local and relative. And if we happened to have a different kind of culture where everyone is around guns and treated them as tools, we might not have the same sort of issues about guns, so there are all these sorts of things. At the same time, what you learn from travel is that people are fundamentally the same, which is to say that we can see ourselves in them; they have the same emotions that we have, and the same mix of good and bad that we have. This is an extremely obvious point, and so obvious that it continually gets overlooked, especially in times like these when all of a sudden, on our side of the fence, we're so afraid of Muslims, and, on the other side, people in the Islamic world think that we're all a bunch of arrogant killers, when obviously Muslims are just like us in their degree of culpability, and their innocence and their human ambiguity.

DL: How hopeful are you in general are you that humans can communicate despite cultural and linguistic barriers?
WTV: Well, success and failure will always be partial and temporary. I see no fundamental difference in the way that people relate to each other now—in the success—compared to five-hundred years ago, or five-thousand years ago. There's always some sort of seemingly external force that results from a fundamental drive on somebody's part that separates people; some kind of fear, or greed or hatred, or miscommunication or whatever. There always will be, and there will always be some way of putting the pieces back together in a new and equally temporary way. I think that right now, our country and our culture is in much more serious trouble than most people really grasp. I think the family is in crisis, education is in crisis, the notions of sexuality, and fundamental notions of value—what's right, what's wrong—notions of citizenship, notions of our place in the world, notions of the rights and limits of authority and the individual: all these extremely basic, crucial issues are all up for grabs now. We can be sure that they will eventually reform in some new combination, but our society is increasingly less cohesive and the process of continued deterioration, which will eventually resolve in some new configuration, is likely to be, as always, a painful one.

DL: Do you think that Western society is less happy and more alienated than other cultures and societies have been in the past?

WTV: No, I don't. I think that it is fulfilled and alienated in different ways. I think that what Marx called the "cash nexus" is so central a part of our perception and action in the West now, that we're completely blind to it. I'm always amazed to hear some young person talk about how he has to sell himself or something like this—as if anyone would aspire to sell himself—and (he's) completely unconscious of what he's saying, and the whole notion that, to have a pleasant time, to do something interesting and fun for amusement, what you have to do is spend money. I mean, at this point, people really can't even imagine another way of existence here, and yet the fact is that in so much of the rest of the world, it's not that way. One of the big mistakes that the US has made in Serbia, in Afghanistan, in Iraq, is not grasping that the fundamental value there has much less to do with money, with material prosperity, and much more to do with pride. And does that mean that they are less alienated and better off? In some ways, yes; when I go to a place like Yemen, I admire and envy the certainty and cohesiveness these people have. Everything is fairly certain: there might be some distinction between Sunni and Shia, but basically they go to the mosque, they do the same thing, they believe the same thing, and they have a kinship that we don't, which is really, really great. On the other hand, I feel that in our country, although we neglect and abuse our privilege, we do have the privilege of really following our own individual muse, of arriving at points of view that might be frivolous, unpopular, hateful—right or wrong, whatever they are—but there's probably a wider range of permissible thought here. So, in that sense, we are less alienated.

DL: There's a recurring theme of contact and communication and interaction in your work. I was on the subway today and I noticed that everyone was fixated upon some kind of electronic gadget: cell phones, Game Boys, etc., and it made me think how inwardly-focused we are and how we'd rather look at a gadget than look around us because we are scared.

WTV: It's sad. I think that's one of the many reasons that I hate the car, because the car has really isolated us from each other. That's sort of the normal way to travel, most of the time, and has been for a long time, and, as a result, cities and roads have been developed to facilitate this easy, rapid getting around of all these individuals in hermetically-sealed bubbles, and it means the basic human ability to interact and be interested in each other and relate to each other that children have, atrophies very, very quickly, and it creates this inward quality that you speak of, and I notice it, and I hate it. I really hate it. One of the things that I love about traveling to other countries is that, if I am on the bus or the train, crowded in among all these people, I always have an opportunity to talk and meet somebody. But everything has its price, and I would abolish the car if I could. I would abolish the Internet if I could for the same reason, and other reasons, but it's part and parcel of that individuality I was talking about, too.

DL: What most troubles you about the Internet?
WTV: Well, first of all, I think the notion that there are virtual communities of interest is a fruitful one in some ways, but it's also very dangerous, because it means that you are even more removed from your immediate surroundings; your physical center becomes less important, you have less invested in it, and—it's like your mobile phone—you're less likely to become friends with your neighbors, and I think that is contributing to the decay and loneliness of American society. The second thing that I hate about the Internet and mobile phones as well—and one of the reasons that the paths to individuality we potentially have are being abused—is that suddenly everyone becomes infinitely interruptible. And I think that you can't, really, get anywhere: you can't think about who you are, and what you're doing and where you should be going, if you can be interrupted every second. That's why I don't have email, I don't have a mobile phone, I don't have a fax; I don't watch television for the same reason: I hate the interruptions, the commercials. On the Internet you get exposed to all kinds of ads and, in the meantime, people who mean you no good are tracking your movements, your buying patterns, your interests, and making it all the more likely that the interruptions in your life will be more and more seductive, therefore more and more effective, and keep you from being yourself.

DL: I read that Google's new Gmail system will scan the text of your email and tag ads to your email which refer to words in the actual message.
WTV: Yeah, that sounds like a natural development and wouldn't we all just be better off without that garbage? So many of my friends are sadly saying, "Well, you know I have to check my email messages again today, I probably have twenty or thirty messages and a bunch of spams," and I think, "Who wants to live that way?" But obviously a lot of people think it's great.

DL: A lot of people don't feel they have a choice about how they live . . .
WTV: That's right. And of course we always do have a choice. We have the

choice to say no, we don't have the choice to say yes, sometimes. If you're in a relationship with another person, let's say, (and) both of you are decent people, if one says "no," let's say to having sex, or one says "no" to continuing the relationship, that's it. No is stronger than yes. It takes two to say yes, but only one to say no. And I think that's true really of any social contract: when you get to the point where you want to say no to the Internet and you're not allowed to say no to it, that's going to be really, really sinister and horrible, but fortunately we're not quite there yet. My publishers are always saying, "What do you mean you don't have email?" And they get upset, but what can they do?

DL: You are in the position where you can say that . . .
WTV: Well, I am in that position because I set out to be in that position, and anyone else can set out to be in that position, too. One of the most insidious things about mobile phones and email, and part of the interruptability, is that the whole world now wants the power to change its mind about any number of things at the last minute, so decision-making occurs over shorter intervals of time, and the results are less effective. I remember when one of my books went into a new printing: they were able to email everything to a designer and do it quickly and on the cheap, and so the end result was that even though it had been fine before, in this printing, my name was misspelled on the spine of the book, not on the front cover, and that's because everything happens so quickly and everyone can say, "Let's change the color of this tomorrow. Here's some guy who can do that—let's send it to him, it's done." There's less time for oversight and it's less likely that you can make some kind of a good plan and really think about it. So many people now expect that plans are going to change, and you can fine-tune your plans as you go and so on and so forth, which to me is like a recipe for disaster. I would rather think to myself, "Ok, I'm going to make the best plan that I can, and people I'm working with will sign off on it and then they're not going to be able to reach me until I complete my plan." Then I have the freedom to really throw myself into it and do the best that I can, and they've agreed to it, and they can't, halfway through, say, "No, we want you to do it a different way." I'm better off and I think they're better off, too.

DL: The emotion of fear plays a major role in your writing. Your message seems to be something along the lines of "If you go out there and experience the world, you'll find it's not necessarily as scary as you might have thought."

WTV: I think that's true. I think people can benefit from being afraid, feeling that fear and then thinking, "Ok, this isn't the end of the world, what happens next?" Last week I had, basically, a minor stroke, and I'm fairly young for this stuff to happen. And it was somewhat disturbing and upsetting, and at the same time, I have faced death before in my work, and so I'm basically recovered now, but if this were to happen again and finish me off, I think I'm ready. I think I have thought a lot about what I want to do, and I'm trying to do it, and fear is a very useful goad, it really is there to remind you: I don't like what it is that I'm fearing: what *do* I like? What is it I want to be doing? And when the inevitable happens, of course I'll regret the fact that I'm going to disappear from the scene, but everyone is going to regret that, so, more fundamentally, do I regret the fact that I wanted to do X when I did Y?

DL: Was the stroke encouraged by the various experiences you've put yourself through so far?
WTV: I don't think so. I'm not really sure what caused it, and I feel fairly healthy and happy and so forth. It could have been a little bit of stress. It could have just been some physical accident. Who knows? And that's life.

DL: I read *The Royal Family* a couple of years ago, and I personally think it's a classic; would you say you are you underrated as a writer? Is it perhaps due to your treating themes a lot of people are uncomfortable with?
WTV: I would say that I'm satisfied with my audience. If I had a wider audience and I could make more money, since I too am a slave of the cash nexus, of course I would appreciate it, but other than I don't really care, Daniel, if nobody reads my books. I just write for myself and I feel fairly lucky that I'm able to support myself doing it, and a lot of these things that seem to disturb people, don't really disturb me. I mean, I look at them, sometimes they make me sad, but it's interesting to explore why they make me sad and sometimes when I delve into them a little bit more, they turn to be really less sad than they seemed on the outside, and that's often my experience with the world of street prostitution, for instance. You see some stinking, abscessed, confused human being and you think, "What a wretched life." And then you start meeting her, you get to know her a little better and you see, "Well, let's see, she has happiness every day, when she gets her drugs. She has her dreams which are just as rich and just as valid as ours. She has a certain amount of freedom, and she has these incredible adventures which make most of our lives look pretty tame." She lives really, really rapidly; she ages a lot, it's a very risky, bleak sort of life. It's horrible in a lot of

ways and it's also not without its own drama and glamour. And we're very, very foolish if we just relegate her to this category of an abject, exploited being, because she is, as are we, but she would probably be offended and we wouldn't be doing her justice if that was the only way we looked at her. So I guess *The Royal Family* was an attempt—well, probably my whole work is an attempt—to try to understand the Other.

DL: Why do you think most people are scared, don't want to go there and are happy with the prejudice they might have? It's easier to think a whore is doomed and damned and wretched and it makes the person saying that more comfortable with their life . . .

WTV: Yes. Well, really, to try to get to know the Other is a project that is fraught with effort and discomfort and, even in marriage, when you're picking your partner, you think, "This is the person I am most likely to succeed in getting to know and benefiting from getting to know." There are all kinds of unexpected difficulties, problems, drudgery—how much more so than with other human beings who are more likely to be alien? It's completely understandable and really forgivable that most people avoid making that effort—always have and always will—and it's the job of communicators of whatever kind, whether they're novelists or social reformers, or religious prophets, to do some of that work and inspire people to do a little bit more of that work.

DL: Have you got used to putting yourself in uncomfortable situations because you know you might gain some insight from it?

WTV: Absolutely. That's the reason to do it. When I was younger, the thrill of the exotic was much stronger and my emotions, my sadness and empathy and excitement and gratitude—all those sorts of things that I felt when people let me into their lives—were more immediate, let's say, and, now, as I'm middle-aged, there are fewer surprises and so things are less immediate, but I feel like I'm gradually becoming more effective, and, I'm not saying that one stage is better or worse than the other, (but) I'm gradually getting more successful at perceiving underlying patterns.

DL: Have you become more of less hopeful for humanity's capacity for empathy and understanding and happiness and that sort of thing?

WTV: I would say neither. I would say I'm no more or less hopeful than I ever was. I don't think that the human situation has changed (or) is going to change anytime soon. And I know that so many people, in the era when I was finishing *Rising Up And Rising Down*, were convinced that it was going to be a great world and all the problems had been solved and things were just going to get better and better, and I never really bought that, so a lot of people thought I was kind of gloomy; and now, of course, so many people think that we're in this *terrible* situation and I don't quite buy that either. There's nothing that is fundamentally new. This so-called "War on Terrorism" we're having: Some attenuated version of the experiences that most people in most of the world have always had, and we used to have, say, during the Indian Wars.

DL: Isn't it disappointing that humanity doesn't seem to learn from its own mistakes?

WTV: Well, after all, Daniel, how could it? Children are not wiser or more fulfilled than their parents. If they were, in a way, that would be kind of a tragedy. Then I think maybe I would be jealous of future generations, but I think you have to look at everything from the standpoint of your individual life. And Heidegger talks of us being thrown into a world not of our own making, and our fundamental way of relating to the world is just "being there" and gradually falling toward death, falling away from this mysterious "thrown-ness" and every choice that we make closes off other choices, obviously, so this is really the fundamental constituent of human *being*, and there's nothing we can do about it. That being the case, with all this necessity and all these arbitrary circumstantial limitations on our being and our fulfillment, we're going to make certain kinds of mistakes. They may not be the same mistakes that our parents made, because circumstances will be different, they might be different mistakes, (but) they'll still be mistakes. Our ability to perceive is always going to be limited. Our capacity to mature is always going to be quite small; when you look at it that way, you see that we are very, very small beings, and we can despair at that fact or we can try to be sort of easy on ourselves, and say, "Given how heavily the deck is stacked against us, we should be proud of any little thing we can accomplish."

DL: *The Royal Family* is an archetypal book about men and women as different species, asking how they can understand each other and how they can relate; have you got any closer to understanding that?

WTV: I think so. And that is definitely one of the activities in my life that has given me some of the most fulfillment, just trying to understand some of the differences between men and women and trying to see woman as the

Other, and trying to relate to woman in that way. It's a wonderful and end-lessly exciting, surprising project.

DL: What haunts you most of all the things you've seen? Are their images and situations that come back to you and you still can't make sense of them or come to terms with them?

WTV: It varies over time. I remember I went to Iraq in 1998 and, seeing that the sanctions were still in effect then, and seeing how deeply they had bitten into people's lives, how they were killing people, and then coming back here and talking to my neighbors and finding out that they didn't have a clue that we were still at war with Iraq, when the Iraqis were saying, "How much longer are you Americans going to be at war with us?" that was very haunting and disturbing. And months before the Second Gulf War, when all the newspapers and magazines suddenly started saying, "When are we going to war with Iraq? What's going to happen next?" None of them said, "Should we go to war with Iraq?" and I kept talking to people about it, and they all thought that I was an idiot to put it that way; that was very, very disturbing and upsetting to me at the time, and that sort of haunts me now, and I remember being in Yemen in 2002 and this one guy, a business man, told me "Of course you Americans are going to attack Iraq. I know that you will, and once you do, we're all going to join Al Qaeda, (and) we're all going to get you." And it was just so sad, and so depressing, and I knew what was going to happen and we haven't even seen the half of it, and that, I guess was haunting to me.

DL: What music do you like?

WTV: I like Scarlatti a lot. And Shostakovich, and, let's see, I like some of the so-called ethnic music. Did you ever hear the *Mystery of Bulgarian Voices*, those CDs that were popular in the '80s? Those were really beautiful. It's all female choral type singing, beautiful voices. I like some of the Muslim singers, but probably what I like the best is Western classical music. How about you?

DL: I like rock music. Heavy metal for the most part.

WTV: Oh, good for you. Well, I have been known to crank up the volume with David Bowie and The Who and stuff like that, but I don't go to the music store that often, and, since I don't listen to the radio, I don't watch television, I'm out of touch with a lot of music. But I'm happy with what I listen to.

Art and Freedom in Time of War: A Conversation with William T. Vollmann

Andrew Ervin / 2005

Portions of this interview appeared in *Rain Taxi* (Summer 2005) and *The Journal News* (March 20, 2005) ©Andrew Ervin. Reprinted by permission.

Europe Central is a bit of a departure for Vollmann. Like Danilo Kiš' masterpiece *A Tomb For Boris Davidovich*, an acknowledged influence, *Europe Central* contains a series of self-contained pieces that gel together to form a novel. Here, however, the stories come in pairs—common thematic and moral concerns repeatedly unite two separate narratives. Furthermore, Vollmann lined up eighteen of these double, mirrored tales so that every one seems to reflect the others in beautiful, startling and bizarre ways. The line between fiction and fact is a blurry one. The end of the book features a long list of the sources Vollmann referenced in order to get his historic details as accurate as possible. Set mainly in the mid-twentieth century, *Europe Central*'s characters include Adolf Hitler and Josef Stalin as well as artists Käthe Kollwitz and composter Dmitri Shostakovich. The most memorable figures, though, are two opposing lieutenant-generals: Russian A.A. Vlasov, forced to defend his homeland from invasion; and his nemesis, the German Friedrich Paulus. Then there's Kurt Gerstein, the SS officer who risked his life to save the very people he was supposed to murder. The result is without question the most profound fictional—if it can be called fictional—account of World War II since Pynchon wrote *Gravity's Rainbow*. Last week, on the ides of March, I phoned Vollmann at his home in Sacramento, California. He was obviously suffering through a nasty cold but graciously spoke at length about the origins of *Europe Central* and how in wartime good people end up committing horrific deeds.

Andrew Ervin: How did *Europe Central* come about?

William T. Vollmann: I've been really interested in the subject of totalitarianism since I was in elementary school. I remember seeing one of those film loops about the first arrival of the G.I.s in one of the concentration camps. And later on I realized: well, I'm part German and my relatives are probably involved. What does this mean? How could they have done this? So I read a lot of books about Nazism, in the seventies, and then I gradually got interested in Stalinism as well. Then in the eighties I read Wassily Grossman's *Life and Fate*, which I think is one of the great books of the twentieth century. That was the first place I really saw the clear equation of Nazism with Stalinism. Up until that time most people, myself included, tended to think "Of course Stalin was bad and killed a lot of people, but Hitler was worse." And Grossman said it the way it was.

AE: Do you mean to distinguish between different types of murderers?

WTV: When I researched *Rising Up and Rising Down* I realized that in fact Stalin was a more effective killer than Hitler, you know for one thing he was on the winning side of the war. He died probably of old age. And he killed maybe five times as many people as Hitler did. So he was highly successful at what he did, and as I say in *Rising Up and Rising Down*, the twentieth century was really the century of Stalin. Hitler in a way was more of the self-destructive ideologue with the artistic temperament and Stalin was a murderous bureaucrat.

AE: Are there degrees of evil?

WTV: When I wrote *Rising Up and Rising Down* I got more and more interested in various moral dilemmas, soluble and insoluble. And I started thinking of these people in the stories as tragic actors, people doing the best they could. Good people or indifferent people, sometimes evil people fighting for evil regimes. Whichever regime won or lost, the people were still going to suffer and yet they had a certain amount of moral choice all the same.

AE: Do you find it strange that your readers may very well sympathize with the plight of Nazis? Of Stalinists?

WTV: I think of somebody like Kurt Gerstein or for that matter Vlasov or even Paulus and none of them were probably bad people. Gerstein was the most heroic of them all but the other two were probably really doing their best. And if they'd happened to be, let's say, American generals they would be more or less effective and they wouldn't have had their various, kind of sad ends.

Vlasov's story always haunted me. I first heard about him when I was reading volume one of Solzhenitsyn's *Gulag Archipelago*, which must have come out in the late seventies. And he just mentions Vlasov very briefly. I thought, how strange—how could this possibly be, this Russian guy fighting for a supposed liberation army under Hitler, against Stalin? Very little was written about Vlasov and every now and then I'd go to the library, there'd be nothing. And then finally I went to a graduate library and there were five or six books. Even those didn't say that much about the guy, but I got some sense of the circumstances. But it was like writing a piece of science fiction in a way. You know that Jupiter has a certain gravity and probably atmosphere and you extrapolate and try to imagine what life on Jupiter would be like and you do your best but you don't know that much.

AE: *Europe Central* toys with the distinction between fiction and nonfiction. Did your meticulous footnoting and recording of every source you consulted interfere with your artistic freedom?
WTV: I feel like I had more freedom with this book than I do with the *Seven Dreams*. There's a lurking supernatural element in this book, which of course is found in the *Seven Dreams* as well, but only because there are various Native American myths and so forth that I'm drawing on. But I wanted Germany and Russia to represent these superficial oppositions, while at the same time they're really the same place. The Germans and the Russians during that war, because it was such a brutal war, saw each other as the evil, monstrous other. And at the same time they were both under these totalitarian regimes and their thoughts were controlled and everything else. So the differences were more superficial than they seemed. So I set up some oppositions that are superficial oppositions, and sometimes play on the supernatural. In these stories, it's usually winter in Russia and it's usually summer in Germany. In the story about Käthe Kollwitz ["Woman with Dead Child"], when she goes to Russia it's summer in Berlin when she leaves on the train and a few days later for some unexplained reason it's snowy when she gets to Moscow. So I had fun doing stuff like that.

AE: After dedicating *Europe Central* to the great Danilo Kiš, specifically mentioning his *A Tomb for Boris Davidovich*, what gives you—or any artist—the right to ask people to read your book instead of picking up a proven masterpiece?

WTV: In one sense, there's nothing new under the sun and there never has been and there never will be. So it doesn't really matter. Just because Shakespeare wrote *Romeo and Juliet*, we're not barred from writing a story with the boy-meets-girl theme. In the case of *Boris Davidovich*, yeah—it is a masterpiece and the stories are written by somebody who knew what it was like to live in not exactly a strict totalitarian regime but let's call it a soft totalitarianism regime, the way it was under Tito. And he was a Slav. He probably had more access to the languages involved, the culture, the history was more immediate. So he was probably better when it came to writing about the Komintern than I could ever be, in a lot of ways. On the other hand, I have the liability and the virtue of writing at a distance. Therefore I can be kind of evenhanded about German and Russian characters. I can play them off against each other and at the end I can inject the American element. Just as Tocqueville could see certain things about America because he was a European, I like to think I can see certain things about Europe as a result of being an outsider.

AE: Got an example?

WTV: The Käthe Kollwitz story, for instance. It would be very hard for a European to write that story. A German would either write her off or talk about what a great proletariat artist she was. And [her] trip to the Soviet Union would probably make the German a little bit uncomfortable and so he probably wouldn't make it the focus of the story. Whereas to me, it's the ambiguity of that trip that the whole story is all built up to. Here's this person who has devoted her life to creating images that would make us feel for poor people and she's going to the country of the proletariat. This is sort of the dream of her life, this is where what she stands for has come into being. And yet she gets there and she dimly senses that maybe she's being used. She goes back to Germany and never talks about the trip, really. That's something that an American or another outsider can look at and say, "How peculiar, what was going on here?" And I can see it probably as more significant and I have less invested in it. I think that she was a great artist and that some of her work is incredible. I've been to her museum in Berlin a couple times. Some of my Berliner friends tell me that everybody from East Germany just hates her because she was so widely copied. That she's like this kitschy cliché.

AE: You mentioned the "soft totalitarianism" that Kiš lived through. Do you see a parallel with what's going on now in the United States?

WTV: I think that we're—

AE:—I can leave this out of the newspaper if you prefer.

WTV: Oh, I don't care. I'm not afraid. I think I told you that my phone has been tapped since about 2000 and this call's probably being recorded not only by you. So what do I care? I think we live a—how would I describe it?—I suppose the most appropriate phrase would be soft fascism. I don't know if I told you that I was detained coming across the border? Five hours. They called in the FBI. My mail has been opened quite often since then, all my international mail. Often it's opened with razors, so if there are books from my French publisher maybe they'll send me five and I'll get two of them. And the two that come, the covers are damaged with the razors and so on and so forth. They're not being at all careful. It's almost as if they want to give me some kind of a message. Or maybe they're just clumsy, who's to say?

AE: You don't sound intimidated.

WTV: Well, the interesting thing is that basically, with the Patriot Act, they can do whatever they want without telling anybody. There's no real accountability anymore, there's no law, and most people are really okay with that. And most people have always been okay with that. When I was in Taliban Afghanistan, they said to me, "Look, if I have safety now, then maybe it's okay if I can't listen to music on the radio and I can't watch television." And I think that most Germans probably felt that, "Hey if Hitler's going to make Germany great again, and get us lots of jobs, and get the Treaty of Versailles abrogated we can put up with a few restrictions." And people now are thinking, "Oh, it doesn't really matter that there were no weapons of mass destruction in Iraq," that maybe now we'll go into Iran. Bush seems to have lied about that. The whole social security thing is a lie, and Halliburton is ripping people off, and god knows what torture we're committing in Afghanistan and Gitmo. No one that I know is that worried about it.

AE: So to most people you think the means are justifying the ends?

WTV: They think, "Well, hopefully we're being aggressive, and we're doing the right thing, and we're getting Al Qaeda off our backs, and if a few mistakes are made, so what?" It's very disappointing to me that the clear proof of torture has not made more difference. If Al Qaeda were to have another successful atrocity in the US then that stuff would be *completely* irrelevant. In the Gerstein story ["Clean Hands"] I talk about how Gerstein's father was so afraid and could hardly imagine what was going to happen if Stalingrad is lost and then what's going to happen, and so on and so forth. For somebody like that, and probably for so many Germans, the end which became simple national survival would have justified any means. That's really true for most people because self-preservation and national preservation are both very selfish. Most people would probably gladly countenance torture and other atrocities if they thought their way of life could be preserved.

AE: Would the Democrats be any better?

WTV: No. Kerry had his chance and it was close. I definitely would have rather had him win. I think he was somewhat more honest. But I doubt that he would have had the guts to undo all the things the Republicans have done. I think we are in a very bad time and I don't know whether it's worse than it was during the fifties or not. I was born in '59 so I can't really say. I'm sure that in the fifties if you'd gone to a town meeting and said, "I'm a communist and I read pornography, and I think it's great to smoke marijuana," and you kept saying it, you probably have gotten investigated. Maybe you would have gotten arrested, I don't know.

AE: Following the model of your Kurt Gerstein story, what is your responsibility as an artist in this political climate?

WTV: I think that if you are called upon to do something that you can do, that will make a difference, you should do it even at the cost of your own life. I don't think that you should romanticize what you can and can't actually do. There's nothing wrong with throwing your life away in a good cause without accomplishing anything. On the other hand, you're certainly under no obligation to do that. I have been asked a couple times to go to Iraq, and I would go back there but only if I really thought that what I wrote could make a difference to people. If I did think that, I would go immediately and probably I would be killed there, because I think that to really do it right you would have to talk to Iraqis about what's going on. That means getting away from American supervision and control, and we have committed so many war crimes and destabilized the country so much that there's a lot of hatred, and I imagine that it would only be a matter of time before somebody came and shot you or cut off your head. In the meantime, I think we have an obligation to publicly stand up against this wicked administration, and denounce the war crimes that are dragging our country down into shame, and it's a country built on some really wonderful principles. When I was doing the book tour for *Rising Up and Rising Down* I felt that every time I was on the radio and the conversation came around to current politics I had to say, well, I think that the president is a war criminal. A lot of these stations, even NPR, seemed very uncomfortable when I said it. I'm sure I didn't do my career any good, but so what?

AE: So an artist should take a stand for what's right, whatever the risks?
WTV: That's one of the reasons I admire Käthe Kollwitz. And it's so interesting too to see that as a result of doing these very brave, subversive, dedicated things and just following in this path that was good, for so long, she became ripe to be duped. So that's a cautionary tale. You can do something that is right, and keep doing it, and at some point it might not be right. But for now, clearly publicly standing up to this administration is the right thing to do and it's a scary thing to do, but a little less scary than it was a year ago.

AE: What did you leave out of *Europe Central*?
WTV: There was some material at the end of the book which I have removed and will be in a different book. There is an occasional reference in *Europe Central* to an imaginary Eastern European country called Turvakia. There is a memoir that was in the end of *Europe Central* which is written by the crown prince of Turvakia. He becomes a Nazi puppet and then he destroys a Nazi base on the moon with a death ray. It just gets weirder and weirder. He eventually comes to the United States and he manages to come into the White House and he finds out that the president is this huge black vulture or possibly eagle. It's screaming and picking at people—it's very surreal. I'll save that for it's appropriate time. Right now it's about fifty or sixty pages. It'll probably be a little bit longer when it's done.

AE: Would it work as a stand-alone book?
WTV: It'd be awfully short.

Interview with William T. Vollmann

Ben Bush / 2006

Portions of this interview were published in *Poets & Writers* (March 30, 2006), *The Fanzine* (May 18, 2006), and *Bookforum* (July 10, 2014). ©Ben Bush. Reprinted by permission.

William T. Vollmann's most recent book, *Uncentering the Earth*, examines the social impact following Copernicus's discovery that the earth was not the center of the universe. It is a story of the complexities and imperfections of the natural world butting heads with the elegance of ideology. I spoke with him over the telephone from his home in suburban Sacramento.

Q: With completing *Rising Up and Rising Down*, I've heard you say that your research into violence which you had thought of as your life's work was coming to an end and that you wanted to move on to other projects. Is that how you're feeling still and how are those other projects coming?

V: Hold on one second, Ben. My little girl is here and she is playing with all my old boy scout mess kits. I'm just telling her that it's okay for her to use them as a drum. I will vacate the room. [*Laughs.*] Hey Lisa, spread out that stuff and you can bang as much as you want. I'm going to talk to Ben downstairs. Anyway, when I think of the things I'm working on now, I'm interested in other aspects of human experience as well. This book I'm writing about Noh theater is a very, very happy book even though many of the plays are tragedies, but it's focusing on what makes art beautiful and how to best represent feminine beauty. So, that's something I really enjoy. And then my book about the California-Mexico border, of course, it has some sad moments and so forth, but really it's just very relaxing and tranquility-inducing for me to be studying the price of green beans over a hundred year period. It's a lot of fun to think about and to see parables about America and the way that agriculture has altered and changed over the last century. For instance, the ideal in Imperial County used to be the small family farm and then pretty soon the homestead itself wasn't sufficient. People wanted things like washing machines, so they had to raise extra crops and sell them to get the cash to have these conveniences. And now raising the crops and so forth is basically for money and so it's these huge agribusinesses involved and the end result is that the land is so fertile and the technology has gotten so successful that there are constant crises of overproduction. During the Depression they were taking truckloads of stuff from the Imperial Valley and dumping it in the ocean while people were starving.

Q: *The Grapes of Wrath.*
V: Exactly.

Q: I read the piece about the rafting trip down the most polluted river in America. I've heard these legends of you firing blanks at literary readings, is that true or is that unsubstantiated rumor?
V: Oh, that's true.

Q: What prompted you to do that and what sort of reactions did you get?
V: Writing is the score, let's say, and the public reading is the performance of the score. If you're trying to distill let's say a 1,000 page book into a thirty or forty minute reading, you take different sections. You're going to pick sections that possibly that contrast with each other or reflect on each other somehow. Since they're pulled out of context they're going to create a different impression than if you read them all the way through in a book. Sometimes in the course of abridging and isolating things you want to increase the dramatic tension or you want to punctuate what you've done, particularly if the pieces have to do with something suspenseful or violent or whatever. It's entirely appropriate, I think. There's this one piece that I used to read; it's called "The Back of My Head" from *The Atlas*, and it was about an experience that I had in Sarajevo where I was constantly being shot at, as was everyone else, going through sniper fire and this and that, and I went to the morgue and saw all these awful things, people shot. And at one point I was outside, near the front line with a friend of mine and suddenly I felt a very sharp impact on the back of my head, and I was sure that I'd been shot, and I reached up and I touched the back of my head and my hand came away all wet and I thought "Oh, this is really bad." And I saw that actually the stickiness wasn't red and I realized finally that someone from a tall apartment nearby had thrown a peach pit down at the back of my head. So when I read the story, when there are shots, I often pull the trigger, so there's a loud bang with the blank and so on and then for that

last experience when I describe that sudden impact, I pick up the pistol and I cock it and people are kind of bracing for the shot and so forth when I read the part about the peach pit, it turns out nothing happened and I put the gun down and I don't fire it. So that's one example of how I think the gun can be effective and helpful to magnify the perception that I'm trying to convey, but for a lot of the books, like for the Copernicus book there's no reason to shoot off the gun.

Q: Get an astrolabe out in front of the audience instead?
V: And smash it to bits.

Q: One of the things I thought was interesting in your work and what I've heard you say about it, is that you consider the journalistic pieces as they get published in magazines, less true and less beautiful than the uncut versions, but the interesting thing is that the uncut versions end up in books that are categorized as fiction. Do I have that, right? Some of the stuff in *The Atlas*—non-fiction, right?
V: Yeah, *The Atlas* is categorized as fiction legitimately because some of the pieces in it are short stories and some of them are prose poems and then there are some pieces like "The Back of My Head" which are reportage. And as the James Frey scandal reminds us, if there's any fiction in a book, why not call it fiction? But the books that I label non-fiction for instance *Rising Up and Rising Down* contain nothing but the truth to the best of my knowledge and there were times that it would have been easy for me to make something up. No one would have ever known the difference and the story would have been better and so on, but I'm proud to say I never did it.

Q: A lot of those areas you were in there was probably not a lot of fact-checking going on. A while back I was reading through volume five of *Rising Up and Rising Down*, I was trying to figure out what my understanding of the Vollmann approach to journalism might be. Here's what I came up with: interview the most villainized people in the world with an open mind, include as much uncut interview as possible, so they can defend their cause themselves, assume people have good intentions until proven otherwise. Don't believe anything until you see it. Does that sound about right to you?
V: That's right and not just the most villainous people, but everybody because everybody is interesting, everybody has a story and if we go somewhere and we are bored by another person then we have failed. That's one of the fun challenges of this *Imperial* book—writing about the prices of string

beans; it's a place where you go and it's flat and it's hot and seems incredibly boring and it seems as if nothing has ever happened. And nothing ever has and nothing ever will. And in the meantime, because people live there it's just teaming with human drama and so that is true. Each person is all things. And that's what we need to remember. Hitler was very kind to animals. That doesn't make him less evil, but it makes him more human. It makes it possible to start thinking about where he was evil, because obviously he had the capacity to be nice in certain areas of his life. So, to me, that's a fruitful approach and it doesn't just trap us in some kind of moral relativism.

Q: You sometimes insert nonfiction sections into your fiction. In *The Ice-Shirt* you put a section on modern drag queens getting ready for a night out in the middle of a gender-bending Inuit creation myth. What do you see as the purpose of inserting a nonfiction section in the middle of a fictional story?

V: When I wrote *The Ice-Shirt*, I could have written something like *You Bright and Risen Angels* without ever going to any of those places and that would have been okay, but the task that I set myself was to represent reality, but to represent it through symbols and be poetic. The main thing was that I knew reality was much greater than I was. That there's so much out there that my art could only be enlarged and benefited if, instead of staying in my head, I went out of my head. So, I felt that I wanted to go to Greenland and Iceland, which I did. I went to Newfoundland, where the Viking settlement was and tried to hike by myself and went to the Baffin Islands, and I felt like I had some understanding of these incredible landscapes that the Vikings must have seen with similar emotions. So, then when it came to this legend of elder brother and younger brother that you mentioned, why not continue to do that and try to indicate that this is a real archetype, you don't just read it and think "Oh, how quaint and how peculiar that they would think that." Gender-bending stuff is all around us and here was an example of someone turning into a woman before my eyes. That's something I've always been interested in. I'm extremely heterosexual but I love women and I like thinking about female beauty so much that I have a lot of respect and appreciation for transvestites and that's one of the reasons that I have embarked on this Noh project. Now, here's old, kind of dumpy men, who turn themselves into beautiful young girls even though they still are waddling around in their stocking feet and you can see their jowls moving under their masks, they're really, really beautiful. So, I guess that's a long answer to your question.

Q: Long answers are fine. You often seem a little frustrated with the direction of contemporary American literature. Is part of that because you feel like a lot of writers are kind of locked up in their heads like that?

V: Well, the general level of literacy for writers and readers is far below what it used to be. And we now commonly see books in which people can't get their possessives right. Publishers send out catalogues and you read the copy and it's full of grammatical errors. In my parents' generation and in my grandparents' generation people really were much more connected to the written word; I won't say that they were more intelligent or better educated necessarily because I'm sure that they knew far less about what's going on in other parts of the world and diversity and tolerance and the ecosystem and so forth and these are very important things, but there was a sense that most people with a basic education could read and take some pleasure in reading and now people like to write and express themselves but they often resent the work required to express themselves well or even to read books by dead people. It's often been said that we're midgets standing on the shoulders of giants and if you step off the giant's shoulder you're going to be that much shorter. So, I think it's pathetic that readers and writers today are as ignorant as they are, as ignorant even of foreign writing. In the seventies, there used to be this Penguin "Writers from the Other Europe" series and I read a bunch of those books; that's how I got introduced to people like Borowski, Kundera, Konwicki. It blew my mind; I thought they were great and when I talk with my editor at Viking I always say "Paul, why can't you guys you reissue those?" and he says, "It'll never happen, there's just no market for those." And of course, Dalkey Archive had brought a couple of them back and so forth but it's really sad, it's really disturbing and it helps explain how people who are fundamentally good-hearted and well-meaning and sincere as Americans are, could re-elect a president who is a war criminal, who is a torturer, who has dragged and is dragging our name through the mud. And we can still find people who think that he's the greatest and it's because people here are so ignorant and so isolated. And I blame readers and writers for that.

Q: Almost your entire back catalogue is in print except for *An Afghanistan Picture Show*, I thought that was interesting because it seems suddenly very topical again and I was wondering if there's a hesitance to republish that because you were fighting on the side of people who have become associated with the enemy?

V: Yeah, I don't know why. It was recently published in German and in Italian, Europeans tend to get a kick out of it because the main character is a naïve blundering American and that's one of the hobbies of Europeans is to look down on Americans, and not always without good reason.

Q: In your journalism, how do you get people to trust you and to what extent do you think of yourself as chameleonic, adaptable?

V: I like to think that I have more integrity than many journalists because if it's a choice between getting the best story or trying to be a good person, I will choose the latter. I don't betray confidences. If somebody tells me something on the record and then later changes his or her mind, that's a different story, but I at least think about the person's reasons for changing his mind. I think the main thing is to be open and generous with people. To be very up-front about your project and to rely on and defer to local knowledge whenever possible and respect local perceptions which many journalists are not very good at doing. When I was in Serbia, I said "Alright, I need to find out what the Serbian point of view is." And so my Serbian interpreter liked me whereas some of these other Western journalists would come in and in the Foreign Media Center they would be loudly talking about how the Serbs were all war criminals. Well, of course, a lot of Serbs were and are war criminals. But if you say that in front of them and that's all you say, chances are, you're not going find anything out. When I was getting ready to go to the Taliban Afghanistan I was thinking, "Well, probably most people hate the Taliban and they're this awful tyranny, but I'll just keep my mouth shut and listen." And I was amazed to hear people, including women, saying the Taliban are the most perfect government ever and other people were saying, "Well, the Taliban are making mistakes. But that's because they're ignorant. All they know is war and the little education they've had is studying the Koran in the Madrasas so they're doing the best they can," and I think there's some truth in that. If I had just gone over there and said "I think all the Taliban are assholes," first of all, I wouldn't have gotten my visa and no one would have helped me, and second of all, I probably wouldn't have seen the more complicated picture.

Q: For *Uncentering the Earth*, what got you fired up on the project? Was it an early interest in sci-fi?

V: Well, I used to like H.P. Lovecraft when I was in high school, and I remember that one description of him was he was called "a literary Copernicus." I think that was from Fritz Leiber. And the reason was that he took horror and he took it from the human heart—*Wuthering Heights* or whatever—where it was all internal, and he moved it way out into outer space, where human beings were insignificant and just the prey of Cthulhu and all these very powerful aliens, and I always thought that was interesting, and, when I got a little older and was capable of thinking about things a little more seriously, I was like, "What was it like to suddenly relegate the Earth from the center of the Universe to an orbiting planet?" And so I was very curious to learn more about Copernicus and, as I looked into it, of course, it turned out that it wasn't sudden. Like most people in history, Copernicus had predecessors and he did part of the job but not all of the job, but to me that just made him all the more human and believable and a little bit more endearing in a way. But I'm very impressed with this shy, reclusive guy who never saw a planet in his life except as a point of light and nevertheless worked out this mathematical system that wasn't completely right, but which was better than anything before and couldn't really be explained away. So he did this amazing thing and then was kind of worried about what it was that he had done and what the implications might be, probably to himself personally but maybe also to his Catholic faith, and kept quiet until his death bed and then afterward people really suffered because of Copernicus.

Q: I wanted to ask who the astronomer Eric Jensen is who you frequently mention assisting you through the book.
V: Norton found him for me. I told him that I was a non-scientist and I wanted to do my best. I wanted them to find some professional astronomer who could vet the book and save me from my errors. And speaking of which, Norton has introduced two egregious errors beyond the proof stage. Two diagrams, I think they left out a deferent circle in a diagram in which the deferent circle is very important. And they're probably not going to be sending errata to book stores, because they say that book stores don't comply. But if you want to, feel free to call up Norton and ask them about those two errors.

Q: Did you go out stargazing working on the book?
V: Just on my computer. I have the Starry Night Pro software.

Q: I'm sort of shocked that you didn't go out and look at the night sky. It seems up your alley.
V: I thought about doing it but I thought that wouldn't have been what Copernicus could have done. What I did do is—I love astronomy books and for years I had one beautiful book of planets after another, and I like looking at those and thinking about those. Copernicus says the moon is perfectly

round and made out of perfect imperishable superlunary material—and here's a picture of the moon with all of its craters and it's beautiful in a way, but very different from what Copernicus could have imagined. It's very interesting to think about that stuff.

Q: In the book there's a certain sorrow that we'll never have a world view that orderly.

V: It's true, and I guess that's part of maturity that you think things are a certain way, and the way they are makes so much intuitive sense, and so it's going to continue to work probably in poetry and in myth, where things don't have to be rational. But outside of art, at some point it seems like we have to put the notion of meaning at some distance from us. We don't want to get rid of it completely because it is still valid, but we don't want to say that because somebody looks a certain way that he has a certain kind of personality, or a certain kind of temperament or that he's good or bad. That would be the sort of thing that the Nazis might do; it's also the kind of thing that poets might do or that writers might do. They want a name with a certain significance, and when you're constructing as much meaning as possible in a poem or a work of fiction, the kind of thing Nabokov does, to play those games and discover that. It must have been immensely satisfying to live in that earth-centered cosmos where observation seemed to perfectly confirm the Bible and vice-versa, and yeah, of course, it's sad to leave that stuff behind.

Boxcars, Shostakovich, and the Poor: William T. Vollmann Talks with *Bookforum*

Donna Seaman / 2007

From *Bookforum*, Vol. 13, Issue 5, February/March 2007. ©*Artforum*. Reprinted by permission.

William T. Vollmann has traveled to unforgiving and turbulent places in search of insights into the human condition, conducted exhaustive research, and written epic works that commingle genres, deepen our perception of history, intensify our sense of empathy, and complicate our moral equations. Feverishly prodigious and protean, Vollmann is fascinated by symbiosis and the pairings of opposites, and he himself projects a complexly bifurcated sensibility. He is saintly in his devotion to people who are marginalized and maligned and is martyrlike in his zeal to write to the point of physical debility and spiritual exhaustion. Yet there are intimations of lustfulness and showboating in his work, as well as the scholar's obsessiveness and the scientist's practiced detachment. Vollmann can sound simultaneously wise and naïve. His books, especially the all-encompassing, multivolume *Rising Up and Rising Down* (2003) and his epic historical novel of totalitarianism, *Europe Central* (2005), are phenomenally erudite and panoramic and at once exacting and impressionistic in their analysis of ethical conundrums and the wilderness of ambiguity. Clearly, Vollmann is tough, intrepid, audacious, and pragmatic. Yet in conversation, he is kind and restrained. Humble, if bemused and curious. Charming. No wonder he can get so many unlikely people in diverse cultures to talk to him and welcome him into their lives.

A year after receiving the National Book Award for *Europe Central*—an ascension into acceptability that few among the readers of his off-the-radar early works would have imagined—Vollmann presents a concise (for him) work of socially conscious nonfiction titled simply and provocatively *Poor People* (Ecco). A mix of nervy oral history, candid philosophical inquiry, and self-critical personal reflection ("How could I be fatuous enough to hope to 'make a difference'?"), *Poor People* draws on Vollmann's sojourns in Thailand, Yemen, Colombia, Vietnam, Afghanistan, Iraq, Pakistan, Kazakhstan, Bosnia, India, Russia, Mexico, and Japan. In each place, he asks people why they are poor, what the best way is to help them, and what their greatest hopes are. He seeks to understand how oppression, environmental degradation, prejudice, and sexism result not only in deprivation, shortened lives, and illiteracy but also in, to use his terms, invisibility, deformity, unwantedness, dependence, accident-proneness, pain, numbness, and estrangement. As Vollmann attempts to gauge these "dimensions of poverty," he asks himself the always-unsettling and age-old question "What do I owe the poor?"

The author "has no use" for the Internet and consequently doesn't use e-mail. Nor does he carry a cell phone. When we spoke on a land line about scheduling an interview, Vollmann was about to set off on a train adventure. Not only wouldn't he be reachable during his journey, he also wasn't sure exactly when he would return to his hometown, Sacramento. We ended up reconnecting just before Thanksgiving. His parents had traveled to California from their home in Switzerland to visit him, his wife, and their young daughter. As it happened, my parents were also visiting from out of town. And so our conversation was subtly influenced by all the emotions family gatherings arouse and a sense of gratitude for the good fortune that allowed us to talk about books.

Donna Seaman: You just returned from riding freight trains, jumping into boxcars, and all that?

William T. Vollmann: You bet. I'm writing a book about riding the trains, and I've been doing it off and on for about a decade. I really enjoy it. It makes me feel like a self-reliant nineteenth century Emersonian. Everything that my grandfather used to do for fun is now illegal. People are now discouraged from doing everything my father used to do. We're ruled by safety nazis and safety monkeys. How nice it is to briefly escape them and to have the illusion of a little personal freedom.

DS: Are you finding kindred spirits out there?

WTV: There are fewer and fewer. In *On the Road*, Kerouac talks about entire flatcars filled with hobos reading the funny papers. It's not like that anymore. When I go to homeless shelters, I meet old guys who have done it and who tell me great stories about it. But most of the people I meet on the rails are schizophrenic or alcoholic, and even they're few and far between.

DS: You spend time speaking with homeless people?

WTV: Sure. Why not? People who have suffered tend to have interesting stories. That was how Dostoyevsky made his living, writing about suffering.

DS: You examined violence in great detail in *Rising Up and Rising Down*. In *Poor People*, you focus on poverty.

WTV: Yes, but more modestly. In *Rising Up and Rising Down*, I wanted to develop a moral calculus. Although it's flawed, I do think I achieved something. With *Poor People*, I thought, I don't really have the right or the capability to figure out how to eradicate poverty. I think most other people don't, either. But if I can describe what the experience has been for some people, maybe we can learn something from that. If not, at least we can open ourselves up to people who suffer. We can think about them, and that's probably good for them and good for us.

DS: You make the crucial point that poverty isn't strictly about material deprivation; it also involves the impoverishment of people's inner lives.

WTV: That's one of the really sad things. In speaking with people for *Rising Up and Rising Down*, I would often hear eloquence. When you talk to poor people, you often meet people whose minds and spirits have been starved like their bodies, and so they're not capable of eloquence.

DS: In 1990, you published a set of rules for writers, and the first is "We should never write without feeling." How do you balance the discipline required to report straightforwardly on the lives of those who are suffering with the urge to express your concerns or your political beliefs?

WTV: Nabokov always used to say that any book that tried to teach him something, particularly some sort of political thing, he immediately banished from his bedside. And whether or not he wrote with feeling, I admire his work very much. Of course, he did end up writing in one way or another about dictatorship and exile. To read Nabokov is to think about some of the problems of totalitarianism and the Soviet Union and class privilege. So it's always there.

DS: In *Europe Central*, you fictionalize the lives of real-life artists, most extensively the composer Dmitry Shostakovich. Why is Shostakovich at the hub of this novel?

WTV: I admire the guy, and I feel sorry for him. I think he succeeded in most of what was actually possible for him. It's easy to say that he was morally compromised. He joined the party; he denounced Sakharov and Solzhenitsyn. That's really, really sad. But at the same time, he survived, and he helped others to survive. And he was able to write this extremely beautiful, complicated, transgressive music that could have gotten him executed. And I'm so glad that he did. It's incredibly beautiful music that repays years and years of listening.

The other fascinating thing about Shostakovich is that, I think, he started off as a true believer. He believed communism was a solution to, at least, the conditions in prerevolutionary Russia, and possibly to the problems of the whole world. After he suffered and got some sense of how horrible Stalin was, I'm sure he lost a lot of his idealism. But it's still very possible, we just don't know, that he still thought that some form of socialism was really the best solution. He never had very many kind things to say about the US or about the other Western countries he visited. While he didn't take a spiteful or jealous tone, there is a sense that he felt that our way of life was a failure. When I think of how he has been criticized for not speaking out more—which probably would have caused him and his family great harm—I tend to think that within his own context, he was very successful and admirable. By keeping his head down a little bit, he was able to get some things done. I can identify with him in some ways—it's impossible not to compromise yourself as you make your way through life. I let magazines alter my articles in ways that I believe hurt the words that I've written. I continue to live in a country that I have always loved but that now has an administration I absolutely despise. What am I going to do? If I can't hold myself up to a higher standard, how can I judge him harshly?

DS: You also portray the German artist Käthe Kollwitz, whose work is compassionate but was appropriated by the Soviets.
WTV: Yes, I thought a lot about her. Here's someone who was such a great artist and believed in helping others and was so committed, and therefore it was very easy for the Soviets to manipulate her. There's a lesson here: Most of us, if we're lucky, are good at one thing. Maybe we're good at two or three things. So should we be held responsible for the fact that we're not good at everything? Maybe we should be. It's very hard to say whether Kollwitz failed or whether she was taken advantage of. In either case, it doesn't affect the greatness of her work. The art continues to move people. To make us think.

DS: You specialize in ambiguity and empathy. You embrace complexity. You're a walk-a-mile-in-his-shoes writer on an epic scale.

WTV: There's a Turkish proverb: "Whoever says the truth will be chased out of nine villages." I think that's accurate. To truly consider the other point of view is an extremely dangerous, frightening thing to do. We all think, in the abstract, "Oh, yeah, there's always another point of view." But what does that mean? Are we really willing to consider al-Qaeda's point of view? Or a child molester's point of view? That doesn't mean we have to say those people are right, but it means we have to ask why they do what they do. But when we try to get that close, we find that we have alienated people close to us. When I wrote *The Royal Family*, I put in a character who was a child molester. Some of my friends said, "You know, Bill, this time you've really gone too far. This guy is just too despicable and too disgusting. He makes me very, very uncomfortable." Well, in that case, I've probably succeeded.

DS: You've spent a lot of time in the Muslim world. What are your thoughts about the state of our relationship with Muslim cultures?

WTV: Well, I love those people. I would never be a Muslim myself, but I think a religion that enjoins upon you hospitality to the guest and kindness to the poor makes the world a better place. And I've probably received more kindnesses in Muslim nations than anywhere else in the world. Of course, the extremist Muslims and extremists in our own country have definitely ruined the relationship, and I don't see any hope that it's going to get better anytime soon. It's just going to have to burn itself out. That might take a generation, or longer. And that's very, very sad. I was horrified by the events of September 11 and just sickened by our unjust, criminal invasion of Iraq and by what we're doing in Afghanistan, too. No one is paying as much attention to Afghanistan, but our *modus operandi* there is the same—to gradually increase the pressure and the brutality to get what we want, and that will radicalize the population against us. We'll end up with even more people hating us. That's what we're doing, and that's what we'll continue to do, and that just disgusts me.

DS: What is the connection between your journalism, your real-world quests, and your fiction?

WTV: I think it's extremely good for me to get out into the world as much as I can and vary my experience. That also means going into my head for a while. But not doing just one thing or the other thing. So I have a couple of other nonfiction book projects I'm making progress on. One is a book about the California-Mexico border. In part, it's also about the myth of the family farm, how that has affected what it used to mean and what it now means to be an American. Then I'm looking forward to getting back into fiction for a while.

DS: Will you continue the *Seven Dreams* cycle?

WTV: Yes, I will write a few more of those. Last fall, my father and I did a little bit of driving and walking around as part of my research. I'm interested in Chief Joseph of the Nez Percé, and so we went to the valley in Oregon that was once his home and followed his escape route as far as the first battlefield in Idaho, which is called White Bird Canyon. The Nez Percé went maybe twelve hundred or thirteen hundred miles, depending on how you count their steps. I'd like to cover all of that territory, so that's going to take some time. One of the neat things about the *Seven Dreams* is that surprisingly often, when I go to these landscapes, I can see that they have not been tampered with much. I can still get a sense of what it would have been like in the past—and that's just a wonderful feeling.

DS: You take a lot of photographs. How important is photography to you and your work?

WTV: Photographs can be very important. One of the things I love about archives is that you can see in great detail ways of life that no longer exist and, of course, people who are dead. There is a certain kind of immortality there. One of the reasons I dislike and distrust the Internet is that you might go on and search someone's website, and a year later, the statement will have been modified, the picture will have been replaced with something else. It's like a memory hole in Orwell's *1984*, the little grill in the desk where the documents were dropped down to be burned and replaced with something else. So I don't like digital photography because there is no guarantee of permanence as of yet. A compact disc or DVD has a very limited life. When I was photographing the street prostitutes in Sacramento, I used my 8 × 10 camera and made some platinum prints that should last for hundreds of years. It makes me happy to think that these poor prostitutes, whom no one ever gave a damn about, whom people spat on and did terrible things to, will have a certain amount of immortality. Long after they're gone, if these prints are taken care of, say, four hundred years from now, people can look at their faces, and they deserve that.

DS: In *Poor People*, you write about being surrounded by people who can't read your work. You're a writer and also a publisher [Vollmann's CoTangent

Press publishes limited-edition artists' books]. What place do you think the book holds in our society?

WTV: I think that readers and writers are now simply an interest group. A relatively powerful interest group, but their influence is waning year by year. The good side of that, I think, is that it becomes increasingly likely that people will read and write only for the love of it. And that's a very, very good thing. It's likely that throughout history, most people have never been particularly well educated, and the world has gotten by somehow. Independent thinking is a category that almost by definition applies to a small number of people, because the great majority of people tends to think alike. So I can't say I even find it that alarming that more and more of the people I know don't read. It's a little sad for me personally, but that's only because that's what I like to do. As I travel all over the world, and I meet people, let's say in Yemen, for whom the only book that is at all important is the Koran, I think, well, they have very rich and interesting lives. Who am I to tell them that they should be any different? The average person is as smart as he or she needs to be. And that if we get in some terrible mess, then people are going to wake up and try to figure out what needs to be done.

I really love the novel *World Light* by Halldór Laxness. He is a great writer, and in that book he writes about a guy who is a true poet. He's got this incredibly gifted sensibility; he really appreciates all the beauty around him. The only flaw happens to be that he writes terrible poems. So nobody can appreciate any of the stuff that goes on in his head. Maybe we're all that way.

DS: In the new book, you often ask the men, women, and children you speak with, "What is your greatest hope?" What is *your* greatest hope?

WTV: I would like to continue to have the great life that I have, to be able to investigate the world and try to see and create beauty. And at the same time, I would like to do something of significant service for my fellow human beings. I don't feel that I've done nearly enough, and I don't know what that service would be. I have considered going back to Iraq. I very much admire the late Margaret Hassan [the British head of CARE's Iraq operation who was kidnapped and murdered in late 2004]. Maybe if enough people went over there and let themselves be decapitated or tortured or whatever, that would undo some of the evil things that are being done there. Maybe there is an easier and better way to act. I don't know. I want to live as much as anybody. I don't really want to go over there and put myself in harm's way. But I would consider it.

William T. Vollmann:
The *Powells.com* Interview

Jimmy Cline / 2010

First published on *Powells.com*, April 19, 2010. © *Powells.com*. Reprinted by permission.

For his recent book, *Kissing the Mask*, Vollmann's focus was the ancient Japanese artistic tradition of Noh theater, with some added thoughts on subjects ranging from Kabuki theater, geishas, Yukio Mishima, Andrew Wyeth's Helga Testorf drawings, transgender prostitutes, and the classics of Japanese literature. This is one of the first books on Noh theater in decades, as well as an insightful meditation on the various aesthetic manifestations of beauty throughout the world and what it is about them that personifies femininity. Jimmy Cline talked to William Vollmann before his reading at Powell's City of Books, on April 6, 2010.

Jimmy Cline: In past interviews, you mentioned traveling to Japan and learning about Noh Theater. How long ago did you start working on this project?
William T. Vollmann: I first got really interested in Noh in about 1977. There was an independent bookstore in Bloomington, Indiana where I was going to high school. It was a really nice place. There was a New Directions paperback. It was the Pound/Fenollosa book, *The Classic Noh Theatre of Japan*. [*Powell's* Editor's Note: *Ernest Fenollosa was an Italian scholar who studied Japanese art during the late 19th Century. From his notes, Ezra Pound finished translations of fifteen classic Noh plays.*]

Cline: I've read that.
Vollmann: It is still in print, which is so wonderful. I thought, "These are so strange and eerie." I kept thinking about them. The first chance I had to go to Japan, which was in the early nineties, I went to a Noh play. I thought, "This is very, very slow." I noticed lots of people falling asleep. I didn't really

know what was going on; I was getting a little sleepy myself. Then the more I studied it, the more fascinated I got. I guess I started writing the book in earnest in about 2002.

Cline: In the beginning of the book, you interview Umewaka Rokuro. He's part of a dynasty of actors, from the great Minoru, who was acting in the late nineteenth century, and saved Noh, in a way.
Vollmann: That's right. One story that I have heard is that, strange to say, Ulysses S. Grant helped out. I don't know if you read that, too.

Cline: Yes, in 1879 he saw his first Noh performance.
Vollmann: Yes. I've read his memoirs. He was a great strategist. He didn't seem like a super-educated man. He was sort of semi-literate. It was amazing that he said, "This is really terrific. You Japanese should preserve this." They thought, "Well, we are under the Americans' thumb. If they are telling us that, then maybe we had better pay attention."

Cline: Like Fenollosa in a way, but it seems like Grant maybe had more pull.
Vollmann: Yes. Fenollosa is loved and revered in Japan. But he couldn't have really been an authority figure.

Cline: The book is ostensibly about Noh theater. Even toward the end you bring it up again amongst various different allusions and references. But it is also clearly about understanding feminine beauty and grace—understanding the beauty behind superficial layers of illusion, like the mask.
Vollmann: That's right.

Cline: How do you feel like the book balances out as a technical book on Noh Theater, and also a kind of abstract meditation on understanding what it is to be a woman? Do you feel like they have equal weight within the book?
Vollmann: Probably Noh itself has a little bit less weight. It certainly has much less weight than I imagined when I started to write the book. I quickly found that what interested me the most about Noh was the representation of femininity. Because Noh is also tied up with the dangerous addiction of attachment to anything while you are alive, I needed to bring in the warrior plays and some of these other plays as well.

But once I started watching these actors turn into women, then I thought, "Wow. How are they different from a tea girl in a kabuki show, making herself up? She still has the penis, but she is out there as a prostitute. People are paying her because she is pretty and sexual. How is she different from a geisha?" I started hiring geishas, and it is $1,000 to $2,000 an hour to have a geisha pour you a little sake and very, very slowly dance for you. What about transgender people here, and what about g-girls (genetic girls)? Is there any sort of commonality to all of this? I knew that the biggest mistake I can make would be to answer the question, especially as a man. But precisely because I'm a man who is attracted to women, there may be some things that I have to say as a spectator of feminine grace that women themselves may not be able to see. I quote this one friend of mine named Shannon in the book. I asked her, "What is it like for you? You have all this power over men." She said, "I'll tell you how it is. You are constantly checking. You're repairing your lipstick. You're worried that your high heel might be breaking. So while you're young, you can't enjoy it. Then you start to get old, and then you're just really sad, because it's gone." That is her perspective.

I think that to ask the question and realize what an incredibly deep question it is can maybe encourage everybody to appreciate beauty in his or her own way. That's sort of my intention.

Cline: In terms of Noh plays in English translation, there's book by Arthur Waley. Donald Keene is a really famous Japanese scholar that did twenty different Noh plays and put them together. There's the Fenollosa and Pound book.
Vollmann: And the Royall Tyler too.

Cline: I have not read that one.
Vollmann: I think actually his is the best. I was very impressed reading those. He also did a neat translation of *The Tale of Genji*.

Cline: Your first introduction to Noh plays was through reading them. This book is going to introduce a pretty large audience of Western readers to them in another light. The way Keene describes a lot of the plays, he says that they have some literary value to the Western reader, but they do really absolutely no justice to understanding how a Noh play functions.
Vollmann: Exactly. Yes, it's like reading the libretto to an opera and never seeing it performed. That's exactly how it is. But what makes it even stranger is that Mr. Umewaka told me, as you might have read, that for him the mask is always most the important. Then Fenollosa and Waley were saying that actually it's the music that is most important. Or the dancing. So nobody even agrees on what it is, what's the most important aspect.

But Mr. Umewaka was laughing at me. He said, "Actually, you know more of the words of these Noh plays than most Japanese who come to see me. The words are really not very important." But he was still kind of pleased that I was trying to be a good white boy. He enjoyed talking about the plots, and explaining them to me. I really enjoyed that because they are so way out there.

Cline: There is a part on Mishima Yukio, which seems like a pretty important part of the book. Given the nature and the content of most Noh plays, it is about a Japanese concept for death, which you use quite a lot. *Mono no aware.*
Vollmann: Right.

Cline: Accepting the transient nature of existence. I've read Mishima's plays, which I thought were great.
Vollmann: They are so different from the others. They are fascinating.

Cline: They're almost cynical in a way. I read this part out of Donald Richie's journals. He was friends with Mishima, and he talks about the suicide in such a distant manner. It seemed like he was pretty familiar with his friend's motives for doing it, and it seemed like Mishima just couldn't accept or deal with the process of aging. He basically wanted to end his life because he couldn't bear the thought of himself as an old man.
Vollmann: Exactly, which is why he became a body builder, to try to make his body beautiful. But I think there's even more to it than that. Mishima showed an almost unexcelled knowledge of the Heian aesthetic, which really informs so much of Japanese culture today.

Cline: The Heian period was when Lady Murasaki was writing?
Vollmann: Yes, it was; she was in the middle of it. Because it was so oriented toward culture and maple viewing and all kinds of things like that, probably to the detriment of its administration—but still, it must have been a really, really amazing highbrow court. Then all the centuries of war afterward made people look back upon the Heian period as this kind of golden age, and everything they remembered about it became better even than it could have been. So, in these Noh plays, like the Noh mask has high eyebrows and black teeth. That is a copy of the way makeup was for Heian women and some of the Heian courtiers as well. Mishima knew all this, and he could allude to it, but he couldn't feel the beauty of it.

Have you read *Sun and Steel*?

Cline: No.

Vollmann: That's his literary testament. He talks about how words are like ants, eating holes in the wood. He could only experience these words, no matter what they were, as corrosive. That's why his figure of Kabachi, for instance, is really quite disgusting.

Cline: It's much, much different from the classic version. It's a Zeami play, isn't it?

Vollmann: It might have been. But yes, it seems like Mishima had very little appreciation for women. I don't know what it was like for his wife.

Cline: Does he stand in the book almost as an allegory on beauty, that his attachment is futile? It contrasts to basically stepping back and trying to appreciate it and not completely understand it. That seems like an aim of your book—and a lot of your previous books, too.

Vollmann: Yes, that's right. As you were saying, this whole idea of *aware*, this melancholy awareness of transience, makes beauty more special. When you see a beautiful woman and you know she's not going to be beautiful forever. Or you see a great play or a great dance, and you think, "In a few minutes, this is going to be over forever." Or you're making love with someone and you know that, pretty soon, you're both going to climax and get out of bed. We might have another great time tomorrow, but this time is never, ever going to come back.

For Mishima, it was almost as if the knowledge of the transience was so horrible to him that he wanted to throw everything away and say, "Let's face it. This is all just deceitful. It's all about death. So let's get right to the point and die. All these beautiful women, they're very, very dangerous, and poisonous, and evil, and they're going to make me forget what's really going on."

Cline: You use a few non-Japanese allusions or examples in the book. The Norse sagas and Andrew Wyeth's Helga Testorf drawings.

Vollmann: I love those.

Cline: I got a chance to look at them. They are really beautiful. Also, there are transgender women that you interviewed. What made you decide to fit in non-Japanese examples? Because the book uses primarily Japanese examples, especially Noh theater, which is intrinsically Japanese.

Vollmann: That's right. And I imagine that some of the people who read it will be Japanophiles and they will be annoyed, and maybe disgusted by these intrusions. But the way I look at it, Zeami was such a great artist, and

Noh was such a profound art form, that maybe what it says about beauty is universal, in which case let's try talking about some things that are very un-Japanese in these same terms and see if it makes sense.

Cline: They translate the point, and show it in a different light. I don't think they're out of place. I think it's more illuminative. You've done that in your work a lot. It always has an international appeal to it.

Vollmann: I think it's nice to see coherence out there, because so often people narrow themselves. With Norse beauty, for instance, it seemed like the common element, the metonym of a beautiful woman, was her white arms. If there's any one metonym in Japanese culture, it is probably the black hair. So you start thinking maybe that is one thing that beauty has to do when it's performing or manifesting itself. It's going to have a certain shorthand. You think, "Oh yeah, white arms means she's got to be beautiful." So some girl wants to look beautiful and she's going to try to make her arms white. It's kind of simple.

I'm curious whether that's how it is everywhere in the world, and it might be. It probably is. Because people are in a hurry. They like to symbolize things in a convenient way.

Cline: Were you overwhelmed? You probably had to cut some examples and representations of beauty that you wanted to use in the book, especially Japanese ones. For example, you could have used the women in the films of [Yasujirō] Ozu. [Kenji] Mizoguchi's women, too.

Vollmann: Sure, I did. I thought when I was writing *Rising Up and Rising Down*, I wanted to be as comprehensive as I could, because it's a book with a utilitarian purpose. It strives to help people to think about various cases of violence and whether or not they're justified. But I think if you had an immense book about beauty, you would be beating people over the head and they would stop appreciating the beauty in it. You know?

Cline: Yes. It seems like maybe that's why it was even shorter. You could exhaust the point after a while with such a delicate subject like that.

Vollmann: Yes, for me it's a very short book. The whole Japanese admiration for understatement is something that makes sense here, I think. Especially because, after all, you can't ever get beyond the mask.

Cline: Even when you describe how the actors feel when they are on stage, what constantly comes up is they respond, "Well, I strive to feel nothing when I am on stage."

Vollmann: Which is so different from what an American actor would say. I was fascinated. Maybe that's how it is to be a woman, or to be a man, or to be anything completely. You do it so much and so well that you don't think about it. It just expresses itself through you.

Cline: Is there a translation date set for a Japanese edition? How do you feel about how the reception might be in Japan?

Vollmann: I'm going back to Japan at the end of the month. I'll dress up in a monkey suit and wrap up copies of *Kissing the Mask* in red paper, maybe, and bow and give them to all the people who helped me. There's some talk about translating it. I think the only book of mine that's been translated so far is *The Rifles*. The woman who translated that actually helped fact-checking for this. She's translated a chunk of it for a magazine over there. So yes, I think there's a good chance it'll happen.

Cline: As far as Japanese culture goes, do you feel like you'll continue with that interest?

Vollmann: Yes. I feel like after years of writing non-fiction, I'm finally ready to write some fiction set in Japan. Maybe some historical fiction.

Cline: There's a wealth of information to use for historical background.

Vollmann: Such crazy stories, yes. I might enjoy writing some ghost stories set in Japan because their whole idea about the spirit world is so interesting.

Cline: Was *Kissing the Mask* ever intended as a piece of fiction?

Vollmann: No. It was sort of like when I wrote *Imperial*. I thought first, "Well, maybe I could write some long, Steinbeck-like novel about illegal aliens crossing the border." Then I realized, No, I don't have the knowledge to do that. And I never even pretended to myself for a second that I had the knowledge to do that. With *Kissing the Mask*, I don't know that I could write anything fictional about a Noh actor. But I could probably write something interesting, something fictional, about a spectator at a Noh performance. Maybe I could write some fiction about a geisha. I felt very, very comfortable with the geishas and I learned a lot from them.

Cline: What were the Noh actors' reactions when you were asking questions about such an abstract artistic tradition that some Japanese probably don't even feel too confident about completely understanding?

Vollmann: Mr. Umewaka was extremely kind and helpful always. Mr. Mikata—who is a little less well known but I think he's a really, really wonderful actor, he's a bit younger—maybe the first time he was a little bit suspicious, but he warmed to me, and was so kind and open. There are some photographs of him in there. And Mr. Kanze, who was probably Mr. Umewaka's rival for the number one spot, I don't think he had a lot of use for me. It was kind of annoying to him, probably, to have some guy badger him. But he did give me one interview before he died. I got to see some of his performances, which were amazing.

Cline: Did Mr. Umewaka give you a pretty good bit of information about his family? How does he feel about that? You also describe the development of a Noh actor. It is very difficult as they are growing up trying to grow into their flower, as Zeami puts it.

Vollmann: That's right. I tried not to talk to him too much about his non-public life. He was kind enough to have me over to his home and meet his wife and so forth. But I never wanted to presume that I was his friend, or that I was entitled to ask him anything that was too intimate. What he was telling me was, in a way, so intimate as it was: how he feels when he is getting ready to become this or that character. That was fantastic, as far as I was concerned. My hunch is that, if you asked him or any Noh actor, and even some of the geishas, about their training, they wouldn't say that much. It's just a lot of drill, drill, drill, what they call *muga*, the selfless repetition of a hammer stroke or a dance step or something like that. It can't be very much fun.

Cline: As was the case with *Imperial* and *Poor People*, you approach difficult, abstract, pretty general questions, but they seem to come out of struggling with a lot of these different questions. It seems like the process of writing it out and trying to understand it a little better and comment on it—it seems like it's a cathartic process for you. Do you feel more distance in a good way from understanding beauty after finishing the book?

Vollmann: I want to learn more, which is how I feel about *Imperial*, too. Speaking of transience, I'm fifty years old. I've already started to experience some of the losses that happen with aging. At the same time, I've been incredibly fortunate, mainly thanks to my journalistic work, to have gotten to see so many different parts of the world. I've had the leisure to read a lot and think a lot, and so forth.

So there are all these questions that I have about the world. If I don't investigate them now, I never will. I feel more urgency, I guess, in trying to understand reality than I ever have. I want to go back to Imperial and write some stories there. I can hardly wait to go back to Japan. I have all kinds of other projects that I really want to accomplish while I still can.

She Who Is So Lovely Is Drinking in That Loveliness I've Drunk

Carson Chan and Matthew Evans / 2010

From *032c*, Issue #19, Summer 2010. Reprinted by permission.

It is said that the American author William T. Vollmann has a peculiar way with people, that his heedless sincerity in attempting to comprehend others is as startlingly foolish as his literary renderings of them are complex and involved. None of this we would know, however, because we've never met him. Vollmann didn't want to be photographed and refused a live interview. So we decided to become pen pals.

Carson Chan and Matthew Evans: In *Imperial*, you write: "It may be that, since this southeast corner of California is so peculiar, enigmatic, sad, beautiful and perfect as it stands, delineation of any sort should be foregone in favor of the recording of 'pure' perceptions, for instance by means of a camera alone; or failing that, by reliance on word-pictures." How do you view the finished work in relation to the field research you've conducted for it? Is *Imperial* the book capable of communicating the Imperial that is "perfect as it stands"?

William T. Vollmann: *Imperial*, like Walker Evans's and James Agee's 1941 book *Let Us Now Praise Famous Men*, is simply an honest effort, and as time goes by, and *Imperial* alters, as has the sharecropping South observed by Evans and Agee, my failures may indeed be slightly mitigated by the fact that both they and *Imperial* itself are farther away, more of a piece, both woven into the fabric of their time. I swear that if I had had more money and more years, I would have done better and more. How sad I feel not to have learned more about the various Indian tribes! How much I would have longed to send an army of spies into the *maquiladoras* for ten years!

Chan/Evans: You've mentioned that *Imperial* is America, and that *Imperial* is the world. One can't help but wonder whether you chose this particular place as a symbol for "the center of the world" because of its name.

Vollmann: You have a point. What an eerie name, for Germans and Americans alike! Bismarck's honest *Realpolitik* is more comprehensible to me than the strivings of American idealists who proudly rejected the hierarchicalism of the British Empire, thought themselves democratic and free, wrote a beautiful Constitution, which I will always love, widened the dreams of Wordsworth, Blake, and the French Revolutionists—and meanwhile cheated and hunted down Indians, tried to keep yellow and brown people in peonage, praised small, self-sufficient homesteads while proudly giving birth to giganticism . . . And none of this was hypocrisy. It was what Orwell would call "doublethink." It was Imperial. On the Mexican side of the border, Imperial has a more pompous grandiosity. My friend Larry [McCaffery] always says that, for him, Mexican Imperial is two great pillars and a huge sign and a driveway leading to an abandoned building site. On the American side, Imperial is a self-defeating idea of infinite individual enrichment. When the riches get big enough, the corporations come in. When the farms are rich enough, the price of farm produce goes down. And everyone takes water for granted, until there's not enough of it.

Chan/Evans: What can we gain from trying to understand the world through *Imperial*?

Vollmann: We can gain an appreciation of the beautifully and horribly arbitrary nature of delineation.

Chan/Evans: Does this project of mapping the world have failure built in as an outcome?

Vollmann: Of course any mind is finite and reality is infinite. Therefore, all of my projects must be failures. The more I hope to accomplish, the worse I must fail. But this is no excuse not to be ambitious.

Chan/Evans: Does admitting failure negate its effects?

Vollmann: Unfortunately not. However, admitting specific failures may help somebody else to improve upon my most egregious weaknesses, so that, over time, failure may be lessened—until further time passes, and my projects come safe into the harbor of irrelevance.

Chan/Evans: But it's easier for your readers to see your books as masterpieces—works that demonstrate this unbelievable ambition and calculation—than not. What do you strive to achieve through writing books, and such lengthy ones at that, if not works of greatness?

Vollmann: I long for my sentences to be beautiful and for the things which have moved me to be preserved for as long as possible, for their own sake, not for mine. The loveliness of a sunny Arctic day, with mosquitoes singing in the moss and ice shining like rainbows, what can I do to memorialize this as the Arctic melts? The people I've loved, can I write them epitaphs before they and I melt, so that someday someone might wish to have met one of us? And now as I get old, and begin at last to see political patterns in their naked horror, I think: Can I record any of the lessons I'm learning, in hopes of sparing some future soul from making or suffering from certain mistakes?

Chan/Evans: Is the naïveté and lofty grandeur so present in The Young Man from *An Afghanistan Picture Show* becoming more difficult to engage after so many years of field research?

Vollmann: I expect less but hope just as much, and long even more than when I was young to do good.

Chan/Evans: What were some of the most striking differences for you in visiting Afghanistan in the early 1980s and then again in 2000?

Vollmann: In 1982, Afghanistan was an occupied country. I felt its fear and desperation as I came over the mountains with the mujahideen. We were vulnerable to enemy planes; there were bomb-husks everywhere. I admired the mujahideen who were willing to sacrifice their lives for their country and their faith. In 2000, the Taliban controlled most of Afghanistan. The parts I visited were safer and better off. There is no question that, for all their ignorance and repression, the Taliban were vastly superior to the Soviets, and probably better than the feuding warlords and bandits in the immediate post-Soviet years.

Chan/Evans: Would you ever write about a place without having been there first?

Vollmann: I would prefer to visit in most cases. But I could imagine writing about some fantastic or alternate universe in which anything goes. Such was the nineteenth-century America at the beginning of *You Bright and Risen Angels* [1987]. Such might be my vision of a Jovian landscape.

Chan/Evans: You purposely leave out autobiographical details in your books, yet there is an undeniable relationship between your books and your life. One particularly poignant example of this is the elaboration in *The Atlas* [1996] of your two companions' death in Bosnia. Why did you choose to photograph them right away?

Vollmann: Because I knew that my gaze was not rational at that moment, but the camera's was and always would be. I knew that later on I would want to look at those pictures and try to understand exactly how and why they died. I expected that the matter would be obfuscated by the forces which killed them, and I thought that the photos might be evidence of the truth, whatever that might turn out to be.

Chan/Evans: Why be objective?

Vollmann: Philip K. Dick wrote that reality is the thing which, when you stop believing in it, refuses to go away. When we refuse to acknowledge reality, we put ourselves at risk and we cheapen ourselves.

Chan/Evans: How do you justify your tactic of paying your interviewees?

Vollmann: Many critics find it journalistic blasphemy. I am proud to practice the principle of fair exchange as I understand it. I disapprove of journalists who simply take a story from people and leave them with nothing.

Chan/Evans: Do you think money can bias a story?

Vollmann: Absolutely. So can anything else, including knowledge itself. It is the journalist's job in all cases to expose the bias in his interviewees and in himself.

Chan/Evans: In a recent article in *Bookforum*, you critically quote Ariella Azoulay from her 2008 book *The Civil Contract of Photography*: "Studying a photograph that allows a reading of the injury inflicted on others becomes a civic skill, not an exercise in aesthetic appreciation." You discuss the negotiation between the artistic/subjective use of photographs and their objective/archival importance. Do you consider the photos you take to illustrate your books works of art or photojournalism?

Vollmann: They are works of photojournalism. They are meant to say: "Look! Please do look! This is really how it was, or how I sincerely thought it was. The camera thought so, too. Now, what do you think it means? What can or should we feel or do about this? You have seen this picture, so now your opinion means something on this topic."

Chan/Evans: But do you think that fiction can more truthfully, if not more accurately, portray history?

Vollmann: Nonfiction can sometimes go deeper (as in the case of *Imperial*), by eschewing the sometimes dangerous luxury of "readability." Statistics are important; physics and chemistry and economics help us approach reality. On the other hand, fiction can say: "I imagine that the situation, and the person in that situation, was thus. I am going to imagine him as well as I can, and try to make him live. Then you may be able to feel the life of this bygone time as I did. Of course, my imagination may be a spurious one. So take me with a grain of salt—just as you would a page of water statistics."

Chan/Evans: The secret Chinese tunnels under Mexicali are the subject of a central chapter of *Imperial*. Can you talk about the relationship between physical and literary structures? Are these mysterious, subterranean structures below the city a spatial or urban cognate of the relationship between fiction and reality? That we build upon a ground that remains mysterious seems to be an idea operating in your work.

Vollmann: They certainly can be. I love the Jungian notion of the unconscious "shadow" which represents the other, the forbidden, the opposite, the evil, the erotic, the new. I made some use of it in *Europe Central* [2005]. Equally fascinating to me is the Marxist notion of a material substructure which allows the cultural superstructure to operate. Do you remember H.G. Wells's *The Time Machine* [1895]? The subterranean Morlocks keep things running so that the hedonistic Eloi can enjoy the sun and make love. In exchange, the Morlocks get to eat the Eloi. Whatever lies beneath the surface may indeed devour what is above, especially if it goes unrecognized. Secrecy is power. This paradigm is what makes the best work of Poe, de Sade, and Lovecraft so haunting. Secrecy is also power in Orwell's *1984* [1949], when Winston and Julia have their (so they believe) undiscovered love nest, where they can be soft and naked.

Chan/Evans: You've mentioned before how your biggest literary weakness has had to do with plotting. How are you improving this?

Vollmann: By living longer, which means ageing and changing, and seeing other people and places do the same. A baby has the same personality he will have as a grown man, and as a senile inmate in a nursing home, and yet certain aspects of that personality flower and then wilt; some fundamental idiosyncrasies are sharpened with age, or modified by others; and of course all things pass. We are all dying and in the process of losing everything. But there will be a different everything tomorrow. All this is obvious, but I am finally beginning to feel it and perceive it as well as merely think it. Isn't that what plot is about? A lovely example is *The Tale of Genji* [an 11th-century

Japanese literary work, often considered the world's first novel], whose story continues at the same level of excellence after its protagonist's death.

Chan/Evans: Many of your readers have bemoaned the fact that, despite their length, your books end suddenly. What sort of structure do you use, if any?

Vollmann: This is hard to answer. The *Seven Dreams* books need outlines, at least mental ones, since they are based on specific historical incidents. As for the others, I guess I would say that they end when their words strike in me some chord of fulfillment.

Chan/Evans: You often eschew conventional structures in which narratives have a beginning, middle, and end.

Vollmann: To me, they all have beginnings, middles, and ends.

Chan/Evans: Is there a difference between how you write nonfiction and how you write fiction?

Vollmann: When I say a work is nonfiction, then I try to make everything in it literally true. When a work is fiction, then I am free to blend truth and lies as I wish.

Chan/Evans: Editing, or lack thereof, is a source of much criticism about your work. Can you talk a bit about your self-editing process when you write?

Vollmann: I edit my books until they seem done. When I was a child, other children mostly did not like me (perhaps because I read more than they did). This was sad at the time, but it gave me strength, so that if reviewers think my books too long, if readers are offended or bored, if editors remind me of the increasing price of paper, well, I wish I could please them, because I do like to please people, but in the meantime, like Leonard Knight in *Imperial*, I will just keep doing things my way.

Chan/Evans: You've criticized the tendency in postmodern literature to focus too much on language games instead of trying to communicate in the most sincere way possible. However, you've used complicated structures, images, varying typefaces and other typically postmodern devices. How is your approach different?

Vollmann: I fondly (fatuously) imagine that my language games are means to an end, that my typefaces enhance the reader's ability to visualize what I describe. I hope and believe that even ambiguity can be sincere.

Chan/Evans: In the past, you've mentioned that you don't find postmodernism to be a very useful name for the context in which writers since the late 1970s onwards have found themselves. How do you see yourself within the context of your peers?

Vollmann: Of course, like each of us, I imagine myself to be a very special, unique sort of person, deserving of everything that I want to have, and therefore confounded by "unfairness." And of course, like each of us, I resemble Tolstoy's Ivan Ilyich, who is very proud of the decoration of his home, which resembles the homes of anyone of his class and time. So what is my context? I am me; I am you; I am nothing.

Chan/Evans: Prostitution is continually celebrated in your work as if for the transgressive way it lays bare the fundamental dynamics that drive culture: sex and money. In the Netherlands and Germany, prostitutes are given insurance packages—does this not completely dampen the transgressive or culturally revelatory power of prostitution?

Vollmann: I wish that all prostitutes could be given insurance. I hope for the day when prostitution will not be stigmatized, when there will be many types of licensed prostitutes: therapeutic, recreational, artistic (heterae-courtesans)—and when unlicensed ones won't go to jail. Like all human beings, I am fascinated by the transgressive, but that will always remain in one form or another, so I would rather see prostitutes safe from violence than be compelled by their very existence to provide it. (You want transgressive prostitution? Go to a dominatrix.) In the meantime, I wish we could mature into a more realistic, wholesome attitude about our erotic needs. Even those who find sexuality an unpleasant topic ought to see that we cannot wish, say, defecation away, that we need toilets, sewers, etcetera; and the same line of reasoning goes for our other corporeal and psychological aspects. *The Royal Family* [2000] and *Whores for Gloria* [1991] derive much of their sadness from the fact that in my culture prostitution is considered sordid and even criminal.

Chan/Evans: Unlike America, could the Dutch or German state, then, be the equivalent of the Queen of the Whores, the caretaking character you've developed in *The Royal Family*?

Vollmann: Why not? I would rather drink my social contract from the breast (or vulva) of an affectionate female than receive my sustenance from an indifferent bureaucrat or worse. On this topic, why has the German state so often been termed "paternalistic" while Germany's not so distant neighbors speak of Mother Russia? How happy I would be to live in Sweetheart America!

Chan/Evans: American mythology is founded on being able to change who you are—perhaps one of the strongest cultural incarnations of an Ovidian ethos. Do you think that we've lost that capacity?

Vollmann: The overt emergence of transgender people is an exciting, indeed astounding, hallmark of American Ovidianism. I love it. And I sincerely believe that we are making measurable progress in transforming ourselves away from racism. The election of a black President, the increasing freedom of interracial couples to go where they please without nasty consequences—these are very wonderful things. But it may be that, in general, the transformations encouraged by American individualism take place more in the symbolic, mental, cybernetic realms than in "physical reality." Social Security numbers, the Patriot Act, concern about legal liability, the decay of the cash economy, all these things make it more difficult to check into a hotel room with a secret lover. And changing homesteads and professions, how big a deal is that when every state has similar fast-food chains, and when bank tellers, pharmacists, construction contractors, and so many others are for better and for worse less autonomous each year.

Chan/Evans: In *Europe Central*, you write that "one of life's best pleasures is reading a book of perfect beauty; more pleasurable still is rereading that book; most pleasurable of all is lending it to the person one loves." Do you distinguish between reading for pleasure and reading for research?

Vollmann: Reading is always pleasure for me, but there are many different kinds of pleasures. Sometimes the pleasure comes from teasing out a pattern (even a horrible or frightening one, in which case the pleasure is submerged in ghastliness) or discovering a provisional answer. Sometimes it comes from the utter joy of the beautiful sentence, image, story, or world. Sometimes it comes from the unexpected. Sometimes it comes from increasing my understanding of the world, as when I dip into my old college ecology textbook.

Chan/Evans: Is there a larger project behind mapping the world through fiction? Do you desire to chart your whole world through writing?

Vollmann: For my answer, I refer to you the prospectus for my *Seven Dreams* series. I wrote this about twenty years ago, but it still gives a fair idea of what I am trying to do with landscapes.

William T. Vollmann: The Self Images of a Cross-Dresser

Stephen Heyman / 2013

Portions of this interview appeared in the *New York Times* (November 13, 2013). ©Stephen Heyman. Reprinted by permission.

In July 2013, I visited William T. Vollmann at his writing bunker in Sacramento, a squat white building surrounded by a tall fence and barbed wire. Outside the studio, a homeless man slept under a tree; Bill encourages drifters to camp out in his empty parking lot. The bunker used to be a cheap Mexican restaurant. Inside, the walls, the chairs, the doors, even parts of the ceiling were covered in Bill's expressionistic paintings and woodblock prints: mostly images of women looking slightly alarmed. In his entryway was a major work, "Homage to the Vulva," which consists of seven netherviews of a Bangkok prostitute whom Bill visited in 2001. He had a small bedroom brimming with books, and, in the corner, a series of wigs on Styrofoam heads that are propped up on poles. Each foam face was hand-painted—sloppy lipstick, bulging eyes. One looked a bit like Gene Simmons. "Whatever woman comes in here, I always say, 'Now, those are your rivals,'" Bill told me. "They kind of freak out."

I had come to Sacramento to profile Bill for the *New York Times* in connection with *The Book of Dolores* (powerHouse, 2013). This catalog of Bill's experiments with cross-dressing includes paintings, photographs and prose. "Dolores" is Bill's female alter ego and all her trappings—dresses, giant sealskin boots, Double-D silicone breast-forms—were stored in a giant walk-in refrigerator, formerly the Mexican restaurant's meat locker. "Dolores likes to put her breasts on and have them stick to her chest and sleep with them," Bill said, "which is against the manufacturers' instructions." On a long, hot day, in which we drank beer and whiskey and ate barbecue, Bill explained the origin of Dolores. He told me how he first discovered cross-dressing among prostitute friends in the Tenderloin District of San Francisco and how his curiosity developed into a passion—one that he indulged sometimes while drunk or high, sometimes as part of a strange vision quest for his mind-bending fiction, sometimes just because he liked the feel of a satin dress against his ankles.

SH: Why do you live in Sacramento?

WTV: I've lived in Sacramento for nearly twenty-five years now. And I got very fond of it. I like to ride the freight trains. This is a great place to do that. And there's this neat old Chinese town in the [San Joaquin River] Delta called Locke. It has all these ideograms on these crumbling old buildings. It's kind of cool. And people in Sac are not that into reading and writing so I can just walk around and be Bill and no one bugs me.

SH: Whereas if you were in San Francisco that wouldn't be the case?

WTV: Yeah, that's right.

SH: And why did you pick this neighborhood?

WTV: It's called Alkali Flat, and if you can, don't put my exact address in there because I like to keep my privacy. I try to keep the building looking somewhat abandoned on the outside. Whenever the homeless show up in my parking lot, I say, "Stay all your life, bring all your friends." The city doesn't like me too much for that. But I figure, let them stay.

SH: Do they take you up on your offer?

WTV: Oh, sure they do. I had one prostitute who stayed here for a couple years until the police finally arrested her. Her mother actually came all the way out from Mississippi because my parking lot sounded so good to her. I thought that was pretty sad. I guess her daughter told her, "Come out, no one is going to bother you." If people stay for a day or two, they make a lot of trash. But if they realize I'll let 'em stay, they start to sweep up, keep it clean. The city has an anti-camping ordinance; you're not allowed to stay in your own backyard for more than one night. So they're always after me.

SH: To the extent that any one book, any one collection of writing or pictures, is significant to you, how important is *The Book of Dolores*?

WTV: I have to say it makes me very, very happy that these pictures are coming out. I had so much fun and I really felt free to play. I also have a certain amount of fear and dread about the publication of the book. And I'm thinking I may not want to go to the Middle East anymore. Maybe they'd cut off my head? [*Laughs.*] But who knows.

SH: Who is Dolores? An alter-ego?
WTV: There are really two of them. One is just me, in a dress, having fun. And then the other is the character of a novel I wrote who is much more sad and desperate and extreme. In part, she's based on some of the t-girls I met.

SH: T-girls?
WTV: Transgender girls, prostitutes. And I just started to imagine what it would be like if, instead of a mode of playacting, it was an expression of true gender dysphoria, and I would give everything to be a woman. Maybe I wasn't as privileged as I am, so I would have to get hormones on the street and maybe become a prostitute and this and that. I thought, you know, it probably would not have a very good ending—although it might. I just interviewed some more t-girls in San Francisco a week or two ago. Two of them were in their seventies. They were quite happy, quite successful about who they are.

SH: The novel about Dolores, called *How You Are*, hasn't been published yet, has it?
WTV: No, and I'm not sure it will. I showed it to my editor at Viking and he was like, till now, the marketing people really liked you but I don't know whether they can handle this. I thought, well, maybe he's right. Maybe I'll just keep it on the shelf for a few more years. But I had a lot of fun, imagining this alternate universe.

SH: Can you give me an abridged version of the story?
WTV: Well, there are so many ways in which people can be transgendered. Let's just talk about male to female. A man might be gay and he thinks this is a good way to attract male sex partners who don't want to say that they're gay. Or a man might really feel like, deep down inside, he is a woman and he'll do whatever it takes to become a woman. Or a man might have what's called *autogynephilia*: he's sexually aroused by the idea of himself as a woman. And a lot of the t-girls I met are both very inspiring and occasionally somewhat narcissistic. Because you *really* have to be into yourself one way or another to do this kind of stuff. And so, in the novel, Dolores is so determined to become a woman that she leaves her child—I have a child; I would never do that—and she engages in a bunch of relationships and gradually becomes a drug addict, a prostitute, and eventually hangs

herself. One thing I found: Street prostitutes can be desperate sometimes, and t-girl street prostitutes can be desperate with male muscle. Sometimes they can be a bit opportunistic. I've had t-girl male prostitutes make me up and sometimes it's very different from being with g-girls—genetic girl prostitutes. Sometimes they'll say, "Oh, you know, you look so beautiful Dolores, let me just try to grab a little kiss." And you think, Oh, this must be what it's like to be a woman and get sexually harassed or groped or whatever.

One of the most interesting things about actually trying to be Dolores myself once in a while is the fear. I've always heard women say, "I don't like going out at night by myself." I've heard it, but I never really *got* it. Until I went out in a relatively welcoming place—San Francisco—tottering around on my high heels without my glasses because, unlike me, Dolores is a little vain. She's staggering around, can't see a thing. Cars are roaring by and guys are yelling things at her and she feels quite frightened. I feel like I identify a little bit more with women as a result of this experience.

SH: Obviously, you've interviewed and spent lots of time with prostitutes over the years but at one point you became interested in these transgendered prostitutes and then thought to experiment with cross-dressing yourself?
WTV: That's right. Well, you had asked me to pull out some things about the origin of Dolores. I'll bring a couple of photos over.

SH: Great. This beer is really nice.
WTV: Oh, yeah—nice and hoppy.

So in the '80s, I started writing a septology called *Seven Dreams*. In the very first volume, *The Ice-Shirt*, there's an Inuit myth about the origin of the human race. There were two brothers and the younger brother eventually gets changed into a woman. And that's how humans reproduced. And I thought, how interesting—but how could I really understand that? And in the Tenderloin at that time, the t-girls were just called transvestites. And through a friend, I knew a couple of them. And they said, "Oh, you know, we can make you up." So I went down. They had some orange peels. They cut an orange in half. They took the orange and dried the orange peels—two boobs. And a dress and a wig—it was very, very simple.

My friend Ken Miller took some pictures. [*Shows the photos.*] See, that's Miss J. And Miss Giddings. Miss J is long dead from AIDS now. And I don't know what happened to Miss Giddings. Miss J explained that she was just a "light positive," so she could have sex with me. I said, "Oh, that's so nice of you, I'm heterosexual, so . . ." Anyway, that was so long ago.

SH: So that was your first experience with cross-dressing?

WTV: That's right. I didn't think twice about it but then when Ken gave me copies of the pictures I thought "Wow, this is so much fun." Have you ever done any of that stuff yourself?

SH: No. Perhaps I've put on a wig for a Halloween party. In your case, do you feel a kind of frisson, is it titillating for you on some level?

WTV: Yes, it's titillating and very, very eerie. I write a lot about Native Americans. Sometimes, if I feel like engaging in some sort of a vision quest, I might stay in the studio in the dress and wig with the breast-forms for two or three days—and I'm the only one who has a key to the place—and I might not eat, I might just drink some booze, and maybe around midnight, I'm slowly walking down here, in the middle of the night, it's very, very dark, and actually it can be a little spooky here at night, and with my little flash light I see this faint gleam in that mirror down there, and I get close enough to see this very, very weird, frightening woman in a wig looking at me. It's a great way of scaring myself.

SH: But do you always have, in the back of your mind, this notion that this is a performance, a means to an end—and that end is going to be fiction or a series of photographs?

WTV: It's interesting that you use the word performance. Not too long ago I wrote a book called *Kissing the Mask*. I go over to Japan quite a bit. And originally I thought this book would just be about Noh theater. After looking at these Noh actors, I got a chance to watch them put on their masks and so forth. And then I started thinking, I wonder what it would be like, since they're performing femininity in a way, to see Geishas do it. I had such a great time—photographing the Geishas as they were getting ready. [*Shows photos.*] These three or four pictures cost me around $700. Geishas are very expensive.

SH: Just to be able to get access to them?

WTV: Yeah, that's right. They measure time with incense sticks. When an incense stick burns down, it's a quarter of an hour—three hundred bucks. When I saw the amount of work they went through—I had always imagined femininity as what you're born with, what's between your legs. And then I realized: no, it's a performance. Here's a very young geisha in Kyoto dancing for me. These movements take years and years to perfect. And I thought, "OK, so it's not just about how you look, it's about how you move, all the things you do to get ready." [*Shows another photo.*] This is a t-girl prostitute in LA.

I guess one of the big disillusionments in this whole thing, you know, I just imagined when I started doing this again, in about 2007 or 2008, that I could just put on a wig and some breast-forms and I would look just like the Dolores from the 1980s. I had forgotten of course that I had aged, so I looked like this horrible old Elizabethan courtier. Anyway, I went to this place in Tokyo one time where cross-dressers pay—another seven hundred or eight hundred bucks—for this woman to make me up. Most of them just get made up there and have a little tea with the woman and then they wash it off there and go out. Because it's a big secret.

SH: You mean, they pay just to be transformed . . .

WTV: . . . in that one place. Yeah, that's it. They pay to be there for an hour and then they just go home and no one knows. There's a lot of shame around it. I felt some shame too, once or twice. Someone's thrown a rock.

SH: Around here?

WTV: Yeah. So I don't go out dressed up here. And the cross-dressing stuff might be coming to an end anyway.

SH: Do you feel like that phase has resolved itself because you've written that novel and you've produced this series of photographs?

WTV: It's possible, yeah. You know, I tried to make my mind and my personality sort of blank when I'm writing, so I can be any number of things. My work is all about trying to empathize with the other. When I was writing my novel *Europe Central*, I got to be Shostakovich and Hitler and Akhmatova and all kinds of people. And when I wrote *Fathers and Crows*, I got to be this seventeenth-century Indian hero named Amantacha. So it's been great to be Dolores. And I have a bunch of props. Maybe I'll continue to dress up from time to time, but the thrill of it has lessened for sure. And that's what a lot of long-term cross-dressers say. At first, it's so exciting for them and they can hardly wait to buy a new slip and look at themselves in the mirror. Then after a while, you say, "Well, I am this or I am not this, so what's the big deal?" Your wife doesn't get too thrilled when she puts on her slip, that's just what it is.

SH: Part of that is because, as you keep on doing it, it feels less like transgression?

WTV: That's right, yeah. And I'm sure part of it is my generation. Very likely, unless we swing way to the right, in another twenty years, people will say, "Oh, so there's a man who puts on a dress, who cares?" And that will be great. But in the meantime, probably this will have lost some of its narrative power for me as a novelist.

SH: But if you met just kind of a typical, normatively straight guy in a bar who was trying to understand the appeal of cross-dressing, is there a way to explain it to him?

WTV: I guess I would say to another heterosexual male. "You probably enjoy watching the woman you desire stripping down to her lingerie and you might enjoy buying her lingerie. And, so, wouldn't you feel even closer to her if you put on lingerie yourself?" Most of the t-girls that I talk to don't feel that way. They say, "Oh when I was three-years-old I used to steal my sister's underwear and play with little-girl toys. I always felt like I was a girl and I got punished and I had to hide it but finally I did it."

SH: And you can't relate to that part of it?

WTV: It's not my story. I can easily imagine it. As a novelist, I can imagine myself into anything. They say that some men become women to attract what they desire and others to be what they desire.

SH: How does someone who has autogynephilia become fulfilled?

WTV: One way is to take hallucinogenic drugs, to go on some kind of vision quest, where eventually you can split your personality. As happens in the novel. Maybe the male self actually can see and even have sex with the female self.

SH: It would be some kind of drug-fueled masturbatory fantasy where it actually feels like you're having sex with another person?

WTV: But of course the way I imagine it in this novel, Dolores would never really like somebody like me. She's a young girl, relatively young. That's actually a very interesting thing, too. When people transition, at first they're like young girls, then they're like teenagers, then they're young women—no matter what their chronological age. And so Dolores is a relatively young woman trapped inside this fat, aging male body, with pouches under my eyes. And sure I've bought the old bitch a bunch of clothes, but she's not grateful. She would like to get rid of me if she could. At least in the novel.

SH: The t-girls you've met—they don't have these split personalities with different ages, do they?

WTV: Everybody's different. One of the people I interviewed last week was a guy who often performs as "Donna Persona": he dons a persona. He said, "Now Donna, she can get away with saying all these things that I can't. I would be considered so rude and mean if I let myself say these things. Everyone likes Donna, even though she's this and she's that." It was so fascinating. And it worked for him. A lot of the t-girl performers just really let themselves go. No one takes it too seriously. And then others really do a great job and look exactly like who they are. There are probably as many different types of t-girls as there are women.

SH: The name Dolores, where did that come from?
WTV: Oh, yeah, a woman named me. She said, "Dolores is sadness and pain," and she has sort of sad eyes, so I think that's a sort of appropriate name for her. At first it seemed a little strange and then I got used to it. And I consider myself a relatively happy person, but if there were a Dolores she would probably feel not very happy at all to be stuck with me.

SH: When you put on the clothes and the makeup, you take off your glasses, so you can't see that well, and you look at yourself in the mirror, and you imagine that you're younger, that you're beautiful. Then later when you look at the photographs you're upset.
WTV: What a great experience! This is what my fantasy is, this is my reality. I can either ignore reality or I can accept it. And that doesn't invalidate the fantasy. I can always be whoever I want in a watercolor or a drawing or a novel, but I can't be whoever I want in real life. I'm getting older and older, someday I'm going to die. It doesn't matter. I don't have to make a big deal out of it, I can just have fun and play.

[*I ask Bill to give me a tour of the art-making area of his bunker, where he has a power engraver—he was working on a suite of Norse block prints when I visited—and where he prints his Dolores photographs using an arcane nineteenth century method called gum bichromate, which takes up to twenty-eight days to produce a single print. Then Bill leads me to a large walk-in closet that was formerly the Mexican restaurant's meat locker.*]

SH: What's in here?
WTV: This is the meat locker, where Dolores's parts are. When the electrician wired it up, he asked, "What do you use this for?" I said, "Oh, that's just where I keep my victims." There was a long silence. . . . She's got her

dresses here and I have my bulletproof helmet and various stuff from my journalism in there.

SH: Have you taken many reporting trips recently?
WTV: No, that seems to be drying up. It seems that the magazines have less and less money. They're mostly interested in domestic stuff. I don't know whether it's to save costs or if they really think Americans are only interested in America. I get sort of sick of it. So there are the wig heads. Whatever woman comes in here, I always say, "Now, those are your rivals." They kind of freak out.

SH: Do you have many visitors or is this mostly a solitary space?
WTV: I have the occasional visitor, yeah. And then let's see. [*Opens the door to the bathrooms.*] I figure the men's room and the women's room ought to connect.

SH: Why is that?
WTV: Well, you know male and female should always get together wher- ever possible. The men's room is the toilet. The women's room is the shower. They didn't used to connect. It was really, really gross when I bought the place. This old restaurant—everything was all rotted out with pee.

[*Bill takes me into another small room.*] And then this is the books and bullets room. I put my phone in the closet most of the time, so I never have to hear it. I got all the extra copies of my books and all the bullets I'll need for my various pistols.

SH: Where do you keep your arsenal?
WTV: I keep them in a safe.

SH: That's good.
WTV: The worst thing would be if someone stole my guns and used them for a crime—I would feel really bad.

SH: I'm curious about the rhythm: reading versus the writing, the painting versus the photographing: is it very programmed?
WTV: No, I just do whatever I want.

[*We leave for lunch. Bill punches a keypad to lock the door to his writing bunker. A short drive takes us to a barbecue restaurant. It's barely noon when we arrive. "A table for two?" the waitress asks. "Unless you're going to sit with us," Bill replies. Later, when we're seated, he asks her, "We were wondering which one of us is more handsome? You are definitely the most beautiful."*]

SH: I heard about your charm with women.
WTV: I have such a great time, I have to say. They can tell that I don't need anything from them. I just enjoy giving them compliments.

[*The waitress sets down two glasses of beer.*]

Here's to you, Steve!

SH: And to you! Congratulations again on the book.
WTV: Thanks, I wonder if I'll be sorry [to have it published]. A lot of friends who could always handle the prostitutes and the drugs were quite disgusted with this. You know, they say that gender is class. The idea of stepping down from the dominant male class to the number two class really disgusts a lot of people, including women. I've been kind of shocked. But I figure, you know, I'm in my fifties, I've reproduced, what's the worst thing that could happen?

SH: What does your wife think of it?
WTV: She's not thrilled but she can deal with it. My daughter is gleeful. She can hardly wait for her friends' parents to hear about this book. Sacramento is fairly conservative, but it's not terrible.

SH: There was a *New York Times* review of your book about hopping freight trains, *Riding Toward Everywhere*, that began basically with the question: What the hell is wrong with you?
WTV: Yeah, I get that sometimes. I figure as long as I please myself, that's the main thing. We're all going to die, and hopefully we're not lying in our deathbeds thinking, I got a terrible review back in 2013. One of the t-girls told me, "I want to die in the arms of a jealous husband." I think I'd like to die of a massive heroin overdose.

SH: Do you still dabble with the chemicals?
WTV: Sure.

SH: What does your doctor wife think about that?
WTV: She has no comment, so that works for me.

SH: Are you able to write after a few drinks?

WTV: Oh, sure. But the best thing to write after is a bunch of crack. Then your concentration is so good. Coffee is kind of like that, too. I mean, crack is just like strong coffee.

SH: You can't feel good afterwards?

WTV: Well, you don't want to do too much. For the Dolores book I figured that she would end up as a meth-addicted prostitute and there was a friend of mine who was editing a book about speed. Not that I know anything about that, but Dolores had a great time on the crystal.

[*We head Back to Bill's writing bunker, where he has agreed to walk me through the process of becoming Dolores.*]

SH: So how do you begin?

WTV: I think it's important to be really clean. So I want to take a shower and shave really well. And usually I almost never bother to shave. Then there's moisturizer and foundation and all this stuff. That was one of the revelations to me: how much women go through. I used to think, this woman looks so glamorous, what nice beautiful long eyelashes she has. And it never occurred to me, she must have spent twenty minutes with her eyelash curler and her mascara. There's this whole science to this stuff, which is appealing to my male self—someone who wants to understand procedures. But the other thing about it that was kind of nice was it gave me a chance to sort of love and take care of myself. If I dressed up, I would take pains with my face. I wouldn't want to just put on some dirty dress but I would work hard and I would feel kind of happy that I actually manicured my body a little bit, something that I have not done for myself. A lot of my female friends, if they're down in the dumps, they'd go with their girlfriends and get their nails done. I never got that before. And so it's just a way of being cared for. Some kind of basic primate grooming, I guess.

SH: Did you spend a lot of time figuring out what kind of cosmetics to buy?

WTV: I had women help me.

SH: Your wife or friends?

WTV: Friends, yeah. They would say, "Oh, you need this. Or, "Let me help you." Or, "This doesn't look good on you." One of the funny things was that they all disagreed. Women in our culture are so appearance-conscious. They say, "Oh, this woman looks so awful." But men could care less. So probably what takes me the longest is shaving. To me the mascara is an incredible hassle. And I don't enjoy it. When I was three, I had an operation on my left eye. I hate having things close to my eye.

SH: How long does it take to make yourself up?

WTV: Dolores takes one to two hours. And after about fifteen to twenty minutes she melts, and I have to go into the shower and wash it off. Kind of sad. When I went to that woman in Tokyo who did makeup for crossdressers, I was shocked. She said that after this $700, it might last twenty or thirty minutes. Wow, now I know why women are always rushing to the bathroom. I had a friend who's now in her early forties. I said, "When you were in your twenties and thirties, you must have had such a sense of power." She said no. "First of all, you don't understand your power until it's too late. And second of all, we're always worried that one of our high heels is going to break. Or we have to rush back into the ladies room to touch up our lipstick. We can never enjoy it." And I thought, how awful. So Dolores has it pretty good.

SH: So the vast majority of the times when you're becoming Dolores it's just to kind of hang out in your studio?

WTV: Yeah.

SH: Occasionally you've gone out, though. Do you think people know that you're a man?

WTV: Probably. I don't think Dolores is too convincing unfortunately. But there's something very relaxing about wearing the clothes. Some women tell me, "Oh I can hardly wait to come home from the office and take off my bra and let my breasts just bob around," whereas Dolores likes to put her breastforms on and have them stick to her chest and sleep with them, which is against the manufacturer's instructions.

SH: Dolores's breasts are not the dried citrus peels, they're silicone.

WTV: 44 double D, silicone, although over the years of sleeping with them they are getting more like pancakes.

SH: Although that happens to real women as well . . .

WTV: That's true! Haha.

SH: Can I see Dolores's breasts?
WTV: Sure. [*Brings out the breast forms.*]

SH: May I?
WTV: Of course. These are "asymmetric breasts with naughty nipples." They cost about $200. If you want to, you can tape them to your chest. It comes with tape. And after a little while they can stay on your chest. And it feels like they're part of you. You're not supposed to sleep in them. But I did and one night I had this horrible experience. Apparently the adhesive had attracted ants and they crawled under my shirt and along my chest, it was quite a disgusting experience.

SH: Do you have a sense that people who are cross-dressers might be grateful to you for doing this book?
WTV: Some of them might. I hope so. People who cross-dress, especially people who go farther than that, suffer a tremendous amount of abuse. There's a very high rate of discrimination and even violence. What's interesting is in our country women can really dress as they wish. And one hundred years ago, that certainly wasn't the case. A woman couldn't walk around and wear pants. When I got married, one of my female friends showed up in a tuxedo, and nobody thought anything of it.

SH: Right, well there's certainly plenty of fashion antecedents for that: Marlene Dietrich, Coco Chanel.
WTV: That's true. Does your wife like to wear men's clothing?

SH: Yes, but for women it's fashionable to play with boyishness or androgyny—it's not transgressive in the same way.
WTV: And how do you think the trend is going for men? I really feel that pretty soon anybody will be able to dress as anything and it won't make a difference.

SH: I think it has a lot to do with geography. Maybe people are more or less tolerant depending on the place.
WTV: Yeah, I was recently in West Virginia. Somebody told me that if people knew I was a cross-dresser they would be disgusted but also that there were so many ugly women in West Virginia that I could probably pass.

Standing Up in Our Small Way:
An Interview with William T. Vollmann

Hannah Jakobsen / 2017

Portions of this interview were published in the *Los Angeles Review of Books* (February 26, 2018). ©Hannah Jakobsen. Reprinted by permission.

This interview took place in person at William T. Vollmann's studio on October 26, 2017.

HJ: You've had a lot of unusual experiences—taken up arms with the muja-hedeen in Afghanistan, been a war correspondent, and hopped freight trains, to name a few. How have you chosen to do the things you've done, and how have they informed your writing?

WV: There are two ways I think, or two reasons, maybe to look for experience for writing, and one is to go out and have some experience that you're curious about and keep an open mind and then decide what you're going to do with it. And that was what Thoreau always recommended, he said it's so important that we never let our knowledge get in the way of what's really much more helpful which is our ignorance. As long as we remember that we're ignorant, we're out there in the world and we can learn things and so, like when I've rid-den the freight trains, I try to keep that in mind. I don't know even where I'm going, what I'm gonna see, who I'm gonna meet, and so I just try to be open, like a child. And then, I have some chance of actually learning what reality is. And the other way to go is, well, I have some situation in my mind, and I want to make it as vivid as I can, and so I want to go out and gather information or local color or a whole experience or something like that for the thing that I'm writing. Are you familiar with my *Seven Dreams* series?

HJ: Mm-hmm.

WV: One of them is called *The Rifles*, and in the nineteenth century all the

Europeans were in a race to try to find the Northwest Passage. Now we have no problems thanks to global warming, but at that time, no one had yet figured out how to go from Europe to Asia, up near the pole, and they thought if they could do that by ship, it would be a tremendous thing for commerce, and all this type of crap, who really cares. So Sir John Franklin tried to complete the Northwest Passage, are you familiar with this story?

HJ: Tell me.

WV: He had made three attempts, and he'd had very difficult times. The first attempt there was starvation and cannibalism. The second time, there was violence with the Inuit. The third time, they got stuck in ice. And it was right before the winter, and they expected to be there all winter, so they were used to it, but then summer came, and the ice never melted, and the winter came. Meanwhile, they were living on canned food, and their idea back then was to seal cans with lead solder. So these guys were all getting lead poisoning, and going crazy, and not knowing why they were acting more and more strange. And we know that because there are some graves of three guys that are actually marked near the beginning of the expedition, and they're perfectly frozen, so they were autopsied, and already, it was only at the end of the first year, there was a high lead content in their tissues. So later on, much, much later, skeletons were found scattered all over the place and there was one place where they were actually hauling a heavy longboat filled with books and not food, these skeletons, just absolutely bizarre things. And they all died. Apparently they built a cairn with some letters, and the Inuit found it and didn't know what paper was so they destroyed it. I wanted to get into Sir John Franklin's mind, and see what it would be like to be all alone, up in the Arctic. So I had a plane take me to the North Magnetic Pole, and I was all by myself, had kind of a rough time of it, which was worse than I expected, but it was great for my book.

HJ: You've spoken about the importance of promoting empathy through writing. And you've written, for example, extensively about sex workers. I'm curious whether your writing about sex work was strongly motivated by the desire to increase empathy for prostitutes and other sex workers.

WV: Well, I first got interested in prostitutes because I was a customer. My fiancée had left me, and I tried and tried to get a girlfriend, but, you know how it is like when you see someone who's really sad and pathetic, you tend to think, do I really want this needy person to drag me down? So that's what all the girls must have thought. And finally, had a call girl come, and it wasn't even physically that great but, it just kind of made me feel like a man again, that I could be with some woman. And so then I started thinking about what the whole experience is like, what it all meant, whether it was good or bad, whether these women were exploited, empowered, all of the above, none of the above. And so I made lots of stories and drawings and photographs of prostitutes, and it took me a long time to actually decide what I thought. So that was more like the first thing, about riding the freight trains, as a customer and then more and more as a friend, and someone who listens. I try to understand them. And then I was able to say "Well, this is what I think."

HJ: That surprises me a little, because a lot of topics you write about feel so relevant to the big sociopolitical conversations of our time. I'm thinking of your portrayal of the experience of the economically disenfranchised in *Poor People*, or of migrant workers in *Imperial*, and the work that many of your books do to explore the circumstances of sex workers. So it's interesting to hear the role that pure curiosity plays in your writing.

WV: Reality is always relevant. And so, if you were to go out somewhere and try to find out something about a place or people that you didn't know, and you were to write about it honestly and beautifully, then five hundred years from now if there are still people, people would want to read what you had to say, and it would touch them somehow. But if instead you said, "Well, alright, I'm going to write something about the homeless and I'm gonna make up some script and I don't need to really meet them but here's what I think"—then it might be sort of interesting as a document that revealed you or your times or something like that, but it wouldn't be as compelling. That's my feeling anyway. So, what do you think?

HJ: About why a person should write about something?
WV: Yeah.

HJ: I dunno, I mean I think so far in my life I personally have mostly had the experience of writing about things out of necessity, but . . .
WV: What's been the saddest thing in your life?

HJ: My life so far?
WV: Yeah.
HJ: Let me think. I mean, I feel like I've been pretty fortunate to never have ever had to deal with anything truly sad happening to me. Like, there are

moments when I feel very depressed, but it's not because anything has happened to me. So I think that the moments where I've felt the saddest in my life are not because anything has happened to me.

WV: But because you didn't get what you hoped for or?

HJ: No, just because of my own reflection about life and like, just not because of anything. What about you?

WV: Well, let's see. Probably the saddest thing was my little sister's death. She drowned when I was a kid, and I was nine, she was six, I was supposed to be watching her, and I fell down on the job and that was really hard for me, and for my parents, and I wish it had never happened. On the other hand, since it has happened and that was back in 1968, I've tried to let it define me. I'm somebody who as a little kid screwed up, and so how can I possibly not be empathetic to other people who screw up? Here I am sitting in the same room with a rapist or a mass murderer, or somebody, and I think okay, this is my brother or my sister, cause we've both screwed up. And I don't have to like the person. I might even think, this person deserves to be put to death. But still, I have to listen and remember that we're brothers and sisters.

HJ: So, does it make a difference to you that what happened in your life was an accident, whereas raping someone or committing mass murder is a purposeful act?

WV: Oh, you know, it's all a slippery slope, right? So I met a guy in Sarajevo and I forget what the details are. There are three different nationalities, so most likely say he was a Muslim married to a Serb or something like this. So, the Serbs said, "Alright, you're a Muslim, we should kill you, but here, you go ahead and you kill these women, these Muslim women. If you do, we're gonna let you go. If you don't, we're gonna rape your wife and then kill her." So, what's the right choice there? Either way, you're a murderer, and you either murder the person you love, or you murder some strangers. What's worse? So there's no answer right, and that means, that guy's a victim, whatever he did, and so there's someone who's murdered someone who has a reason. People always have reasons. What about somebody who's demented, just crazy? He can't help himself because the demons made him do it or whatever. It doesn't make it right, but all you can do is listen to these people. Or what about all of our soldiers? Right now. All the American people say, "Oh, hurrah for our soldiers, they're protecting us." Well what are they doing? Since the war on terror began, we've killed, what? Maybe a couple hundred thousand people? We've had maybe two thousand people died on September 11, something like that, and maybe, what, another ten thousand since then, we're killing others. Can we say that that's right, can we say that that's wrong? When we talk about war and what's justified, the two issues are proportionality and discrimination. So, proportionality means if you're on the other side and you killed a hundred people on my side, I might have the right to kill 99 or a hundred people on your side, but not ten thousand, and discrimination means you went out and you killed my brother because he had a gun and a uniform and he was trying to kill you but you didn't kill my little daughter, who didn't do anything to you. That's discrimination. So, those are some of the ways we can look at this stuff and decide to what extent this person who's doing these wicked things, or, committing violence, we don't have to call it wicked, he's like me, and to what extent he isn't. And I think you can examine it and it's worth examining but it's a very painful process, trying to go through all that and come to an accurate judgment about what a person is and what should happen to that person. I think it's possible to say for instance that probably both of the president Bushes were war criminals. Maybe Obama was too, unfortunately. And it looks as if Trump is going to be, unfortunately, so it's probably worth doing that, although, what do you do with that information?

HJ: It's interesting to think about this idea of relativity in terms of the way that your books—and I'm thinking in particular about *Europe Central*—humanize characters. Have you considered writing about President Trump?
WV: It'd be very different, yeah. Hopefully, if you woke up tomorrow in President Trump's body, you would say, there are a lot of things that I'm not going to do. But what if you woke up and you had all the life and conditioning that he did? You always got to do whatever you wanted, you could rip people off and people thought that was great. Your father was a jerk, and a racist. You might or might not have been a racist, you might have been fine with blacks and gays and everything else, cause you were happy to take money wherever it came, but suddenly, "Oh now I've gotta be president, so I'm gonna lash out against them," and so forth. If you can understand, I don't know, what kind of a little boy Trump was. I don't know, actually, that much about him, because I find him such a dreary person, that I wouldn't really want to know. I guess if he commits enough evil then I'll have to really think about him, try to figure out where he comes from, but it'd be interesting to imagine him as a very sweet little baby, and then what went wrong, like how did it go wrong, and where does his identity come from. That's our job as writers.

HJ: Yeah. It sounds like you think who people are is very determined by their circumstances.

WV: I think, yeah, I think that's very true, and of course it's also true that some people determine their circumstances. Marx would say we're all products of our circumstances, and Tolstoy said that in *War and Peace*, that Napoleon thought that he was in charge, but really he was just like a piece of bark floating down a river. Both the person and the times are important. Suppose you woke up tomorrow and you were in the body of, let's say, a German boy who was eighteen years old and it was 1939, and all you'd ever learned in your education was from Hitler Youth, and then suddenly it was war and the radio said, "Oh, the British and the Polish and the Jews, they've all attacked," and what are you going to do? Is it your fault? When they hand you a gun and say, "Go off to the front line and defend your country," you wouldn't know better. How could you possibly be blamed for that?

HJ: True, but people who come from very similar situations sometimes turn out really differently. I feel like people's bigotry is often ascribed to their circumstances, for example.

WV: Dr. Spock in his book about kids said that little children are like scientists—so the baby drops her bottle, and just to see whether it's going to fall, the hundredth time as opposed to the ninety-ninth, and it always does so after a while, she kind of learns something about gravity. And we're only as good as our powers of deduction, from our observations. My grandfather only had a high school education. He worked on the Union Pacific railroad, and he worked with a lot of other disadvantaged people. He came over from Norway when he was three, and he would get his mouth washed out with soap in elementary school for speaking Norwegian. So, those were the assimilation days.

HJ: Where did he move to from Norway?

WV: To Dresser, Wisconsin. And then when I knew him he was in Omaha. But he could never speak Norwegian, it was washed right out of his mouth. So here's some guy who had a very, very poor difficult life. He was a machinist at the UP and it was pretty crummy there. He never learned very much about things of the mind, he'd watch TV and sports, and he became a racist, and part of it was, he got burgled one time, and it was by a black man. And he said, "You know, Bill, up until that time I never had any anger against the blacks. But after that . . ." And if you look at it from somebody's perspective who doesn't have a lot of education, a lot of tools . . . well, of course this guy had something bad happen to him. And so he's making a generalization to protect himself. And his generalization is you'd better watch out for black guys. And that was shorthand for something true, which was you'd better watch out for disadvantaged men. And a lot of disadvantaged men are black. And it wasn't right, but you see that's how people come to these ideas, of fear and hatred.

HJ: So you don't hold someone, your grandfather for example, you don't hold him responsible for those views?

WV: Well, he did his best, never had any money, took good care of my grandmother and now he's dead. Can I say that he was a bad man? No. Was he as bad a man as the black guy who burgled his garage? He never burgled a garage. He said some hateful things, but he never said them in public. And maybe we're all haters, and racists, and misogynists or whatever, to some extent. But we live long enough and had things are going to happen and we have to remember that the person who is maliciously hurting us represents himself or herself and doesn't represent that gender or racial group or whatever. And a lot of people don't have the tools to make that effort. And especially with this crappy educational system and this crappy system of so-called news that we have, where all the poison is reinforced, it's more and more like the Nazis. That's what I think anyway. So we have to stand up in our small way and know that it doesn't do any good but that doesn't let us off the hook. What do you think?

HJ: It's hard. Like a lot of people, I find myself applying different standards when I think about what certain people say, like older people for example, and I'm not sure how I feel about that.

WV: Right, yeah. I remember once sitting on this Greyhound bus next to this nice old baker, and we were riding together for five or six hours. We passed Manzanar, and he was saying it was so terrible what they did to the Japanese. He said, "Well, what if only they did it to the Jews? Hitler was so right, they should have burned all the Jews screaming," and I was just so sickened. I just got up, and I changed my seat. And I wouldn't talk to him anymore. Now I'm thinking, was that wrong? Maybe what I should have done . . . this is probably what I'd do now—is say, "Oh really, why do you think that? I want to understand why you think that." That's what I try to do with my friends now that are on the right. Instead of saying, "Oh fuck you, you voted for Trump; I don't want there to be a civil war," I think, "Hey, I want them to still like me, and I want to like them, and not let this come between us." 'Cause if we just completely sever relations, how can anything good come of that? We have to try and find some common ground, so what does that mean? Does that mean we tolerate evil? Should I have tolerated that guy saying those wicked things? There's no right answer, all you can do is try to be mindful. My best friend Ben always says, "Remember, Bill, whatever you do is going to be a mistake. As long as you know that everything's a mistake, you can cut yourself some slack. You're never going to do anything right." And that's kind of comforting. I wish it were otherwise. I wish everything I did were perfect.

HJ: You've written about people having a certain responsibility as Americans to, say, understand the Vietnam War. Do you also feel as a writer and as a person that you bear responsibility based on other factors, like race and sex?
WV: You know the saying "To whom much is given much is expected"? It's no credit to me that I have a talent for writing. I've worked very, very hard, but I've always loved doing it, so it's not even really work. And it's no credit to me that I didn't come from a broken home and I was able to get enough money, and my parents had enough money for me to travel a lot and so yeah, we can say I'm privileged and you're privileged and so, if we care about our brothers and sisters, then we want to help others and ideally it should make us happy to help other people. When there's some guy out in my parking lot and I know that the day after he leaves I'm going to be out there cleaning up his poop, but I'm out there talking to him and it makes me really happy that I'm defying the anti-camping ordinance and giving him a place to stay for a night or two, then I feel really good about myself. And if there were no anticamping ordinance, and there were something else that I had to do, I would do it. It was never something I wanted to do, but after I bought this place, I can't escape it, and so that's one of the things I've been called to do. I could either say, "You know what, fuck off, don't make a mess in my parking lot, just get the fuck out of here." That's how all my neighbors talk to them. And I'd be saying that every single day. Or instead I can say, "Oh, you know, come and stay and try and keep it clean for my sake, please." And if you don't bring a lot of stuff it's going to be a long time before the neighbors complain and call the police and, really, it amounts to the same thing in the long run. They get moved on, but at least I'm trying to do something good. Gandhi said you have to scrupulously resist the desire for results. And César Chávez said something like that, too. And if there's some guy or some poor woman sleeping in my parking lot and I let her stay, how much credit can I take? I can't take credit 'cause I have the parking lot. But I know I would

be ashamed if I said, "Get out of here, I'm not gonna allow you to lay down your head in my cold, wet parking lot."

HJ: Switching gears—you've written about the effect of, in certain places like Afghanistan and Iraq, pulling out your Quran and showing other people that you take some sort of an interest in what's important to them.
WV: That's right.

HJ: Do you have any thoughts about religion generally? I think a lot of people would never read a religious text that's not from their own religion.
WV: Right, well, I don't know very much about it, but here's what I will tell you, that when I'm in the Middle East, and all the men call each other brother, and when it's prayer time they all stop at the side of the road wherever they are and they go and pray together, and I don't, I feel that I'm missing out on something, and I think it's very, very sweet to watch them together. And I'm sure that it's the same for women; when there's a wedding in the Muslim world, you would get to be with the women, but I'm out in the street where all the guys are dancing around and the bridegroom comes and kisses everybody on the cheek . . .

HJ: I've been to the women's section of a Muslim wedding.
WV: So you know how it is right? Yeah, it's wonderful.

HJ: I always wondered what the men were doing.
WV: Yeah, that's right, and now we both know a little, right? But, when I first went to Pakistan, I was just a kid, really . . . I guess I was exactly the same age as you. So wherever I would go, people would say, "Oh, let me buy you a Sprite," or, "Hop on the handlebars of my bicycle and I'll wheel you wherever you want to go," and I said, "Oh, but why?" "Oh, because you're a guest of my country and it's my duty to God." And I thought, how wonderful. So to the extent that religion encourages us to love the other and help the stranger and be kind to the poor, that's a wonderful thing. I've met Marxists who do just the same thing, who are atheists and that's their religion, so I guess the only other thing I can say is that when I was in Bosnia in '94, and my two friends were shot, and I was in the backseat of the car and they were killed, I thought I was about to die, and I thought, "Well, you know, I could pray, oh please God let me stay alive, you know," that sounds pretty fake, I'd never go to church.

HJ: Did you grow up religious?

WV: No, my mother is a Christian scientist, my father was a Lutheran but after my sister died he rejected God. And I just thought, "The only thing I can really say is that I'm grateful for my life." And my two friends, one of them had bought a bunch of oranges that day, they were all rolling around in the back seat where I was, and I was lying down, ducking down so I wouldn't be seen, it was like eleven in the morning and I really ha to pee, so I was thinking, "I have to wait until nighttime and then try and crawl out in the darkness without being shot," and I opened up one of those oranges and ate it. "This is probably the last orange I'm going to eat; I'm probably going to be killed before the end of the day; it just tastes so good, I'm grateful for that orange." And after I did survive my father said, "You know, Bill, I'm worried about your mental health, because you seem unnaturally cheerful these days after what happened." I said, "Dad, I'm just so grateful to be alive." All these things that I used to be so upset about, I don't know whether my friends would give anything to be in my place, or whether it doesn't matter because they're dead. But I don't want to be in their place, and I just have to be grateful. And so, that's my religion. Being grateful.

HJ: I also wanted to ask your opinion on movies. I know you're not a fan of television but do you like movies?

WV: Yeah, I do.

HJ: Which ones?

WV: I think that *Berlin Alexanderplatz* is the best movie ever made.

HJ: I've never heard of it.

WV: It actually came out as a series of TV programs. It's something like fifteen, sixteen hours long. It's based on a novel; it's far better than the novel. And it's like life itself. When you watch it, at first it's very, very slow. It's also quite painful to watch. It's about a guy, a pimp, who beat his girlfriend to death. He just got out of prison. He's trying to go straight. And his landlady adores him, lets him right back into the old room, that she kept for him all the time he was in jail, and all these other girls are so happy to see him. And so he's, it's kind of like what we were talking about. He's this awful guy, he's a murderer, and he's also like this very, very innocent, childlike guy, and he's just kind of completely in the moment, he doesn't mean any harm, he's just totally brutal in this innocent way, and he's trying to go straight. So you see him like for one whole episode he's out there like trying to sell lapel pins on street, he doesn't get any. Then he tries to sell the Nazi newspaper. And bit by bit he's slowly drawn back into the life of crime. It's just really incredible, it's really sad.

HJ: Have you ever seen *Sophie Scholl*, a movie about Hans and Sophie Scholl?
WV: No I haven't seen it, but I'm very interested in them.

HJ: Well it strikes me that there's such a contrast between what you were describing earlier about having certain beliefs because of your circumstances.
WV: Right. They overcame their relative privilege, and they achieved nothing, died for their beliefs, and it turns out that in a way they did achieve something. Because here we are, talking about them, more than half a century later, and thinking that they were inspiring. Did you ever hear of the writer Hans Fallada?

HJ: No.
WV: I think the name of the book I'm thinking of is called *Every Man Dies Alone*. It's a fictionalization of the case of this couple who tried to something a little bit like that. They would go around and leave little typewritten messages like that, like "The Führer wants to kill us all," and "Nazis are murderers." All they could do was type it out once and stick it into a public bathroom or something. And they survived for two or three years, and of course the Nazis were ferociously looking for them. They finally caught them and killed them. It's really interesting. I don't know what the real story was. In the novel, they sort of woke up once their son was killed in France. It could have been something like that. Sort of disheartening to think that if there were an American couple now and their son were killed or their daughter were killed over in Afghanistan, instead of gaining more consciousness they'd probably say "Oh! those goddamn terrorist ragheads!"

HJ: That's probably true. That German couple could have also easily had a very different reaction.
WV: Of course. But, they say that when the Kaiser started WWI, everybody was cheering and thinking, "Oh, we're all going to be back by Christmas," and then when Hitler went into Poland, people were almost silent and did not want to. They remembered the suffering and defeat of the previous war,

and it wasn't that they were necessarily nice people, but they understood more how it might play for them. And so, some parents in West Virginia, their son gets killed, they don't think, "Oh, well, that brings closer the time when the Muslims are going to land and overcome us and there'll be Sharia everywhere": that's a joke, no one really thinks that that can happen anytime soon. But the Germans knew that they could lose and be defeated and occupied again. I think that's the only real difference.

HJ: You seem to think that it's really essential that Americans have some sort of an understanding of the Muslim world. Have you ever endeavored to study Arabic?
WV: No, I never have. And I'm not very good at languages. I actually have some cassettes for how to learn Arabic. If I was going to focus the rest of my life on the Muslim world, then I would try, but there are a lot of things I'm interested in, too.

HJ: Yeah, and Arabic is not a quick learn. I want to switch gears a little. You've compared prostitution to a lot of other jobs—do you also see a relationship between writing and prostitution?
WV: Of course, yeah. We're all prostitutes. even every little child is a prostitute. You do something because your parents will reward you if you do and punish you if you don't, not because you want to. What I'm against is nonconsensual prostitution, in the same way that I'm against nonconsensual anything. All you can really say is that we can't say what sex is, we can't say what prostitution is, and we can't even really define consensuality, except in our own current normative mores. So if I saw some big kid raping a little kid would I intervene? Of course I would. If there was some woman on the street renting out her pussy would I intervene? Probably not. I'd think it belongs to her, she gets to do what she wants. If on the other hand I saw some pimp in the background saying, "Make me money, bitch or I'm gonna kill you," well then I'd intervene. But it's like when you were asking me about somebody committing murder. You have to consider everything before you can say for sure. And it might be that like if we really knew everything about Trump, we'd feel sorry for him and we'd like him. I can't say that I wouldn't. I don't think that I would. It's hard for me to imagine that there's anything in his personality that excuses him, but who am I to say?

HJ: I feel like a lot of people in writing about you focus on this idea of you being an outsider, in terms of like prostitution and drugs or whatever. Do you have any feelings about being thought of or referred to as an outsider all the time?

WV: Yeah, my feeling is I don't care. I don't care what people think of me.

HJ: Really?
WV: I mean . . .

HJ: You seem really like remarkably self-assured, especially in terms of—I think a lot of people, myself included, need to be told that something we did is good or that we're good at something to really believe it.
WV: Well, what would you most like to accomplish in your life?

HJ: I really wish I knew.
WV: Well, if you don't know, maybe what you most want to accomplish is to be a good person and to have a happy life, and in a way those are the best two accomplishments that you could possibly succeed in doing. I would say if you're not driven to do something, you're very, very lucky. Five hundred years from now, you and I are going be dead, and it's not going matter whether I ever wrote a single book. You know, all that will matter . . .

HJ: I think your books will exist five hundred years from now.
WV: Well, that's very nice of you, but it probably won't matter to me. You never know.

HJ: Well, you'll be dead, so of course it won't matter to you.
WV: Exactly. You know, I'm so grateful that I'm Lisa's father.

HJ: Did being a father make you think differently at all about things like your own purpose in life?
WV: Well . . . I became more certain, I would say. It used to be, people would say something and I would think "Well, yeah maybe that's true, I don't know, I can't really argue with it 'cause I'm not sure." And then suddenly "Oh listen, Lisa needs this, or this would be great for Lisa. This would be bad for Lisa. I know that, I know that in my bones, and I'm going to stop it from happening, I'm going to do whatever I can to do the right thing." And then you have to be careful to not go too far in that direction; just cause that was the greatest thing for Lisa doesn't mean it's at all useful to anybody else. That's the human thing, we generalize based on insufficient experience, and that's what a novelist does, too. You bring this character alive and they say, "Oh

yeah, the heroine of this book, she's so much herself, she's so perfect," and that's fine, but you know she never existed, and the reason she's so perfect is because the author has distorted reality. No one's like that, so we have to be careful.

HJ: That makes sense. Do you have the same amount of self-assurance in your visual work as you do in your writing?
WV: Oh sure. But that's because I'm only trying to please myself. And so, when I do it right I please myself. When I don't please myself I have to keep working on it, and then all my life people have told me, "You know, Bill, you'll never get published or your stuff is awful, or it's too wordy."

HJ: People have told you that?
WV: Yeah, or people will say, "Oh, your art is so perverted, and obscene, and this and that" . . . so it's like, what do I care, I just do what I'm going to do.

Could You Do Any Better Than We Did?

Ted Hamilton / 2018

Portions of this interview appeared in *Boston Review* (April 11, 2018). ©Ted Hamilton. Reprinted by permission.

William Vollmann was in New York for a stop on his *Carbon Ideologies* book tour when we met at the Hugo Hotel in SoHo, where he was staying. He'd read the night before at the Strand Bookstore; hoping to get out of the hotel, he asked where I'd like to go, and we turned the corner to a sleek, minimalist café. He bought me coffee and asked the barista how his day was going. The following conversation took place over about an hour.

TH: Well, thanks again for taking the time.
WV: Oh, well I appreciate it. I usually don't care at all about publicity for my books. This isn't for me; it's just such an important issue that we all have to do whatever we can, so the more, the better, frankly.

TH: When did you start to care so much about climate change?
WV: I might not have really started thinking about it correctly had I not been a parent. I started worrying about my daughter, and then I think going to Fukushima right after the tsunami and the reactor disaster really made me think.

The tsunami looked and smelled horrible. It was just awful. Seeing the stinking mud everywhere, these temporary graves for people who had to wait a while to be cremated, the crushed houses. By contrast, the nuclear exclusion zone at that time looked almost as if it were just a weekend; people had just gone away days before. There were potted plants that had just started to wither, maybe an umbrella that had fallen down in a doorway, the blinds down, but everything looking pretty intact. And it was as I started coming back and back to Fukushima, watching the weeds grow up through the sidewalks, blinds rattling in the broken windows, vines wrapping around signs, hearing the presumably radioactive boar grunting all over the place—it became a little bit creepier.

The trend for me is to face increasing apparent invisibility. A tsunami is very visible. The radiation becomes so, especially with the pancake frisker, which allows you to have another sense. As my friends always say: suddenly the numbers are pictures. Then you go to a place where there's coal mining, and it's invisible in another way, and people deny climate change and they turn their backs on the visible scars of the mining. They don't want to face the acidification of their tap water. And you certainly find that all of these resource extraction companies wanted to be invisible. The ones that I call "the regulated community" are so adept at the art of "no comment."

TEPCO is by far the nicest. They actually met with me. And so you think, "All right, here's stuff like tap water that's going to rot people's teeth in West Virginia, and no one talking about it. So why should you trust them to have our interests at heart when it comes to climate change?"

They say that there are two characteristics of interest to a scientific hypothesis. One is that it can never be proved, only disproved. We can't prove that CO_2 causes climate change, just as we can't prove that there's a law of gravity. But the other thing is that if the model is good, you can make accurate predictions. So I can predict with some confidence that if I let go of this cup it's going to fall on the floor, because it's always done that before and it will probably do that this time. And the climate change model has made certain predictions that are coming true. So back in 1965 there was a man named Roger Ravel who predicted that by 2000 the CO_2 concentrations would go up by 25%. He was a little bit off: it wasn't until maybe 2010 or 2014 that we actually got up close to 400. He also said that the seas were going to rise, and that eventually that rise would be catastrophic. And we have about one hundred and fifty years' worth of tidal gauge measurements, and since 1990 we have satellite measurements as well, and we found that throughout most of the twentieth century the seas were indeed rising by something like 1.7 millimeters a year. After 1990 it was more like 3.2 millimeters a year. So that suggests that we are seeing some validation of the climate change model. Then there are all kinds of things lately—things like the fact that the glaciers have been receding all over the world for twenty years, and so on and so forth. So people have to become more and more stubborn to deny that this is likely so.

TH: A big topic in *Carbon Ideologies* is expert knowledge and the connection between knowledge and responsibility. Having immersed yourself in this material for so many years, I'm wondering how much of your own job you see as finding the truth and telling the truth.

WV: Well, I would like to think that I could do that. I'm not best suited to do that, because I'm not an expert, and the math and science stuff doesn't come naturally to me. I've done the absolute best that I can, and I hope that I have most of the numbers right. What I am decent at doing is describing people's experiences and motivations. So I can reel off some of the predictions of the Intergovernmental Panel on Climate Change, what's going to happen in the next few years. And I believe them because there are many, many scientists in that organization, and they're not paid to advocate for any particular thing. Whereas the people who argue against them are so often shills of the resource industry, and what they'll do is argue that the measurements aren't valid or something of the sort, but they don't propose any measurements of their own.

That having been said, what I think I can do better is talk about the experience or ideology, if you will, of these different fuels. The people at Fukushima who used to say, "Thanks to TEPCO, a lot of us people in these small towns actually have jobs." And in West Virginia there was a waitress who told me that in McDowell County, "You're either a coal miner, you work in a prison, or you're in prison." All this kind of stuff. And the last thing that we want to do is blame ordinary, fairly powerless people for hindering us from going forward to stop climate change. The fact is that electric power is something that we accept almost as a human right. It's easy for me to say, "Well, I'm willing to fly less and not turn on my air conditioner"—but what about the poor old lady in Bangladesh who's carrying all these shocks of corn in her hand, and she's feeble and exhausted, and wouldn't it be nice if she had some electric help? Who am I to say?

That's the real tragedy of the whole thing. It's a combination of short-term greed, monetization, frivolous use of electricity, and the legitimate aspirations of poor people to have some of what we have. When I was interviewing those two oil tycoons in the second volume, I found myself quite sympathetic to a lot of what they said. Archie Dunham, the former CEO of Conoco, said, "Look, Bill, there are all these people in the Third World, and they want to have a hot shower, too, and they're going to do that whether or not we like it."

I can't say that he's wrong. And in a way, of course, that makes me all the more discouraged.

TH: Do you think it's important to assign blame or apportion guilt?

WV: I think it's important to assign blame to people who have the power to do better and cut safety corners in the interest of making a buck, and delay and delay, refuse to talk, and generally seem very disingenuous, to all of our detriment.

I might use the analogy of vaccination. The parents who say, "Well, for religious reasons I don't want to vaccinate my kids." They seemed to have some kind of an ideological right. But the problem is that if enough parents don't vaccinate their kids, then they create a pool of disease that can hurt our kids. So, when somebody opts out, and that is to everybody's detriment, we have to really, really think: where does that person's right to opt out end?

TH: Then we get into the discussion of the mechanism of control and coercion.

WV: Right. And that's another very, very dismal theme in *Carbon Ideologies*. Because being a product of my time, I very much believe in the freedom of the individual. And a lot of people think that I'm a weirdo, or worse. People disapprove of me sometimes. Like in West Virginia, the Women's Coal Auxiliary was going to let me photograph them in their regalia, and then they suddenly declined without explanation. I'm guessing it's because *The Book of Dolores* just came out and they saw some pictures of me in a dress, and said, "This guy is disgusting." So, I would argue for my right to put on a dress if I want to. And they might argue for their right not to be regulated. So I don't want us to turn into some place like East Germany. But the other thing is that, the longer we wait, the more draconian and centralized the regulations are going to have to be. It's going to be a very, very ugly society, I think.

TH: You address *Carbon Ideologies* to future readers. I was struck by the image towards the end of the second volume, in which you suggest that the book will just be a water-stained relic or a fragment that gets into the hands of the few people who can read.

WV: That seems likely to me.

TH: I'm curious about that strategy of addressing future readers.

WV: Well, Ted, I always liked Thucydides. You know, the poor guy got egg on his face. His military campaign did not go very well. He was in exile for a lot of his life. And so he decided to just write something that he hoped would last for a long time, describing in the most at least pseudo-objective terms—of course, he put his slant on it—what had happened and how this affected or somehow mirrored human behavior.

I find that quite sympathetic. If I were to write for our time—and of course I really have to, because no matter what we write, whether it's science fiction or *Carbon Ideologies*, we're always writing to and about our own time, we can't help it—but still, I would probably be more prone to despair, because things are not going in the direction that I think they should be going. But if I can just say, all right, well let's pretend it's two or five hundred years later, or for all we know twenty years later, and this is what happened. There's nothing we can do about it now. But isn't it kind of interesting and maybe instructive to look back on what our generation did, why we did it? And you from the future, who really must hate us, I want you to take a hard look at yourself, and say, would you or could you do any better than we did? If they can't, in a way it sort of lets us off the hook. It also makes it all the more hopeless.

TH: Do you read much science fiction about what the world might look like?
WV: I love the old apocalyptic sci-fi. I had a lot of fun dropping in epigraphs from this or from that of my favorite old novels.

TH: John Brunner, for example.
WV: Yeah. How about you?

TH: I like that stuff, too. There's an author I just read named Jeff Vandermeer, who wrote the *Southern Reach Trilogy*.
WV: That's right. I just saw the movie of *Annihilation*, which was actually very beautiful, although I would say it's a rip-off of *Stalker*.

TH: In *Carbon Ideologies* there are many scenes of you editing the book, but not many of you writing. You describe in the Acknowledgments how your editing process for *Carbon Ideologies* was different than for your other books because you had to concentrate so much on statistics and numbers rather than on prose style.
WV: Well, for one thing, I felt continually under the gun. I was constantly trying to find people to check and double-check anything from arithmetic to assumptions about greenhouse gases. Pieter Tans at NOAA was extremely helpful, for example. At one point I had a much higher BTU per square foot figure for the warming of CO_2 and he helped me realize that that

was wrong. But it was very, very stressful to look at some large number and think, "Well, all right, so this is a sextillion, but what if it's really a quadrillion?" And to find that many sources disagreed.

I was doing the best I can. I knew that if I just had some kind of rant about climate change I wouldn't really be helping anybody. There are plenty of those out there. But if I could somehow give people the tools to make their own cost-benefit analysis, then that would be something new. And as I said, I'm not sure that I was the best-suited to do it, but I sure did my best, so that if someone wanted to, he or she could compare emissions per unit volume of coal to oil, or something like that.

Usually when I edit a book, it takes me very little time. It can be some kind of simple, background process while I'm working on another book. In the case of *Carbon Ideologies*, I turned the book in late and I spent pretty much all of last year doing unpaid editorial labor, so my income was down by about two thirds. My colleagues at Viking, my editor Paul Slovak and my copy editor Bruce Giffords and a bunch of other people, they also just slaved over that book. Bruce was telling me that most of the people he works with there are not numbers people, either, so we're all going way out of our comfort zone. If I and Viking could have afforded to have another six months, then I could have read the book whole one more time and I probably could have improved my sentences a little bit. Some of the sentences are not as good as the sentences in my other books, and there's nothing I can do about it.

But the book has to be a failure in many, many ways. Any such book would have to be a failure. Had I really given each fuel justice, maybe with one volume about each one, then no one would read it and it would also be a failure.

TH: It has to be a failure because it's impossible to reconcile the size of the problem with the size of the book?

WV: And I'm one person, with limited abilities and limited resources. I spent more than I'll make on this book. And what I would have liked to have was an army with sensitive measurement devices equivalent to the pancake frisker, a bunch of FLIR cameras, for instance—that's the Forward Looking Infrared—and with different kinds of FLIR cameras you could photograph CO_2 coming out of a person's mouth, or methane rising up out of a landfill. Each one of these cameras was something like $64,000, and I couldn't even afford to rent one. So, had I been able to do that, since seeing is believing, I think I could have done a better job. There are lots of claims that coal that's burned in a power plant is radioactive to some extent, and with a pancake frisker I couldn't verify that. There's only so much one person can do.

TH: Trying to quantify risks and benefits is something you've done before in *Rising Up and Rising Down*.
WV: Yeah, and I think that someone could carry forward what I tried to begin to do and really consider imminence and proportionality and discrimination to try to quantify the stuff more. Whatever we do, there's going to be some degree of arbitrariness in it, but less so when we're actually talking about science and numbers. Less so with this stuff than with politics.

I think it's Denmark or Sweden that actually makes farmers account for their nitrogen. They're not allowed to spread the nitrogen fertilizers in the winter months when they're not going to do as much good, the crops are dormant, and the chances are that a lot of it is just going to wash off. They say that something like half of all the nitrogen fertilizers just get wasted through run-off, so why on earth would we permit them to just be slathered about?

TH: Seems like wise policy.
WV: Yeah. Then you talk to farmers in the San Joaquin Delta area near Sacramento who are mostly Trump supporters and they feel very, very bitter about constant regulation. And that's what gun owners feel, too. You know, recently I had to turn in my TEK-9 pistol because California had made it illegal. And the police were sorry for me. I didn't really mind that much—I thought, "Well, I had my fun out of it, and it might have been nice if I had been compensated, but I'm not really going to get up in arms about it." But some of my gun-owning friends are furious, and they feel that the regulations never stop, and they get more and more angry.

There has to be a way to make people feel that they're being helped to do better instead of penalized. Why on earth would the coal mining families in West Virginia not vote for Trump when Hillary put her foot in her mouth and said, "We want to just shut all that coal stuff down." What I would have said if I were Hillary, was, "You know, I'm really grateful: to the coal miners and the oilmen and all these people that have given me the electricity that I enjoy. And I still use that stuff, I benefit from it, and so it may or may not be possible for me to continue to enjoy that stuff, but let's try to help them, let's transfer wealth to these people who've gotten kicked in the teeth. And instead of saying, we're going to put you out of work, let's say, hey, how about some solar collectors made out of Appalachian hardwood with

American flags on them that say 'Make America Great'? And we'll help you learn how to make them."

Something like that, that would be a win-win, using the local ideology just as the "regulated community" does. I learned that that West Virginians used to be mostly Democratic voters because, after all, their state is one of the poorest and they receive or did receive a lot of entitlements. So it was quite brilliant of the Republicans to come in there and start talking about family values and [saying], "Well, can't you think about something larger than yourself? Think about all those poor kids who might get exposed to a gay teacher in the classroom. What would that do to our morals? Come on now, stand up for something good." And they fell for it. So I think we have to understand the terms that people think in and we need to help them see what we think is best in our terms and their terms. That's why these so-called carbon ideologies are so important to think about.

TH: But whatever we think about these ideologies depends on whether or not we believe the experts, right? Expert knowledge is a big theme in the book, and it's a pretty bleak time for faith in the experts, considering the rise of fake news and related developments.

WV: Right, and the experts have done it to themselves, too. Let's not just blame Trump. I mean, expert knowledge has always been and always will be abused. I remember as a little kid hearing from all the experts that marijuana was insanely dangerous and would lead to hard drugs. All this bullshit. So it's very easy for people to get cynical and say, "You know what? I'm going to believe what suits me."

TH: Shifting gears a bit: many literary critics, including Amitav Ghosh have pointed out that oil has been rather absent from modern literature. Do you think that's an accurate diagnosis, and if so, what would explain the absence of oil from literature?

WV: Well, there was a great writer named Munif, who wrote the *Cities of Salt* trilogy. What a genius, you know? And then there's Upton Sinclair's *Oil!* Have you read that one?

TH: No, I haven't.

WV: It's quite interesting. It begins as a novel and ends up as a tract, but it's still quite interesting. It's about a father and son who start their own little oil company. They hit a gusher and they're doing really, really well, and they've decided that they're going to pay the workers well. Then slowly they get ground down by the big boys who say, "Hey, you can't pay those higher wages because if you do, then our workers are going to be mad, and we're not going to buy your oil, and we'll strangle you." And bit by bit the noose slowly tightens, things get worse and worse. It's quite fascinating.

So I would say there's a lot of great fiction about this stuff. And a lot of work, like J. G. Ballard's *The Drought*, for instance, that, if you want to use the Marxist term about economic substructure and ideological super-structure, you can say is about something going wrong with a resource or a situation that we depend on to be stable. There's something that could easily describe what will happen with climate change where dry places will get drier. So, I wouldn't say that [the claim about oil's absence from literature] is necessarily true. But I also think that there's always been a disconnect between people like us who work with words and people who work with numbers. And so we have to try to reach out to those people and they should reach out to us, I think.

TH: You mentioned *Cities of Salt*, which doesn't have a main character. In many of your works, such as the *Seven Dreams* series, you bring together a bunch of different voices and jump between perspectives. I'm curious about how you weave all those components together.

WV: Well, in a way the *Seven Dreams* ones are the easy ones to write because I don't really have to invent a story. I just need to start with what the story appears to be and then try to elaborate it, and also to see what part of it is true.

Argall, for instance, is just a very well-known tale of John Smith and Poca-hontas. I started looking into it, and it was a little more complicated, a little darker. I tried to visit some of the sites that were appropriate to the book because that's probably the way that we can get closest to these bygone peo-ple, by looking at some place that they would have looked at with their eyes. And that's maybe why we have this superstitious feeling that we're closer to our dead loved ones when we're right at their graves: maybe that dead per-son is somehow staring up through the earth and looking right at me.

Then I just try to work through whatever primary source stuff I can find. And that includes memoirs, dictionaries, scientific investigations of mate-rial culture, and so on, until I start feeling that I'm in that reality. And of course it's impossible to bring it back, but it's possible to make some plau-sible approximation that doesn't do too much violence to it.

TH: So when you sit down at the computer do you write from start to finish?
WV: No. With *The Dying Grass*, for instance, I must have had five or six

hundred computer files. There would be one about uses of medicinal plants by the Nez Percé, another one about uses of medicinal plants by the Crow because they passed into their territory. I'd have all this stuff, and then I'd go out and look for those plants, and think, "All right, so, yarrow was a very common plant, and something that was often used to staunch the bleeding of wounds." So after the Battle of Big Hole it seems very likely that the Nez Perce women would be out there gathering yarrow. So let's go out and look at some yarrow and maybe even boil some and see what it smells like. That's the kind of stuff that I would do.

TH: You use a variety of characteristic punctuation marks and text features, like em-dashes or small capitals. In *The Dying Grass* you used a new form of indentation. How do you arrive at these tricks?

WV: Well, some books ago I started thinking that, in fiction at least, quotation marks were a crutch. In *Carbon Ideologies*, which is already difficult enough with the numbers, I thought, let's keep things conventional. But ideally, you don't hear quotation marks when someone is reading to you, so you shouldn't need to see them to tell who's talking and when the speech ends. One way to represent that is to have em-dashes to suggest, "Okay, take a breath here." Or, space it a little bit differently, which of course is a form of cheating, it's almost like having the quotation marks back. But I try to do what I can to make sure that the words would still read correctly with the right sorts of pauses no matter how they were laid out on the page.

TH: So you're thinking about what it sounds like read aloud?

WV: That's right. And I do think there's just something kind of easy and juvenile about quotation marks. On the indentation point, I don't want my books to be formulas. So I try to make them all different. I'm starting to run out of rope now as I get older.

But at least with *The Dying Grass* I thought, "All right, well, we know that *Seven Dreams* is a book of North American landscapes, so we want the landscape to speak." So the first couple of years that I was writing *The Dying Grass* I tried to know as little as possible about what actually happened in this or that place. I just knew that, okay, this place is significant, there was a battle here or something like that, so let me go there, try to see that landscape without bringing in the pathetic fallacy. Originally I thought, maybe we'll have these quasi-objective landscape descriptions, let's say in a center column, and then maybe different people will be talking or doing things on either side of that column. I came to feel that that was too rigid and that all I really needed to do was to have indentations to say, "All right, we're going to make it this very fluid, organic thing, and so it's sort of an S-curve as it goes on and on." Someone is talking, at the same time he's thinking something else, and at the same time other people are looking at him or you and I are seeing the landscape that this person is passing through, and it's a way of representing the weird, flickering, simultaneous nature of perceptions in reality.

My guess is that that approximates consciousness. I think that I can look at you and listen to you at the same time, but very likely, if I could really look into my consciousness, I'm flickering back and forth between looking at you and listening to you. I think that's probably how our minds work, that your blind spots are much bigger than we think. And because they're blind, we can't see them.

TH: You mentioned the pathetic fallacy. Often you do the inverse. you'll compare someone's inner state directly to the landscape outside. Is that part of a deliberate strategy?

WV: With *Seven Dreams* it's certainly something I want to do. For the first one, *The Ice-Shirt*, I decided to go to Iceland. It was incredible to stand on that little island on Bridafjord and be wandering through the ruins of Erik the Red's farm, and thinking, "Okay, here are these flowers, there are birds, I'm looking at the ocean and the cloud." And thinking this is probably not too different from what Erik would have seen. To the extent that I can take this stuff in, I'm getting that much closer to Erik. So let's give these things the primary power that they deserve, and in some ways they're going to be the most living aspect of Erik's consciousness in this time.

TH: Is William the Blind different from William Vollmann in *Carbon Ideologies* and your other works of journalism?

WV: Well, he's a bit more of a confused bumbler. I'm a semi-confused bumbler.

TH: Do you have plans for the final two volumes of *Seven Dreams*?

WV: Yes, I do. One's called *The Cloud-Shirt*, and it's about the Hopi-Navajo land dispute in the 1980s. I was actually at Big Mountain in 1986 just as the US government was forcing the Navajo off their land, and it was very powerful and intense and sad. I have maybe two hundred pages written. It's the first part really, and I will go back to that, and try to go back to that place after all these years and see what's happened to these people.

For the other one, my original plan was about the war of the Puritans against King Philip in the Great Swamp. And that's what I will probably follow just because I'm sort of rigid and I laid out that plan, so why not? But I am tempted by the annexation of Hawaii just because that would be so different from the other dreams.

Index

About the Editor

Daniel Lukes has a PhD in comparative literature from New York University and is the coeditor of *William T. Vollmann: A Critical Companion*, the co-author of *Triptych: Three Studies of Manic Street Preachers' "The Holy Bible*," and the author of various articles about literature and music.

www.ingramcontent.com/pod-product-compliance
Lightning Source LLC
Chambersburg PA
CBHW030303060726
47498CB00002BB/482

* 9 781496 826701 *